# GREEK TRAGEDY IN VERGIL'S "AENEID"

## Ritual, Empire, and Intertext

This is the first systematic study of the importance of Greek tragedy as a fundamental "intertext" for Vergil's *Aeneid*. Vassiliki
Panoussi argues that the epic's representation of ritual acts, especially sacrifice, mourning, marriage, and maenadic rites, mobilizes
a connection to tragedy. The tragic-ritual model offers a fresh look
into the political and cultural function of the *Aeneid*, expanding
our awareness of the poem's scope, particularly in relation to gender, and presenting new readings of celebrated episodes, such as
Anchises' games, Amata's maenadic rites, Dido's suicide, and the
killing of Turnus. Panoussi offers a new argument for the epic's
ideological function beyond pro- and anti-Augustan readings. She
interprets the *Aeneid* as a work that reflects the dynamic nature of
Augustan ideology, contributing to the redefinition of civic discourse and national identity. In this rich and lucid study, readers
will find a unique exploration of the complex relationship between
Greek drama and Vergil's *Aeneid* and a stimulating discussion of
problems of gender, power, and ideology in ancient Rome.

Vassiliki Panoussi is Assistant Professor of Classical Studies at the
College of William and Mary. She received her Ph.D. from Brown
University and has previously taught at the University of Virginia
and Williams College. Her research focuses on Roman literature
of the late Republic, the age of Augustus, and the early empire
as informed through the study of intertextuality, cultural anthropology, religion, and sexuality. She has published several articles
on Roman poetry and prose and is currently at work on a book on
women's rituals in Roman literature.

*For my parents*

# GREEK TRAGEDY IN VERGIL'S "AENEID"

*Ritual, Empire, and Intertext*

**Vassiliki Panoussi**

College of William and Mary

CAMBRIDGE
UNIVERSITY PRESS

CAMBRIDGE UNIVERSITY PRESS
Cambridge, New York, Melbourne, Madrid, Cape Town, Singapore, São Paulo, Delhi

Cambridge University Press
32 Avenue of the Americas, New York, NY 10013–2473, USA

www.cambridge.org
Information on this title: www.cambridge.org/9780521895224

First published 2009

Printed in the United States of America

*A catalog record for this publication is available from the British Library.*

*Library of Congress Cataloging in Publication data*
Panoussi, Vassiliki, 1967–
Greek tragedy in Vergil's Aeneid : ritual, empire, and intertext / Vassiliki Panoussi.
p.   cm.
Includes bibliographical references and index.
ISBN 978-0-521-89522-4
1. Virgil. Aeneis.   2. Epic poetry, Latin – Greek influences.   3. Epic poetry, Latin –
History and criticism.   I. Title.
PA6825.P27 2008
873'.01–dc22        2008030568

ISBN 978-0-521-89522-4 hardback

# Contents

# Acknowledgments

This volume began its life as a doctoral dissertation under the supervision of Michael Putnam. My first thanks go to him for encouraging the project and for providing guidance, insight, and such standards of scholarship as I can only strive to follow. Many people and institutions have helped in the writing of this book. My terrific colleagues and students at my new home, the College of William and Mary, make it a joy to go to work every day. During the six happy years I spent at Williams College, my colleagues Meredith Hoppin, Kerry Christensen, Matthew Kraus, David Porter, and Charlie Fuqua offered friendship, unstinting support, and sage advice. Many thanks to Eleni Manolaraki and Erika Nesholm for all our fun conversations on and off topic. Other colleagues and friends, Denise Buell, Monique Deveaux, Tess Chakkalakal, and Olga Shevchenko, contributed much to my thinking and patiently listened to my ideas and worries.

In the years it took me to write this book I have incurred many institutional debts. Williams College provided me with a generous leave, during which most of the writing took place. At that itinerant time of my life, people at various institutions happily offered me a place to work and/or access to their libraries: Gonda Van Steen, David Christenson, and Marilyn Skinner at the University of Arizona; Bill Godfrey at SUNY Stony Brook; Ann Vassaly at Boston University; Gareth Williams at Columbia University; Sara Lindheim at UC Santa Barbara; Peter Knox at the University of Colorado at Boulder; and Pam Esposito, secretary of the Physics Department Theory Group at Brookhaven National Laboratory, eagerly provided administrative help and good cheer. The final revisions of the book were made possible by a Summer Research Award granted by the College of William and Mary. I would also like to extend a heart-felt thanks to the William and Mary Women's Studies Program, and in particular to Suzanne Raitt and Christy Burns, for granting me funds to hire a research assistant.

Portions of the book have been presented at the University of Arizona, Case Western Reserve University, Boston University, Yale University, SUNY Buffalo, Smith College, Drew University, Kenyon College, the University of Virginia, the Williams College Humanities and Social Sciences Forum, and the annual meetings of the American Philological Association and of the Classical Association of the Middle West and South. I am grateful to these kind audiences for their incisive comments and criticism and especially to Neil Coffee, Paolo Asso, and Ann Ellis Hanson.

Chapter 6 is essentially reprinted (with some revisions) from an earlier paper, "Vergil's Ajax: Allusion, Tragedy, and Heroic Identity in Vergil's *Aeneid*," *Classical Antiquity* 21 (2002): 95–134; and a small portion of Chapter 4 has appeared in the essay, "Threat and Hope: Women's Rituals and Civil War in Roman Epic," in *Finding Persephone: Women's Rituals in the Ancient Mediterranean*, edited by Maryline Parca and Angeliki Tzanetou, Bloomington 2007: 114–34.

Several people read parts of the manuscript, helped improve it, and offered much needed encouragement: Antonis Augoustakis, Denise Buell, David Christenson, Andrew Feldherr, Meredith Hoppin, Bill Hutton, Leon Kojen, Brian Martin, Sara Myers, Marilyn Skinner, Barbette Spaeth, Angeliki Tzanetou, and my late dear friend Shilpa Raval. I am deeply grateful to my editor, Beatrice Rehl, for believing in this project and to the anonymous readers for their thoughtful and helpful comments. My copy editor, Russell Hahn, saved me from many an error, while Kate Mertes did the general index with great care. Beth Block, my undergraduate research assistant, cheerfully performed the thankless task of checking references and bibliography with patience and diligence. Of course, I alone am responsible for any remaining errors.

Many other friends and colleagues helped me along the way: Bonnie Gordon, Elizabeth Meyer, John Miller, K. Sara Myers, Sophia Serghi, and Evgenia Smirni did much to inspire and to encourage. Amanda Jablonski, the world's greatest babysitter, provided peace of mind when

I needed it most. Angeliki Tzanetou's steadfast support and generous friendship made this a better book.

My family deserves much of the credit for the completion of this project. My father-in-law, Nikolas Orginos, has helped in more ways than he knows. My husband, Kostas Orginos, and our two precocious children, Nikolas and Anna, offered joyful distractions and pushed me to the finish line. The greatest debt, however, is to my parents, Meletis and Kaiti Panoussi, who did their best to prepare me for this endeavor, endured a long separation, and even provided help with childcare during the last stages of revision. For these reasons, and many more, my gratitude to them is acknowledged on a separate page.

When citing ancient texts, I have used the standard Oxford or Teubner editions. Ancient authors and texts are abbreviated according to the *Oxford Classical Dictionary*, while journal abbreviations follow those of the *Année Philologique*. All translations are my own, unless otherwise noted.

# Abbreviations

| | |
|---|---|
| *D'Anna* | G. D'Anna, *M. Pacuvii Fragmenta. Poetarum Latinorum Reliquiae. Aetas Rei Publicae.* Vol. III.1. Rome, 1967. |
| *Jocelyn* | H. D. Jocelyn, *The Tragedies of Ennius. The Fragments. Edited with an Introduction and Commentary.* Cambridge, 1967. |
| *OCD* | S. Hornblower and A. Spawforth, *The Oxford Classical Dictionary.* 3rd edition. Oxford, 1996. |
| *OLD* | P. G. W. Glare, *Oxford Latin Dictionary.* Oxford, 1996. |
| *PMG* | D. L. Page, *Poetae Melici Graeci.* Oxford, 1962. |
| *Skutsch* | O. Skutsch, *The Annals of Q. Ennius. Edited with Introduction and Commentary.* Oxford, 1985. |
| *TrGF Kannicht* | R. Kannicht, *Tragicorum Graecorum Fragmenta.* Vol. 5. *Euripides.* Göttingen, 1985. |
| *TrGF Radt* | S. Radt, *Tragicorum Graecorum Fragmenta.* Vol. 3. *Aeschylus.* Göttingen, 1985. |
| *TRF* | O. Ribbeck, *Scaenicae Romanorum Poesis Fragmenta.* Vol. 1. *Tragicorum Romanorum Fragmenta.* 3rd edition. Leipzig, 1897. |

# Introduction

IN THIS BOOK I ARGUE THAT GREEK TRAGEDY PROVIDES THE key to understanding representations of ritual acts in the *Aeneid*. I present evidence for the existence of a systematic use of tragedy in the poem, which consists of intertextual and ritual appropriations, and operates side by side with the poem's allusions to Homer. Moreover, the mobilization of this tragic element is linked to the ideological function of the *Aeneid* and illuminates the complex problem of the poem's orientation vis-à-vis the Augustan regime.

The theme of sacrifice is crucial for an understanding of the intricate relationship between the *Aeneid* and Greek tragedy. For example, the sacrifice of the young virgin Iphigeneia, King Agamemnon's daughter, enabled the Greek fleet to set sail to Troy. This well-known episode in the Trojan War is absent in the Homeric epics but is poignantly dramatized in Aeschylus' *Agamemnon* and Euripides' *Iphigeneia in Aulis*. When Vergil in the second book of the *Aeneid* offers a powerful description of Iphigeneia's sacrifice as an instance of the brutality of the Greeks, he departs from his primary model, Homer, and rather follows the practice of the Greek tragedians.

In Greece as well as in Rome, sacrificial ritual normally prohibits the sacrifice of humans. In the Homeric epics human sacrifice appears only once,[1] while in tragedy it is regularly used as a means to indicate that the crisis of the plot is simultaneously a crisis in religious (and, by extension, political) institutions. In Aeschylus' *Agamemnon*, for instance, the

---

[1] Achilles sacrifices twelve Trojan youths at the funeral pyre of Patroclus in *Iliad* 23.175–76.

sacrifice of Agamemnon's daughter Iphigeneia leads directly to his murder, in turn, by his own wife, Clytemnestra. This murder is portrayed
as a human sacrifice. This cycle of retribution, inaugurated by a human
sacrifice, thus brings about a political crisis in the kingdom that is ultimately resolved, in the last play of the trilogy, by the foundation of a
whole new system of justice based on courts and the rule of law. The
*Aeneid* is also rife with human sacrifices, actual and metaphorical, from
its beginning, where we witness the murder of Dido's husband, Sychaeus,
at an altar, to the final slaying of Aeneas' chief antagonist, Turnus, which
is pronounced a sacrifice. The frequency of the motif of human sacrifice
in the *Aeneid* therefore parallels its use in Greek tragedy.

This study does not propose to contribute only to the debate on the
literary pedigree of the *Aeneid*. Rather than studying intertextuality for
its own sake, the book attends to tragedy as a literary model because
it is an ideologically charged choice. Recent interest in the processes
of intertextuality and the centrality of the *Aeneid* as a canonical text
has generated a rich literature with and against which the book works.
Critics focusing on intertextuality have amply demonstrated the ways
in which the poem's systematic allusion to Homer (epic intertext) aims
to establish Vergil as the Roman Homer (Knauer 1964; Quint 1993),
while the poem's reception by contemporaries confirms its unprecedented success in this regard. Homer's imprint thus confers a particular
kind of authority on the *Aeneid* that puts it on an equal footing with
the Homeric epics. Moreover, the poem's importance as a new literary achievement is explicitly connected with an endorsement of the
new political regime because it hails it as the result of a teleological
process rooted in the very beginnings of the Roman nation. I argue,
however, that the poem's systematic engagement with Greek tragedy
(tragic intertext) needs to be read against the epic intertext because it
provides an alternative to the poem's support for Augustan ideology. To
be sure, the *Aeneid* sent a message that met the needs of the dominant
power structure. At the same time, a primary insight of recent criticism on ideology is that ideology is always in dialogue with, and thus
shaped and constrained by, the voices it is suppressing or manipulating.
Criticism on the *Aeneid* has long been divided between those who see it
as a pro-Augustan work and those who see it as deeply pessimistic and
anti-Augustan. My approach contributes to resolving the controversy of

the "two voices" of the *Aeneid* by grounding it in the tension between two generic models, epic and tragic.

The book's attention to ideological matters goes hand in hand with close analysis of intertextual material and suggests a need to broaden the scope of the term "intertextual." The work of Stephen Hinds, Joseph Pucci, and Lowell Edmunds helped the field of classics move away from its rather rigid classifications of allusion and laid fruitful theoretical ground: it defined allusion as a flexible analytical category that encompasses a variety of literary techniques previously ignored or altogether dismissed; emphasized the importance of the role of the reader in activating, retrieving, and ultimately creating meaning; and established that intertextuality in all its complex manifestations is an integral part of all Roman poetry.[2] Allusion, however, is still considered a process strictly embedded in a literary dialogue among authors working within a tradition. In an effort to broaden disciplinary vocabularies, this study builds on these scholars' advances but also employs insights from cultural anthropology and religion in order to interpret ritual representations in the *Aeneid* (Girard 1977; Burkert 1983; Bell 1992). By expanding the term "intertextuality" to encompass ritual representations, I propose that it is no longer a strictly literary process but that it needs to be related to its social context.

Rituals are increasingly thought of as analogous to culturally produced texts and therefore subject to interpretation and manipulation. Ritual representations mobilize the variety of meanings that a ritual experience affords in order to invest them with new meaning. In this respect, intertextual and ritual appropriations can be seen as comparable: just as a battle scene in the *Aeneid* in appropriating elements from a particular Homeric battle scene offers fresh interpretative possibilities, so the inclusion of a ritual description of a sacrifice points to a common ritual "vocabulary" that in turn may illuminate aspects of the text. Viewed in this light, an examination of intertextual appropriations of Greek tragedies in the *Aeneid* reveals that they are intimately bound up with the poem's rich fabric of ritual representations. Since ritual representations in

---

[2] Hinds 1998; Pucci 1998; Edmunds 2001. In the case of Vergil, in particular, valuable interpretations of the allusiveness of the corpus have been and continue to be proposed: Farrell 1991 on the *Georgics*; Conte 1986; Thomas 1986.

the *Aeneid* closely follow the practice of Greek tragedy, they work side by side with other allusive tropes pointing to tragic texts.[3] Recognizing the intricate relationship between intertextuality and ritual is the first step toward understanding the function of the poem's intersection of epic and tragic intertexts.

Once identified, the nexus of intertextual and ritual appropriations is interpreted within the social context of Vergil's own time. Scholars working on Greek tragedy have long recognized tragedy's civic and ideological function.[4] This book, however, does not simply transpose the questions and conclusions of tragedy's critics in the context of Augustan Rome. Rather, it examines how the processes of articulating ideological debate in Greek tragedy are employed and resituates the question of the *Aeneid* as a work that promotes the establishment of a new political regime. In other words, in Greek tragedy, ritual representations, metaphors, and motifs serve as a means of delving into social, political, religious, and ideological issues. I argue that the use of ritual has the same function in the *Aeneid*. Moreover, it is organically linked to the literary process of intertextual appropriation, which is thus viewed as grounded in the social context of Vergil's Rome. In this light, in each chapter I concentrate on issues that are both central to Greek tragedy and fundamental for an understanding of the ideological issues explored in the *Aeneid*: the interconnection of religion and politics as it is manifested in the treatment of the problem of violence in war and sacrifice; the role of the divine in sanctioning and promoting the new state's institutions; the formation of a new identity for Trojans and Latins living together as one people; the values and ideals that their leaders must embody; and the women's

---

[3] The problem of Vergil's relationship with Roman tragedy is an important one but is unfortunately complicated by the serious gap in our knowledge of Republican Roman tragic poets. On the positive side, it is well documented that Vergil knew them, since examples of shared language abound. The broader context, however, is irretrievable, though recent studies by Erasmo (2004) and Boyle (2006) have done much to further our understanding. I have analyzed instances of Vergil's appropriation of Roman tragedies wherever pertinent and possible (see, e.g., Chapter 1, pp. 39–40, and Chapter 6, pp. 214–15), but a greater discussion of their import is beyond the scope of this study.

[4] For example, Vernant and Vidal-Naquet 1988; Foley 1985; Winkler and Zeitlin 1990; Seaford 1994.

engagement in the religious, social, military, and political spheres. Such an analysis demonstrates that the ideological tensions that scholars have long identified as informing the fabric of Vergil's poetry are played out in the poem's epic and tragic intertexts.

Although since antiquity tragedy has been hailed as a constitutive element of the *Aeneid*, this is the first systematic, book-length study of the role of tragedy in the poem.[5] My approach has benefited greatly from the work of critics such as Philip Hardie, Denis Feeney, and David Quint.[6] Hardie has demonstrated the importance of the literary motif of sacrifice for an understanding of the problem of violence in Roman epic; Feeney signaled the need to consider ritual representations in studying Latin texts; and Quint explored the close interconnections between the epic genre and the ideology of empire. The present study brings together these different approaches while at the same time using methods and ideas from cultural anthropology, religion, and political theory (Bourdieu 1977; Thompson 1984; Bell 1992) to signal the importance of placing the literary process of intertextuality in a social context. As a result, the book's contribution is twofold: on the one hand, it demonstrates the importance of Greek tragedy both as a literary source for the *Aeneid* and as a site onto which ideological negotiations of acquiescence and opposition are mapped. On the other hand, it develops a theoretical mechanism for reading intertextuality with attention to the workings of ideology.

The study begins with an exploration of the various ways in which the *Aeneid* represents ritual acts and argues that throughout the epic, Vergil

---

[5] In antiquity, Servius (*Aen.* 4.471, 664) and Macrobius (*Saturnalia* 5.18–19) thought that Vergil knew the Greek tragedies and borrowed from them. In more recent times, the rather impressive volume of scholarship constitutes ample proof: Heinze 1915; Conington 1884.2: xxxv–vi; Pease 1935: 5–6; Duckworth 1940, 1957; Jackson Knight 1953: 133–40; Pöschl 1962 *passim*, especially 60–138, 1978; Quinn 1968: 323–49; Von Albrecht 1970 (although he reaches a negative conclusion); Wigodsky 1972: 91–97; Manuwald 1985; Feeney 1991: 129–87, *passim*; Fernandelli 1996a, 1996b; Hardie (1991, 1993, 1994, 1997) has attempted a deeper and more comprehensive probe into the tragic elements in the *Aeneid*. See also the three doctoral dissertations on the subject: Fenik 1960; König 1970; and Panoussi 1998. On the "tragedy" of Dido, see Wlosok 1976; Muecke 1983; Clausen 1987: 53–57; Jacobson 1987; Moles 1984, 1987; Harrison 1989; Spence 1991; Swanepoel 1995; and Fernandelli 2002.

[6] Hardie 1993; Feeney 1998; Quint 1993. See also Kennedy 1992.

manipulates a representational pattern absent in the Homeric epics and specific to Greek tragedy: ritual corruption followed by ritual restoration. According to this pattern, rites executed incorrectly in the course of a tragic play are ultimately performed correctly, thus restoring ritual purity. The first chapter traces the trajectory of the ritual intertext from distortion to restoration as a means to deploy issues of violence, justice, and retribution. The next chapter attends to Dido's suicide, the killing of Turnus, and the problem of ritual purity and closure. I suggest that the representation of both Dido's and Turnus' deaths is associated with the Roman ritual of *devotio*, although it is ultimately a distorted version of that ritual. Chapter 3 concludes the examination of this pattern by focusing on the divine role in the process of reconciliation and restoration and reveals that divinities willfully follow the same pattern of ritual distortion as humans and undermine any prospect of divine and human *concordia*.

The next two chapters turn to women's engagement with ritual and its repercussions on civic order and the nascent civic identity. Chapter 4 focuses on women's worship of Bacchus and their performance of bacchic rituals, actual or metaphorical. Women's execution of ritual acts is far from ritually correct and fuels the forces of irrationality and war. In Chapter 5, I focus on the contribution of women's rituals to the poem's creation of a new civic identity for Aeneas and his men. Vergil employs the specifically female ritual of lamentation to comment on the impact that grief and loss have on public life and to illustrate proper ways of rendering that grief a positive force for the new nation under Aeneas. Women's rituals are shown to disrupt or oppose Aeneas' mission. Even so, through their ritual activity women emerge as empowered representatives of a point of view that runs opposite to the one that champions victory and empire.

The next portion of the book tackles issues of empire and the identity of the hero therein. Chapter 6 demonstrates that in the *Aeneid*, Roman heroic identity is defined through constant reference to Homeric heroic identity and fifth-century Athenian civic identity as it is deployed in Greek tragedy. Issues of identity and moral action explored in Sophocles' *Ajax* are crucial to Vergil's portrayal of Dido and Turnus, who also find themselves unable to adapt to the social and political structure of Aeneas' new order but also offer themselves as laudable models of heroic behavior.

The analysis presented in these chapters reveals that Vergil adopts and manipulates the conflicts and ambiguities inherent in Greek tragedy in order to express anxieties about Augustus' new sociopolitical order. In the final chapter, I suggest that the problem of the *Aeneid* as pro- or anti-Augustan needs to be reformulated. In an effort to do so, I use insights from recent studies that emphasize the dynamic nature of ideology (Bourdieu 1977; Bell 1992) and argue that it is more instructive to read the presence of Greek tragedy in the *Aeneid* as a means through which ideological points of view of resistance and acquiescence are negotiated. In this light, the generic tensions between epic and tragedy can be seen as reenacting ideological tensions. The failure of ritual to achieve restoration forces the reader to confront the problems inherent in the new sociopolitical order that the poem seeks to assert. At the same time, however, this voice of dissent is instrumental in shaping the poem's celebration of the Augustan regime. The *Aeneid* thus emerges as a text in which these contesting ideologies still struggle for supremacy, with the poem oscillating between endorsing Augustus' new regime and questioning its methods and efficacy. Attention to dynamic processes of questioning and examining as well as of affirming and resolving the new sociopolitical institutions reveals the central role of the poem's generic and ideological tensions and provides important insights into the formation of Augustan ideology and Roman identity.

PART I

# RITUAL

SECTION A

# SACRIFICE

# I  Ritual Violence and the Failure of Sacrifice

et quisquam numen Iunonis adorat
praeterea aut supplex aris imponet honorem?                    (*Aen.* 1.48–49)

And will anyone still worship Juno's deity
or as a suppliant lay sacrifice upon her altars?

JUNO'S ANGER FUELS THE ACTION OF THE *AENEID*, AND SACRIFICE
is at the root of this anger. The performance of sacrifices in her honor
validates her deity; it is a tangible form of worship, the basis of exchange
between gods and humans, and a locus where the power differential
between them is played out. Recent scholarship has amply demonstrated
the importance of the role of ritual sacrifice in the *Aeneid*. The work of
Bandera (1981), Hardie (1993), and Dyson (2001) has shown that representations of ritual sacrifice, sacrificial symbolism and metaphor, as well
as the depiction of various characters as scapegoats, abound in the epic.
One thus may speak of the existence of a ritual intertext (Dyson 2001:
13) operative in the poem.

Building on the insights of these scholars, I offer an analysis of the
*Aeneid*'s ritual intertext, which I examine along with the poem's allusive
intertext. I argue that the poem's ritual representations, metaphors, and
symbols are inextricably linked with the deployment of its rich allusive
program. Throughout the *Aeneid*, Vergil manipulates a pattern of ritual
representations, sacrifice being the most salient among them, absent in
the Homeric epics and specific to Greek tragedy. In many Greek plays,
ritual perversion symbolically represents a disruption of the religious
order that in turn intensifies the conflict and crisis in the tragic plot.

The ritual perversion developed in the course of the play is eventually replaced by a restoration of the disrupted religious order through the correct performance of ritual or the institution of a new cult (Seaford 1994: 368–405). To be sure, the problems, anxieties, and conflicts that ritual corruption brings to the foreground may be far from satisfactorily resolved (Vernant 1988), but ritual correctness is no longer in jeopardy (Seaford 1994: 366–67). In the *Aeneid*, descriptions of perverted rituals often coexist with verbal points of contact with specific moments within Greek tragic texts. As a result, the poem mobilizes a program of sustained allusion to Greek tragedy both through appropriation of specific texts and through the manipulation of the pattern of sacrificial perversion and restoration.

The *Aeneid* does not simply apply the tragic pattern of perversion turned to restoration but transforms it. Viewed through the lens of Greek tragedy, the presence of perverted rituals within the poem creates the expectation of ritual restoration. Yet the poem ends with what I will argue is a poignant moment of ritual perversion and therefore thwarts the expectation of restoration. As a result, the tragic ritual intertext undermines Aeneas' killing of Turnus as an act of retribution and implies the continuation of the cycle of violence. The poem's tragic intertext thus problematizes the very solution necessitated by its appropriation of and engagement with the Homeric intertext.

In an effort to understand the workings of the pattern of ritual corruption and subsequent restoration, the notion of narrative "repetition" as developed by Peter Brooks (1984) and applied by David Quint (1993) in the narrative of the *Aeneid* may be helpful. According to Brooks, narrative is linked intimately with plots of psychic mastery and empowerment. Narrative "must make use of specific, perceptible repetition in order to create plot, that is to show us a significant interconnection of events" (Brooks 1984: 99). For Brooks, narrative is the middle between beginning and end, which is understood as a dynamic "dilatory space of postponement and error" (96). In this "middle," repetitions "bind the energy of the text so as to make its final discharge more effective" (108). Revisiting past moments within the narrative recalls earlier moments and at the same time varies them, thus proceeding to a desired ending, whereby progress and mastery may be claimed (Quint 1993: 51). Repetition thus creates a return to the text with a difference. Yet there is always the risk that repetition will become merely regressive and that the plot will be endlessly repetitious. This dual nature of repetition may destabilize narrative progress and interrupt its forward movement.

David Quint argues that the *Aeneid* plots out such a struggle for empowerment. The second half of the poem repeats events of the first half, with a difference, in order to master them: the Trojans are transformed from losers to winners. The two forms of repetition that Brooks outlines, the negative and the positive, correspond to the dual message of Augustan propaganda, "the injunction to forget the past of civil war (so as to stop repeating it) and the demand that this past be remembered and avenged (so as to be repeated and mastered)" (Quint 1993: 52). This type of analysis can be extended to the poem's ritual text, whereby sacrificial perversion constitutes the middle of the ritual narrative, this space of dynamic delay and detour, working toward "recognition and retrospective illumination" (Brooks 1984: 108). In this light, the epic may be said to deploy the repetition of perverted sacrifice in order to revisit it and master it through ritual purity and restoration. I argue that an examination of this repetition of sacrificial perversion reveals that the ending of the ritual plot fails to attain purity and restoration. In other words, the ritual plot does not end with the positive repetition synonymous with mastery as is the case with the narrative plot.

Actual Roman cultic practice attests to the importance of this psychological need for repetition in Roman consciousness. According to the Roman practice of *instauratio*, a ritual act interrupted or executed incorrectly had to be repeated. Throughout the epic, we witness representations of ritual sacrifices in distorted form. These include descriptions of ritual sacrifices or human deaths cast in sacrificial terms. These sacrificial deaths take the form of failed preliminary sacrifices or failed initiations, criminal acts that require retribution, and the specifically Roman ritual of *devotio*. Each perverted sacrifice thus "repeated" reinforces the expectation of ritual correctness that will lead to a discharge of the ritual plot. The notion of "repetition" is thus helpful for understanding the poem's movement toward resolution and end.

The regular, repeated performance of rituals provides the community with the comfort of control over the ever-unpredictable divine. Similarly, in the context of narrative, repetition provides mastery of past events, which in turn enables progress for the future. Yet repetition within the ritual intertext of the *Aeneid* exposes the failure of ritual, and of sacrifice in particular, to provide such a sense of comfort and mastery.[1] Before I proceed with my analysis of the tragic pattern of sacrificial perversion in the epic, I shall first discuss the different ways in which Homer and Greek tragedy deal with the problem of sacrifice.

## I. HOMERIC AND TRAGIC SACRIFICE

Sacrifice plays an important role in the Homeric epics. The sacrifices performed in the course of the epic narrative involve domestic animals, and ritual elements expressing guilt or anxiety at the killing are notably absent (Seaford 1994: 44). Deaths on the battlefield are never depicted in sacrificial terms, and the verb σφάζειν is used only of animals (Seaford 1994: 47). "[A]nimal sacrifices that occur in the narrative do in fact contrast with killing in battle: the predictable, peacefully ordered process of killing and cooking the animal ends in the joyful concord of the feast, whereas on the battlefield all is uncontrolled violence" (Seaford 1989: 87). The ritual of sacrifice ends with a meal, which thus helps cement solidarity and cohesion among the members of the group (Burkert 1985: 55–59; Seaford 1994: 44) by containing both the struggle of the animal and the struggle among the humans who witness the sacrifice, two types of violence that could be potentially uncontrollable (Seaford 1994: 49). This positive role of sacrifice necessitates the omission of one of the most famous events of the Trojan War, the sacrifice of Iphigeneia. As a result, sacrifice in Homer establishes a desired communication with the divine; it may be said that it is used to reassure in moments of transition into the uncertainty of war and to mitigate the suffering it causes (Seaford 1994: 49).

Sacrificial ritual is one of the constitutive forces of the tragic plot. Human sacrifice in tragedy perverts actual sacrificial practice, which normally prohibits the slaughter of men. In contrast to Homer and choral lyric, death in tragedy is frequently represented in a sacrificial setting (Burkert 1966: 116). Moreover, killings of humans cast in sacrificial

---

[1] On repetition and sacrifice in the *Aeneid* viewed from the perspectives of history vs. reality, see Feldherr 2002.

terms often involve members of the same family, a practice wholly absent in Homer (Seaford 1989: 87). At the same time, the perversion of sacrificial ritual sets in motion the unraveling of the entire religious order, which is eventually restored by the end of the play. As a result, sacrificial perversion stands for the greater social disruption and crisis typical of the tragic plot (Foley 1985: 38).

The sacrifice of twelve Trojan youths (along with the slaughter of horses and dogs) performed by Achilles at the funeral pyre of Patroclus in the *Iliad* (23.175–76) is an exception to the Homeric pattern of sacrifice.[2] It is an act of unprecedented savagery employed to demonstrate the violence of the hero's grief.[3] But this sacrifice differs significantly from those enacted in Greek tragedy. Achilles' sacrificial aggression is directed to outsiders and serves to emphasize that in warfare violence may be uncontainable. But, despite the violation of sacrificial custom, the religious order appears to emerge intact. Instead, the ritual order is threatened by Achilles' refusal to grant Hector burial, and its disruption is eventually averted by his subsequent reconciliation with Priam and the performance of burial rites (Redfield 1975: 210–23).

## II. RITUAL PERVERSION AND TRAGIC INTERTEXT IN THE *AENEID*

In Vergil, the representation of sacrificial ritual often plays the same positive role that it does in Homer: sacrifice is regulated, prescribed, and properly sanctioned by religious custom and law. Aeneas repeatedly displays his piety and technical expertise in a number of such occasions throughout the poem (Bandera 1981: 223). At the same time, Aeneas serves as a paradigm of piety, prefiguring the sacrificial role of the *princeps*

---

[2] In the *Odyssey* (4.535 and 11.411), Agamemnon's death is compared to that of a domestic animal. But it is important to note that it is not described in *sacrificial* terms (Seaford 1994: 63). This comparison, however, reverses the sacrificial principle of substitution that prescribes the death of an animal in exchange for the death of a human.

[3] See Richardson 1993: 188–89. On Achilles' behavior, see Finley 1977: 137; Segal 1971: 13; and Van Wees 1992: 128.

as a symbol of the religious unity of the empire.[4] Ritual and sacrifice
in particular were such an important part of everyday life that images
representing sacrifices came to dominate Augustus' pictorial program.
Images of skulls of sacrificial animals, offering bowls, priests' accoutrements, fillets and garlands, are found in almost every building or monument, even if its function was secular. These images encapsulated the
nation's renewed piety and the "emotional mood of the new age" (Zanker
1988: 115–18).

Yet the narrative of the *Aeneid* also contains descriptions of sacrificial ritual involving human victims, as encountered in tragedy (Hardie
1991: 33; 1993: 22; 1997b). The sacrifice of humans, normally forbidden
by religious law, causes ritual impurity and is a source of pollution, thus
distorting the ritual act. In representations of rituals this perversion may
also be indicated by the depiction of a rite as its antithetical opposite –
the inversion, for instance, of marriage to funeral, as is often the case
in Greek tragedy. The violence of perverted sacrifice thus underlies and
underscores the tragic conflict.

Aeschylus' *Oresteia* offers a prime example of the ways in which perverted sacrifice pushes forward the development of the plot in many of
the Greek tragedies.[5] Reciprocal violence is the central problem of the
trilogy: the murder of Agamemnon by his wife, Clytemnestra, sets in
train the series of events that will lead to the foundation of the court,
which will replace the old vendetta-like system of dispensing justice. In
the plays, the cycle of retribution is cast as a perversion of proper sacrificial procedure. Beginning with *Agamemnon*, all deaths (the demise of the
men at Troy, the feast of the eagles upon the hare, the sacrifice of
Iphigeneia, the slaughter of the sheep by the lion cub, the murder of
Thyestes' children, and the killings of Agamemnon and Cassandra) are

---

[4] Hardie 1993: 21–22. He points out that the equation between Aeneas and the
*princeps* was evident in visual form in the *Ara Pacis*. On the *Ara Pacis*, Augustus,
and images of sacrifice, see also Zanker 1988: 117–18.

[5] There is plenty of compelling evidence that at least the mythical plot of
Aeschylus' *Oresteia* was very well known to Romans. Livius Andronicus has an
*Aegisthus*, while Pacuvius has a *Dulorestes*. Accius has written a *Clytemestra* and
an *Aegisthus* (some posit that they are the same work). Given the number of
plays devoted to this myth, one may safely conclude that Aeschylus' *Oresteia* was
an intertext of vital importance to the Roman tragedians.

presented in terms of ritual slaughter. Within this context, sacrificial perversion effaces the differentiation between pure and impure violence and is indicative of a greater crisis in the cultural order, which Girard has famously termed "sacrificial crisis." All boundaries that have hitherto guaranteed the cultural order collapse: the positive and beneficial animal sacrifices are replaced by human sacrifice; men eat their children; women take on male qualities; the hunter becomes the hunted (Griffiths 1979: 25).

In *Choephoroi*, the cycle of retribution draws to a close: Orestes and Electra temporarily end the sacrificial crisis by hurling themselves against Clytemnestra, a common target. The atrocity of children killing their mother is overlooked through the arbitrary assumption that their right to avenge the murder of their father trumps that of Clytemnestra to avenge the sacrifice of her daughter Iphigeneia. This turning point in the trilogy is expressed by the absence of sacrificial symbolism from the murders of Clytemnestra and Aegisthus (Griffiths 1979: 27; Zeitlin 1965: 484). The inadequacy of this resolution, however, is marked by the return of ritual perversion in *Eumenides*, where Orestes' purification at the temple of Apollo fails to absolve him of responsibility for his crime. The problem of the proliferation of reciprocal violence is eventually solved with the foundation of the court of Areopagus and the conversion of the Erinyes to protective forces for Athens and its people. At the end of the play ritual correctness returns, as the solemn procession performed by the Eumenides attests. Aeschylus' deployment of the myth suggests that reciprocal violence cannot be eliminated but only controlled by the *polis*.[6]

The sacrificial symbolism operative in the *Aeneid* has been noted by Bandera (1981) and Hardie (1993: 19–22, 27–29, 32–35), who have successfully applied René Girard's (1977) theory of sacrifice to explicate Vergil's use of sacrifice as a means to explore the problem of violence in the epic. Girard had used the Greek tragedies as a showcase for his

---

[6] Griffiths 1979: 29. See also Foley 1985: 40–42. The extent of restoration at the end of the trilogy is the object of heated debate similar to that over the end of the *Aeneid*. This is not the place to enter into the details of this debate, on which see Vernant 1988: 29–48; Goldhill 1984: 262–83 and 1986: 1–32; Seaford 1994: 366–67. The point relevant to my discussion is that ritual correctness is now intact, regardless as to how effective it may be deemed to be.

theory, whereby sacrificial perversion is an indication of a greater collapse of the cultural order, only to be restored through the sacrifice of a
scapegoat. This sacrificial victim, willingly sacrificed according to proper
ritual custom, is to take on all the impurities and restore unity within
the community.

Greek tragedy thus provides a useful pattern of analysis that merits
further scrutiny. In what follows I propose a typology of sacrifice that
may also prove a fruitful way to explore the problem of ritual perversion within the poem, as each category is intimately connected with the
major problems that the epic engages. Sacrifice as initiation relates to the
problem of violence and war: the death of the young poignantly underscores the fact that the unanimous community that is to emerge from
the carnage will be deprived of its most brilliant and promising component. Criminal acts that defile normal sacrificial practices underline
the problem of justice and retribution within the context of fratricide;
and the manifestations of *devotio* express in ritual terms the relationship
between the leader and his or her community, while also problematizing
the notion of scapegoating for the greater social good.

## III.  FIRST-FRUITS AND INITIATIONS

### 1.  Iphigeneia

As we have noted, the episode of the sacrifice of Iphigeneia is absent
from the Homeric epics but is central to a number of Greek tragedies,
especially Aeschylus' *Agamemnon* and Euripides' *Iphigeneia in Aulis*, where
it is cast as preliminary sacrifice for the greater destruction of Troy. In
the *Aeneid* too the sacrifice of Iphigeneia could be seen as the starting
point for the thrust of the epic plot (Hardie 1993: 27). Several other
deaths (those of Icarus, Marcellus, Pallas, and Mezentius) follow the pattern of Iphigeneia's death and are represented as sacrifices in actual or
metaphorical terms. The intertextual connection between these deaths
and that of Iphigeneia indicate that they constitute repetitions of this
earlier sacrifice. As a result, these sacrifices too can be seen as preliminary, foreshadowing the greater sacrifice of Turnus. Sacrificial repetition
serves a twofold purpose. As a return *of* the sacrifice of Iphigeneia, it
exhibits the perpetuation of the cycle of perversion. As a return *to* the

sacrifice of Iphigeneia, each instance illuminates a different problem that this perversion and crisis generate: parental responsibility for the loss of children, the problematic nature of killing in war, and the need for a different system to dispense justice and retribution. In this section, I shall examine the ways in which the figure of Iphigeneia launches the intertext of sacrificial perversion in the epic.

The reference to the sacrifice of Iphigeneia occurs as a narrative within a narrative in *Aeneid* 2. The intertext of tragedy thus infiltrates the epic with a reference to an act of ritual perversion, depicting the sack of Troy as an act against religious order and law. Sinon, a Greek, tells a false tale of his escape as he was about to be sacrificed by his fellow countrymen. He explicitly represents his own near-sacrifice as a repetition of the sacrifice of Iphigeneia:

> *sanguine* placastis uentos et *uirgine* caesa,
> cum primum Iliacas, *Danai*, uenistis ad oras;
> sanguine quaerendi reditus animaque litandum
> Argolica. ...                                          (2.116–19)[7]

> **You appeased the winds with the blood of a slaughtered virgin**
> when you, *Greeks*, first came to the Trojan shores;
> with blood you should seek your return and make atonement to the gods
> with a Greek life. ...

This episode, as well as Book 2 as a whole, vigorously deploys the problem of human sacrifice by appropriating the function of sacrifice in Greek tragedy. Sinon's words contain verbal contact with the *parodos* of Aeschylus' *Agamemnon*, which describes the Greek leader's internal struggle as he resolves to sacrifice his daughter Iphigeneia:

> βαρεῖα δ' εἰ τέκνον δαΐξω, δόμων ἄγαλμα,
> μιαίνων **παρθενοσφάγοισιν**
> ῥείθροις πατρῴους χέρας
> πέλας βωμοῦ ...
>
>     ...
>
> **παυσανέμου** γὰρ

---

[7] Characters in bold indicate allusions to *Agamemnon*: characters italicized indicate allusions to Lucretius.

θυσίας παρθενίου θ' αἵματος ὀργᾶι
περιόργως· ἀπὸ δ' αὐδᾶι
Θέμις...                                                                    (*Ag.* 207–17)

[My fate] is hard if I slay my child, the glory of my house,
and pollute with the streams of a **slaughtered maiden's**
**blood** the hands of the father
by the altar...

...

for [the gods] desire with great anger
to **appease the winds with a sacrifice and a virgin's**
**blood**; but Themis
forbids it.

The point of contact between the two texts appears to be the barbaric
nature of human sacrifice, which goes against normal ritual custom. The
play's *parodos*, by dramatizing Agamemnon's struggle to choose between
success in war and his daughter's life, also indicates that his choice to
sacrifice Iphigeneia is not only forbidden by what is right (Themis) but
would also inevitably cause ritual pollution (μιαίνων, 208).[8]

At the same time, the text of *Agamemnon* renders Iphigeneia's sacrifice
even more disturbing by representing it as corruption of the wedding
ritual (223–47). In the *Aeneid*, the same inversion of marriage to death
emerges through the mobilization of another allusive intertext, Lucretius'
description of the same sacrifice (Hardie 1984: 406–407):

Aulide quo pacto Triviai *virginis* aram
Iphianassai turparunt *sanguine* foede
ductores *Danaum* delecti, prima virorum.                    (Lucr. 1.84–86)

How once at Aulis the chosen leaders of the *Greeks*,
the first of men, defiled hideously the altar of Diana
with the *blood* of the *virgin* Iphigeneia.[9]

Lucretius' text focuses on the atrocity of human sacrifice used to serve
political ends in order to denounce the barbarism of *religio* and juxtapose

---

[8] On pollution, see Parker 1983, especially 104–43, and Douglas 1966.
[9] *Virginis* could modify either *Triviai* or *Iphianassai*.

it to the freedom that Epicurean thought bestows on humankind (Hardie 1993: 27). The passage conveys the gruesome atrocity of human sacrifice through verbal contact with the *parodos* of Aeschylus' *Agamemnon*:[10]

> nam **sublata** virum manibus tremibundaque ad **aras**
> deductast, non ut sollemni more sacrorum
> perfecto posset claro comitari Hymenaeo,
> sed casta inceste nubendi tempore in ipso
> hostia concideret mactatu maesta parentis,
> exitus ut classi felix faustusque daretur. (Lucr. 1.95–100)

For she was led to **the altar lifted** by the hands of men, trembling,
not so that, when the formal way of the rites was fulfilled,
she might be escorted by the clear cry of Hymenaeus,
but a pure sacrificial victim at the very moment of marriage,
she might sadly fall in sacrilege slaughtered by her father
so that an auspicious and happy departure would be granted to the fleet.

> δίκαν χιμαίρας ὕπερθε **βωμοῦ**
> πέπλοισι περιπετῆ παντὶ θυμῶι προνωπῆ
> **λαβεῖν ἀέρδην**... (*Ag.* 232–34)

Like a goat [her father ordered] that **they lift her**
above **the altar**, wrapped in her robes,
facing forward...

Lucretius appropriates Aeschylus' vivid description of Iphigeneia being raised at the altar as a young goat. The sacrificial principle of substitution is violated as human takes the place of animal offering. The most salient connective link between the two passages, however, is the exploitation of the horrible reversal of the marriage ceremony as funeral. The shedding of Iphigeneia's blood is commensurate with the act of defloration (Fowler 1987: 191). As a result, the Vergilian text, through the double (or window) allusion[11] to Aeschylus and Lucretius, brings to the

---

[10] Bailey (1947: 615) and Fowler (1987: 192) have also noted the connection between Lucretius and Aeschylus. Hardie (1984: 407 n.9) notes that Lucretius may be expanding on Aeschylus' use of the term *proteleia*. Hardie (1993: 27) argues that Lucretius has made use of Euripides' *IA*.

[11] On that type of allusion, see Nelis 2001: 5.

foreground both the heinousness of human sacrifice and the tragedy of a virgin's death, which negates the woman's transition from adolescence to adulthood.

Iphigeneia's failed initiation into adulthood is closely linked with her representation in *Agamemnon* as a preliminary offering for the eventual fall of Troy, signaled by the naming of Iphigeneia as *proteleia naon* (226). The reference to the *proteleia* – that is, preliminary sacrifices of any kind, but particularly those performed before the marriage ceremony – has particular resonance. The poet employs a word with happy and festive connotations to describe a gruesome act (Fraenkel 1950.2: 41). The young girl, instead of offering *proteleia*, has herself become *proteleia* (Zeitlin 1965: 466). The effect of the word has also been employed earlier, in the opening of the play (*Ag.* 65): the Chorus relate the pains of the war (for Greeks and Trojans alike) before the fall of Troy, since the news of the sack of the city has not yet reached Argos. In this passage too an auspicious term of sacrifice describes men slain in the battles preceding the final destruction of Troy (Zeitlin 1965: 465). The poet thus links the death of Iphigeneia with the deaths of the men at Troy as preliminaries to the "sacrifice" of Priam's city. In other words, the sacrifice of Iphigeneia is going to be repeated on a grander scale that involves the destruction of an entire city. At the same time, Iphigeneia's death is also preliminary to the series of sacrificial deaths that unfolds throughout the play. With each new death her sacrifice returns to demonstrate the perversion generated by a justice system resting on reciprocal violence as a means of retribution.

Iphigeneia's sacrifice as preliminary to that of Troy is also a major motif in the *Aeneid*. Although Sinon casts his own near-sacrifice as a repetition of the sacrifice of Iphigeneia, we eventually find out that he is a human foil to the Trojan horse, consecrated to bring destruction to the enemy. Rather, the sacrifice of Iphigeneia is repeated in the case of Laocoon and his sons. The fall of Troy constitutes a corrupted sacrifice, evident in the description of the death of Priam by his household altar, with the king symbolically standing for the city itself (2.550–58).

In Aeschylus, Iphigeneia's sacrifice is also inextricably linked with the problem of kin killing, which the trilogy explores and eventually resolves with the foundation of the first court. The problem resonates in the *Aeneid*, as the epic also proposes that the problem of civil war will permanently end with the foundation of a new order, represented by Aeneas' new settlement in Latium. The return of the sacrifice of Iphigeneia over the course of the epic relates to the problem of civil war and all that it entails. In the following sections, I will examine the contours of sacrificial perversion in the poem and its subsequent demand for restoration.

## 2. Icarus and Marcellus: Untimely Death and Parental Guilt

Sacrifice paired with the pain and guilt accompanying parental loss are themes that define the episode of Daedalus and Marcellus in Book 6. The death of Icarus may be read as a preliminary sacrifice foreshadowing that of Marcellus. The themes of perverted sacrifice and failed initiation link Daedalus' loss of his son with Augustus' loss of his heir by placing blame for the problem of generational continuity on the figure of the father.

Icarus and Marcellus frame the beginning and the ending of Book 6, both young men whose parents survived their death. The narrative of this dark and complex book begins with Daedalus' settlement in Cumae after his son's demise and the dedication of his wings to the temple of Apollo. Daedalus' loss is connected with that of Iphigeneia through a mobilization of the tragic intertext of Aeschylus' *Agamemnon*:

> redditus his primum terris tibi, Phoebe, sacrauit
> *remigium alarum* posuitque immania templa.                    (6.18–19)

> Having returned first to these lands, he consecrated to you, Phoebus,
> *the oarage of his wings* and built a great temple.

> τρόπον αἰγυπιῶν οἵτ' ἐκπατίοις ἄλγεσι παίδων
> †ὕπατοι† λεχέων στροφοδινοῦνται
> πτερύγων ἐρετμοῖσιν ἐρεσσόμενοι,
> δεμνιοτήρη πόνον ὀρταλίχων ὀλέσαντες...                    (*Ag.* 50–54)

> Like eagles, in extraordinary grief for their young,
> fly around high over their beds
> driven by *the oarage of their wings*,
> having lost their toil of guarding their nurslings' nest.

In Aeschylus, the two vultures that have lost their young and utter mourning cries stand for the Atreidae, who have lost Helen. The theft

of children and the parental cries of mourning also recall the death of
Iphigeneia. Just as Paris is guilty of stealing Helen, so Agamemnon is
guilty of the death of his daughter. By casting Agamemnon as both victim and transgressor, the simile encapsulates the paradox of right and
wrong in the play (Lebeck 1971: 8–9).

Daedalus too, like the vultures in the simile, has suffered parental loss and is partially responsible for his son's death. In Vergil, tragic
metaphor becomes actuality, as Daedalus and his son turn into birds.
Yet parental guilt comes to the foreground with the consecration of the
wings, the father's artifact that caused the son's death. Daedalus' failure
to express through his art his son's passing may be due in part to his
share of responsibility for it, a culpability that emerges through the passage's intertextual contact with the Greek play. At the same time, Icarus'
loss is the last episode in a series of images in the temple constructed by
Daedalus that tell the story of sons killed or sacrificed: the murder of
Minos' son, Androgeos; the drawing of the lot for the yearly sacrifice of
the Athenian youths as retribution for that murder; the love of Pasiphae
for the bull; the construction of the Labyrinth; and the story of Ariadne,
who fell in love with Theseus (20–30). The last three scenes depict events
resulting in the death of another "son," the Minotaur. The theme of children lost or sacrificed thus suggests that Icarus' death is a like sacrificial
offering. Moreover, the presence of the tragic intertext within this framework indicates that it is a return of the initial sacrifice of Iphigeneia. At
the same time, just as Iphigeneia's death prefigured the fall of Troy, so
the story of Icarus is preliminary to the other loss at the end of the book,
that of Marcellus.

The numerous parallels between Icarus and Marcellus have long been
noted.[12] The death of Augustus' successor constitutes yet another instance
of repetition within the framework of sacrifice just outlined. Marcellus,
who died of illness at a very young age (see also Hardie 1993: 92), claims

---

[12] See Segal 1966: 50–54. The passage also shares affinities with Pallas' portrayal;
most notably, they are both referred to as *miserande puer* (6.882 and 10.825, as
well as 11.42). See also Austin 1977: 267 on *egregius* as an epithet describing
Pallas and Lausus (10.435) as well as Turnus (7.473). For Marcellus' loss as the
failure of Augustan Rome to avert the death of the young heir, see Putnam
1995: 116, 164, 90.

a position among these virginal sacrificial deaths through his connection with Icarus (and, by extension, Iphigeneia), as well as with Pallas and Lausus, whose deaths are also cast in sacrificial terms. Ritual vocabulary of sacrifice is found in Anchises' description of him as a gift of the gods taken away too soon (*donum*, 6.871, a term indicating an offering and a sacrifice).[13] In this light, the darkness around the youth's head (6.866) that prefigures his untimely death may also be read as a mark analogous to the *uitta*, the head garland worn by animals about to be ritually slain.

Reading the death of Marcellus in the context of sacrifice is congruent with Roman notions surrounding his death, as a note by Servius (on *Aen.* 1.712) reveals. Servius tells us that in the funeral speech for his nephew, Augustus said that the young man was "devoted" to premature death (*inmaturae morti devotum fuisse*) (Hardie 1993: 29). In Roman ritual, *devotio* is the sacrifice of the leader to the gods of the Underworld so that victory may be secured. Marcellus' death, though due to illness and not the result of a military campaign, still did not prevent Augustus from painting his portrait along the lines of such hallowed Roman leaders as the Decii.

Mourning and guilt appear to cause the failure of Daedalus' art, thus rendering the consummate artist unable to express his bereavement. A father's mourning returns in the case of Marcellus, where ritual at first appears as perhaps a more successful outlet for the expression of grief: Marcellus emerges as the son of Rome, with the landscape of the city participating as a mourner in his funeral lamentations (872–74). Marcellus is also Anchises' son (*o gnate*, 868), who is thus shown to perform the ritually appropriate funerary gestures (883–86). But here too ritual fails to provide relief, as Anchises pronounces its emptiness (*inani / munere*, 885–86). The enjambment emphasizes with particular poignancy that ritual may be the only locus for the expression of grief, even if it is unable to contain it.[14]

---

[13] See OLD s.v. 2. Anchises later names the flowers he offers Marcellus *dona* (885). See also the use of *donum* as sacrifice at *Aen.* 3.439.

[14] See also Austin 1977: 273. The same word is used by Andromache to describe the cenotaph of Hector at *Aen.* 3.304. On the failure of ritual in Andromache's case, see Chapter 5, this volume, pp. 146–54.

Furthermore, as the primary mourner, Anchises assumes a role befitting a mother rather than a father. His lament, placing emphasis on death and the past, is thus incongruent with his task as Aeneas' guide to his Roman future.[15] If Anchises is relegated to the role of a motherly figure, then Augustus emerges as the sole father of the lost Marcellus, the public mourning for a leader lost thus giving way to private grief. Furthermore, the connection with Icarus intimates that responsibility for his death may lie in part with the demands of a dynastic empire.

### 3. Pallas and Mezentius: *Primitiae* as Preliminary Sacrifice

Critics have long noted the depiction of Pallas' death as marriage and defloration.[16] Building on these readings, I argue that the rich ritual symbolism surrounding his killing displays the connection between war on the battlefield and ritual perversion and prefigures the death of another "virginal" figure, that of Turnus. Like other sacrificial deaths in the poem, this one too constitutes a repetition of the earlier sacrifice of Iphigeneia in *Aeneid* 2. Allusion to Aeschylus' *Agamemnon* confirms the tragic origin of this nexus of intertextual links and reinforces the notion that the reader experiences Pallas' death as a return of the death of Iphigeneia. Aside from the motif of marriage to death that Vergil here manipulates, the ritual and allusive intertexts of this episode indicate other important implications of this death. Just as Iphigeneia's sacrifice was preliminary to the greater sacrifice of Troy, so the sacrifice of Pallas is preliminary to the greater defeat of the Latins, embodied in a series of deaths (Lausus, Mezentius), all cast as preliminary sacrifices before the killing of Turnus at the end of the poem. As a result, Turnus' death is foreshadowed in both the narrative and on the ritual plot with the expectation that it will restore the distorted ritual order.

There are both intertextual (Aeschylus) and intratextual (Vergil) points of contact between Pallas and Iphigeneia.[17] Evander's lament at

---

[15] On the mourner as linked with death and the past, see Seaford 1994: 86, 167; Van Gennep 1960: 147; and Chapter 5, this volume, pp. 146–59.

[16] Gillis 1983: 69–77; Putnam 1995: 38–41; Fowler 1987: 192, 194; Mitchell 1991: 227–30.

[17] On the term "intratextuality", see Sharrock 2000: 1–39.

the corpse of his son appropriates a passage from the *parodos* of Aeschylus'
*Agamemnon*:[18]

> primitiae iuuenis miserae bellique propinqui
> dura rudimenta, et *nulli exaudita deorum*
> *uota* precesque meae! ...                                           (11.156–58)

> Wretched first-fruits of youth and harsh initiation to
> a war so near home; and *no one of the gods listened*
> *to my vows* and prayers! ...

> λιτᾶν δ᾽ ἀκούει μὲν οὔτις θεῶν,
> τὸν δ᾽ ἐπίστροφον τῶν
> φῶτ᾽ ἄδικον καθαιρεῖ.
> οἷος καὶ Πάρις ἐλθὼν
> ἐς δόμον τὸν Ἀτρειδᾶν
> ᾔσχυνε ξενίαν τράπε-
> ζαν κλοπαῖσι γυναικός.                                              (*Ag.* 396–402)

> *No one of the gods listens to his prayers,*
> and [the god] destroys the unjust man
> who is involved in such deeds.
> Such a man was Paris, who came
> to the house of the Atreidae
> and disgraced his hosts' table
> by stealing his wife.

The gods' deaf ears to Evander's prayers are intertextually linked with
the gods' indifference to the prayers of (and indeed the destruction of)
an unjust man (φῶτ᾽ ἄδικον καθαιρεῖ, 398) such as Paris. The breakdown
in the communication between man and god as expressed by Evander is
usually the result of human transgression, as the passage in Aeschylus
clearly indicates. Evander's allusive link with Paris seems to attribute to
him some guilt over the outburst of war between Trojans and Latins,
an outburst that Juno has related to the start of the Trojan War earlier
in the book (*quae causa fuit consurgere in arma / Europamque Asiamque et
foedera soluere furto?* [what was the cause for the raising of arms / between

---

[18] Noted by Conington (1884, 3: 332).

Europe and Asia and for breaking their treaty by stealing?], 10.90–91).[19]
Juno's words also point to this passage in the Greek play, with the word
*furto* translating κλοπαῖσι.[20] As a result, this second Trojan War demands
the death of another Iphigeneia, Evander's son Pallas.

The account of Pallas' *aristeia* in Book 10 renders the necessity of his
death all the more poignant, bringing into full view the young hero's
potential as a leader on the battlefield. Like Nisus and Euryalus, however, Pallas also fails in his first foray into the world of the adult warrior.[21] The theme of failed male initiation is brought up by the narrator
(*haec te prima dies bello dedit, haec eadem aufert* [this day first gave you
to war, this same day takes you away], 10.508) and in Evander's lament
over his son's dead body (*bellique propinqui / dura rudimenta*, 11.157). The
themes of virginity, defloration, and marriage to death therefore collude
in order to render Pallas a failed bride, linking his plight with that of
Iphigeneia (Fowler 1987: 192). Pallas' feminization goes hand in hand
with the notion of sacrifice, both expressing his failure to make a successful passage into male adulthood.

Pallas is thus appropriately named *primitiae* in the passage quoted earlier. The word is normally used for the first-fruits, that is, vegetable offerings to the gods at the harvest. Here it is employed to indicate the death
of Pallas. At the same time, as a word suitable for vegetable offerings, it
also denotes the perversion of bloodless offering to human sacrifice. As
a result, Pallas' death is described in vocabulary specifically sacrificial.
Within this context, Pallas' *primitiae* harks back to Iphigeneia's *proteleia*.
That virgin's slaughter constituted a horrible perversion of wedding to
sacrifice; as we have seen, the young girl, instead of offering *proteleia*,
becomes *proteleia*; similarly, Pallas' killing is cast as a virgin's marriage

---

[19] Quint (1993: 50–96) discusses the war in Latium as a positive repetition of
the Trojan War, since the Trojans are now the winners. Juno's use of the plural
in her words describing Helen's theft as a beginning is yet another indicator
of repetition: *soceros legere et gremiis abducere pactas* [choosing fathers-in-law and
abducting betrothed girls], 10.79. For an opposing view arguing for Juno's mis-
representation of events here, see Harrison 1991: 79.

[20] See Fraenkel 1950, 2: 210 on the uniqueness of the use of the word κλοπή, and
Harrison 1991: 83.

[21] On Nisus' and Euryalus' deaths as failed initiations, see Hardie 1994: 24–29 *et
passim* and 1997b: 320–21.

to death (see note 16 to this chapter). The use of *primitiae* also suggests a perversion of normal agricultural procedures and corrupts the fertility of the earth (Lyne 1989: 160): instead of offering *primitiae*, Pallas becomes *primitiae*. In both instances, we have an inversion of the sacrificial principle of substitution: in Iphigeneia's case, human replaces animal offering; in Pallas', human replaces vegetable offering. Warfare is thus shown to pervert both the wedding ritual, with its promise of offspring and continuity, and earth's fertility. Pallas' slaying is a preliminary sacrifice, a repetition of that of Iphigeneia, and it too will generate more sacrificial deaths.

The death of Mezentius, the Etruscan leader fighting on the side of the Latins, repeats Pallas' death in its function as preliminary sacrifice to that of Turnus. This repetition attests to the persistence of the problem of ritual perversion. Pallas and Mezentius may appear unlikely partners in this, yet they embody two contradictory aspects important in the portrait of Turnus: his appearance as at once a virginal figure who fails initiation and as a seasoned warrior and opponent worthy of Aeneas.

The most salient link between Mezentius and Pallas occurs in the opening of Book 11, which picks up at the aftermath of the battle and focuses on Pallas' burial. In the first scene, Aeneas dresses a tree trunk with the spoils of Mezentius and dedicates it to Mars with the following words:

> . . . haec sunt spolia et de rege superbo
> primitiae *manibu*sque meis Mezentius *hic est*.                    (11.15–16)

> . . . These are the spoils and the first-fruits
> from a proud king and *this is* Mezentius *by my hands*.

The use of *primitiae* to describe enemy spoils points to a reversal of rituals associated with peace and war: a term connected with agriculture and fertility, as we have seen, now refers to enemy spoils dedicated to Mars (Lyne 1989: 160) and to a bloody tree trunk that stands for a human body.[22] The equation of the tree trunk with the slain Mezentius can be attributed to Roman beliefs in the animism of trees (Thomas 1988: 263)

---

[22] The description of the trophy emphasizes its relation with the actual human body. See Conington 1884, 3: 318.

and to cultic practice that sanctioned the dressing of a trunk with an enemy's weapons. Macrobius (*Sat.* 3.5.10) tells us that the reference to *primitiae* here looks back to a tradition according to which Mezentius had demanded that the Rutulians offer to him the *primitiae* destined for the gods.[23] Once the recipient of *primitiae*, he has now become *primitiae* himself (Burke 1974b: 29). Again, a word denoting a bloodless offering is used to describe a blood-spattered corpse.

The sacrificial character of the use of *primitiae* in this instance is furthered by an intertextual connection with Aeschylus' *Agamemnon*. Clytemnestra, having just killed her husband, boasts of her deed over his lifeless body:[24]

> ... οὗτός ἐστιν Ἀγαμέμνων ἐμός
> πόσις, νεκρὸς δέ, τῆσδε δεξιᾶς χερός
> ἔργον, δικαίας τέκτονος. τάδ᾽ ὧδ᾽ ἔχει.[25]              (*Ag.* 1404–406)

> ... *This is* Agamemnon my
> husband, now dead, a deed of this right *hand*,
> a just workman. So these things stand.

Clytemnestra's words replicate the epic formula proclaiming the death of the enemy in battle. The transference of the epic heroic code to a wife's gloating over her husband's murder makes the moment particularly horrific. The allusion casts Aeneas' epic boast in a new light as it equates the tree trunk that stands for Mezentius with the lifeless body of the murdered Agamemnon. Aeneas' claim of responsibility for the death and

---

[23] Macrobius informs us that the tradition goes back to Cato's *Orig.* 1: *ait enim Mezentium Rutulis imperasse ut sibi offerrent quas dis primitias offerebant, et Latinos omnes similis imperii metu ita vovisse: 'Iuppiter, si tibi magis cordi est nos ea tibi dare potius quam Mezentium uti nos victores facias.' ergo quod divinos honores sibi exegerat, merito dictus a Vergilio contemptor deorum* [for he says that Mezentius ordered the Rutulians to offer to himself the first-fruits they used to offer to the gods and that all the Latins, out of fear of a like command, said the following prayer: "Jupiter, if your heart desires that we make these offerings to you rather than Mezentius, make us the winners." So because he demanded divine offerings for himself, Vergil deservedly calls him despiser of the gods]. See also Burke 1974b: 29 and Gottoff 1984: 196.

[24] Noted by Conington 1884, 3: 319.

[25] Characters in italics indicate allusions; characters in dotted underline denote textual equivalents.

despoliation of his foe (*manibusque meis Mezentius hic est*, 11.16), a claim appropriate to the heroic code in battle, is implicitly associated with killing a member of one's own family. The casting of Aeneas' killing in battle as a murder within the family is also congruent with the epic's consistent depiction of the war in Latium as civil war.

The allusion to Clytemnestra's words also broadens the sacrificial implications of Aeneas' use of the term *primitiae*. Throughout the play, and particularly in the speech preceding these words, Clytemnestra's murderous act is depicted as a perverted sacrifice. Images of perversion in the realm of agriculture follow Clytemnestra's description of ritual distortion, when she declares that in being sprinkled with her husband's blood she rejoiced like corn rejoices in the gift of Zeus' rain at the birth time of the buds (1389–92).[26] Likewise in the *Aeneid*, perversion of ritual (*primitiae* used to describe a tree trunk symbolizing a human body) and perversion of agriculture render Mezentius' death yet another instance of repeated sacrificial corruption.[27]

In this light, Aeneas' performance of human sacrifice is different from its Homeric counterpart, where human sacrifice threatens but does not ultimately pervert the ritual order (*Il.* 21.27–28). In the *Aeneid*, by contrast, the distortion of the ritual order underlies actions occurring on the battlefield. Upon learning the news of Pallas' death, Aeneas captures eight Rutulians to be slain on Pallas' pyre (10.518–20) and enters battle himself on a killing rampage, mercilessly slaughtering (among numerous others) a suppliant (Magus), a priest of Apollo, and a son of Faunus.[28]

---

[26] The theme of nature's perversion is continued in the Chorus's response to the queen (1407–408). See Conacher 1987: 54. On the perversion of agriculture, marriage, and sacrifice in this instance, see also Goff 2004: 310.

[27] The sacrificial nature of the death of Mezentius is also noted by Leigh (1993: 95–101), who reads him as a *devotus*.

[28] The first killing (536) resembles Achilles' killing of Lycaon in *Il.* 21.34–135, and, as Harrison (1991: 207) has pointed out, it also alludes to that of Priam. The second killing of the priest is Vergil's addition. The vocabulary is strongly sacrificial. Vergil once again makes use of the motif of the priest/sacrificer turned into the sacrificed (see also Hardie 1984: 408 n.12): *Haemonides, Phoebi Triuiaeque sacerdos, / infula cui sacra redimibat tempora uitta, / ... / quem ... / immolat* [Haemon's son, priest of Phoebus and Trivia, his temples crowned by the sacred headband, .... him ... [Aeneas] sacrificed], 537–41. The use of *immolare* is particularly poignant (see Putnam 1994: 185–86). See also Dyson 2001: 186.

As Aeneas' human captives are about to be slain, the narrator emphasizes the violations of proper sacrificial ritual:

> uinxerat et post terga manus, quos mitteret umbris
> inferias, caeso sparsurus sanguine flammas,
> indutosque iubet truncos hostilibus armis
> ipsos ferre duces inimicaque nomina figi.                    (11.81–84)

> And he tied behind their backs the hands of those he would send to the
>     shades
> as funeral offerings, about to sprinkle the flames with slaughtered blood
> and he bids the chiefs themselves carry trunks clothed
> in enemy's weapons with the foes' names attached.

Both the use of the word *inferias* to indicate human offerings and the
sprinkling of the funeral flames with blood are inconsistent with regular
funerary ritual (see Toynbee 1971: 50). Ritual perversion is once again
found side by side with the appearance of *tropaea*,[29] providing yet another
link between human sacrifice and Mezentius' transformation into a *tropaeum*. The practice of dedicating *tropaea*, though ritually correct by
itself, follows the atrocious act of human sacrifice. As in the earlier case
of Mezentius, the animism of tree trunks symbolically casts them as victims comparable to those sacrificed at Pallas' funeral pyre.[30]

---

[29] Dyson (2001: 186–87) demonstrates the connections between sacrificed humans
and *tropaea* as foreshadowing the eventual killing of Turnus.

[30] Another link between the killings of Pallas, Lausus, and Mezentius is visible in
Vergil's use of sexual imagery in the battle narrative. When Aeneas prepares to
give Mezentius the final blow with his sword, the vocabulary recalls the "sexualized" encounter between Turnus and Pallas: 10.896 alludes to 10.475 (and
also to 4.579). So the image of Pallas' "defloration" spills over to Aeneas' killing of Mezentius. The vocabulary of penetration is present in the description
of Mezentius' spoils in the next book as well (11.8–10). The use of sexualized
vocabulary is indicative of the close affinity between the themes of virginity
and sacrifice in the book. The possibility of such a reading in this instance may
be bolstered if we compare Ovid's manipulation of the same phrase (*vagina lib-
erat ensem*, *Met.* 6.551) as Tereus prepares to cut off Philomela's tongue after rap-
ing her. The same phrase recurs at *Fasti* 2.793 right before Lucretia's rape. For
the significance of this use, see Raval (1998: 122–26), to whom I am grateful for
these parallels. See also Richlin 1992: 163.

The designation of Pallas and Mezentius as *primitiae* is related to the issue of sacrificial perversion, as their deaths both constitute preliminary sacrifices for the eventual death of Turnus.[31] In imagining Turnus as a *tropaeum* of Pallas (11.173), Evander's lament provides a connective thread between Pallas and Mezentius.[32] The linkage of these two disparate figures may be explained if we read them as embodying different and even conflicting aspects of Turnus' character. At the moment of death, Turnus' baldric assimilates Pallas' feminine virginity (Mitchell 1991: 230). And just as proud Mezentius undergoes a profound change after the death of his son,[33] Turnus too is a hero violent and proud, yet he too elicits the reader's sympathy at the moment of his final humiliation and defeat.

## IV. CRIME AND RETRIBUTION

The theme of crime and retribution is paramount in the deployment of the sacrificial intertext of the poem. A series of sacrificial deaths illustrates the problem of justice and appropriate punishment in the new order that Aeneas represents. As Aeneas' journey progresses, so does his quest for a system that will guarantee the dispensation of justice in his new-found city. The problem of ritual perversion and of sacrifice in particular illustrates the obstacles inherent in an order that rests in the hands of one individual. Aeschylus' *Oresteia* explores the same problem through the theme of kin killing and proposes as a solution the foundation of the first court – that is, the transference of dispensation of justice from the *oikos* to the institutions of the *polis*. The *Aeneid*, on the other hand, as Hardie has noted (1997b: 317), seeks to reassure the war-torn Romans that where the institutions of the Republic failed, monarchy will succeed.

---

[31] Commentators have been puzzled over the problem of offering *primitiae* after three books of war: "... the offering is here to Mars, as [Aeneas] himself admits, and there is no reason to suppose any direct reference to 'spolia opima,' which could not be won from Mezentius, as he was not the real leader of the enemy" (Connington 1884, 3: 318).

[32] Dyson (2001: 193) argues that Evander's wish comes true, as Turnus, clothed in the spoils of Pallas, becomes a living *tropaeum*.

[33] Putnam 1995: 146. On the "transformation" of Mezentius, see Burke 1974a: 201–209 and Gotoff 1984: 191–218. See also Leach 1971: 86–87.

Within this context, the motif of perverted sacrifice is deployed in order to highlight the problem of crime and just retribution. Intertextual appropriations of the *Oresteia* surface once again within the text of the *Aeneid* and bring into sharp relief the problem of repeated sacrificial perversion and the need for ritual restoration. As was the case with the preliminary sacrifices, the ritual intertext is again marked by corruption that requires ritual purity and restoration. In what follows, I discuss the sacrificial deaths of a number of figures closely linked with crime and punishment, either as blatantly criminal acts calling for retribution or as acts of retribution as atrocious as the crime itself. The deaths of Sychaeus and Lausus are examples of the former, the death of Pyrrhus and the near-death of Helen of the latter.

## 1. Crime: Sychaeus and Lausus

The murder of Dido's husband, Sychaeus, is the first in the poem's series of murders, atrocious crimes demanding retribution, which are represented as perverted sacrifices. The theme of sacrifice in this instance explores the problem of justice within the context of domestic and civil strife. Moreover, these deaths contain intertextual and intratextual appropriations, thus mobilizing the motif of repeated sacrificial distortion in demand of purity and restoration.

The first victim of perverted sacrifice appears in Book 1, where Venus tells Aeneas Dido's troubled story: the queen's husband, Sychaeus, was murdered by her brother, Pygmalion:

> quos inter medius uenit furor. ille Sychaeum
> impius ante aras atque auri caecus amore
> clam ferro incautum superat, securus amorum
> germanae; . . .                                                    (1.348–51)

> Among them [Pygmalion and Sychaeus] fury came about. The former,
> against all piety and blinded by love of gold, secretly murdered
> with the sword unsuspecting Sychaeus by the altar, indifferent to his sister's
> love; . . .

Though this occurrence of domestic strife concerns Carthage, it is also paradigmatic for Aeneas' future course of action in Latium. Book 1 takes great pains to highlight the similarities between Dido and Aeneas as leaders; therefore, the fate of Tyre invites comparisons to that of Troy. Dido's just leadership in the new city offers Aeneas a model of governance. The use of the word *furor* to describe Tyre's political tribulations also has obvious resonance for Aeneas, since the same word describes civil strife throughout the poem. As a result, the reciprocal violence between Sychaeus and Pygmalion should be viewed within the context of violence among kin, a central issue in the poem as a whole. Furthermore, in this case too, as in Greek tragedy and throughout the *Aeneid*, the killing of kin begets sacrificial perversion. Pygmalion's murder of his brother-in-law at the altar, the first corrupted sacrifice in the poem, has a programmatic function and calls attention to the problem of retribution. Dido punishes her brother by leaving, carrying with her the gold that Sychaeus had hidden from Pygmalion. Like Aeneas after the fall of Troy, she founds a new city. In her dying words, Dido refers to her punishment of her brother as one of her life's accomplishments (*ulta uirum poenas inimico a fratre recepi* [I avenged my husband by punishing my brother who is my foe], 4.656). Dido thus avoids the continuation of sacrificial perversion and civil strife by removing herself from Tyre (she may be said to act as a Girardian scapegoat)[34] and by founding a new community where justice is paramount and where the danger of civil conflict is averted.

The poem's emphasis on Dido's heightened sense of justice can be seen in her first appearance in the epic, where she is in the process of giving laws and assigning tasks:

> iura dabat legesque uiris, operumque laborem
> partibus aequabat iustis aut sorte trahebat:          (1.507–508)

> She was giving laws to her men, and was assigning
> the labor of the tasks in equal shares or by drawing lots:

Dido's highly successful way of dealing with crime while avoiding the sacrilege of retribution sets up a model of leadership for Aeneas, which he fails to

---

[34] Reading Dido as a scapegoat in this instance may explain her paradoxical likening to Diana, the virgin huntress, in her first appearance in the poem (1.498–502). In addition, the imagery of virginity suggests that she too, like Nausicaa in the *Odyssey* and Medea in the *Argonautica*, is destined to fall in love with the hero of the poem.

heed. By contrast, the heroic code by which our hero abides dictates the use of violent retribution, whereby sacrificial perversion proliferates. At the same time, Dido's solution to the problem of retribution creates the expectation that sacrificial repetition will eventually provide restoration and closure.

Pygmalion's murder of Sychaeus resurfaces in Aeneas' killing of Lausus in Book 10, thus raising the problems of *pietas*, sacrilege, and justice in times of civil war. After Juno removes Turnus from the battlefield, the Etruscan Mezentius replaces him as leader of the Latins. A bitter fight ensues. When Mezentius is wounded by Aeneas, his son Lausus runs to his aid and loses his life. At the moment of Lausus' death, Aeneas pauses, moved by the young man's filial piety:

> at uero ut uultum uidit morientis et *ora*,
> *ora modis* Anchisiades *pallentia miris*,
> ingemuit miserans grauiter dextramque tetendit,
> et mentem patriae subiit pietatis *imago*.                          (10.821–24)

> But when the son of Anchises saw the dying boy's look
> and his *face*, his *face pale in wondrous ways*,
> he heaved a deep sigh in pity and stretched out his right hand,
> and the *image* of paternal piousness entered his mind.

The scene is rich in implications for Aeneas' role as a son and a symbol of *pietas*.[35] The lines also evoke the language describing the dead Sychaeus, whose killing was the first corrupted sacrifice in the epic:

> ipsa sed in somnis inhumati uenit *imago*
> coniugis *ora modis* attollens *pallida miris*;
> crudelis aras traiectaque pectora ferro
> nudauit, caecumque domus scelus omne retexit.                       (1.353–56)

> But in her sleep came the very *image* of her unburied
> husband, lifting up to her his *face pale in wondrous ways*;
> he laid bare the atrocious altar and his breast pierced
> with the sword and uncovered all of the secret crime of the house.

[35] On Aeneas' *pietas* and the killing of Lausus, see Johnson 1976: 72–74 and Putnam 1995: 134–51. For an opposing view, see Lee 1979: 89–93. The phrase *pietatis imago* also invites comparison with Nisus and Euryalus (9.294), as well as the detail of the tunic (cp. 10.818–19 and 9.488–89) a few lines above.

Like Sychaeus (1.350), Lausus too is unsuspecting (*incautus*, 10.812).
But while in Book 1 the apparition of the ghost of Sychaeus reveals to
Dido the atrocity of a crime, in Book 10 the sight of Lausus' lifeless face
reveals to Aeneas that in the heat of the battle he has destroyed a symbol of *pietas* and thus violated the very quality that defines his person.
Lausus reminds Aeneas of the function of *pietas*, which normally saves,
not takes, lives (Putnam 1995: 135). Furthermore, Aeneas' association
with Pygmalion, the perpetrator of Sychaeus' atrocious murder and a figure embodying the opposite of *pietas* (*impius Pygmalion*, 1.349), implicitly casts Lausus' death as sacrificial and locates the motif of crime and
punishment within the context of sacrificial perversion. The connection
between Lausus' death and that of Sychaeus represents this battle as civil
conflict.

The sacrificial character of Lausus' slaughter and the theme of crime
and retribution are also put to work through intertextual and intratextual contact with the death of Priam. The description of Lausus' dead
body rests on the detail of his hair, now defiled by blood (***sanguine***
***turpantem*** *comptos de more capillos* [**defiling with blood** his hair neatly
arranged], 10.832) which points to the death of Priam as described in
Ennius' *Andromacha*:[36]

> haec omnia uidi inflammari,
> Priamo ui uitam euitari,
> Iouis *aram* **sanguine turpari**.                              (91–94 *Jocelyn*)

> I saw everything in flames
> Priam losing violently his life,
> the *altar* of Jupiter **defiled with his blood**.

In Priam's case the spilling of his blood creates pollution: proper sacrificial procedure prescribes that the blood of the sacrificial victim be col-
lected in a vessel by the officiating priest and then spilled over the altar.[37]
The perversion of ritual incurred through the dirtying of the altar in the
death of Priam has no precedent in Euripides and thus appears particu-

---

[36] Bold characters indicate intertextual links between *Aen.* 10, Ennius, and
Lucretius; characters in italics indicate intertextual contact between Ennius and
Lucretius.

[37] *Jocelyn* 251; cf. also Aesch., *Sept.* 275; Eur., *Ion* 1126–27.

lar to Ennius.[38] *Jocelyn* (252) rightly suggests that Ennius introduces the detail of sacrificial pollution in order to arouse Roman religious sensibility. The allusion has important implications: it casts Aeneas as a double of yet another transgressor, Pyrrhus, who also killed a son (Polites) in the sight of his father (*patrios foedasti funere uultus* [you defiled the father's sight with his son's death], 2.539). Lausus' death is implicitly cast as a corrupted sacrifice similar to that of Priam.

The allusion to Ennius also recalls Vergil's description of the death of Priam at the altar (2.550–53). In the *Aeneid*, the death of the king of Troy is explicitly linked with the theme of crime and retribution: Pyrrhus' sacrilegious behavior is contrasted with that of his father, who respected Priam's supplication and averted sacrificial perversion by granting Hector burial. In his dying words, Priam curses Pyrrhus to find punishment for his crimes, a punishment that eventually comes, as we learn from Andromache in Book 3 (330–32). As a result, Lausus' death in this case too is cast as a crime that requires retribution and restoration of the ritual purity. Aeneas' share of responsibility in the creation of sacrificial perversion demonstrates the inadequacy of violence to resolve conflict, as it is able to transform a hero from a symbol of *pietas* to an architect of atrocious crimes.

Further intertextual borrowing intimately links Lausus' fate to that of Iphigeneia and, by extension, to the major problem of repeated sacrifice of virgins in the poem. Lausus' bloodied hair evokes the sacrifice of Iphigeneia in Lucretius:

> Aulide quo pacto Triviai virginis *aram*
> Iphianassai **turparunt sanguine** foede.                                    (1.84–85)

> How once at Aulis [the Greeks] **defiled** hideously
> the *altar* of Diana **with the blood** of virgin Iphigeneia.

Iphigeneia's death not only underscores the notion that the theme of sacrificial perversion is here at work but also places emphasis on the guilt of the perpetrator of the sacrilegious act. Though the Vergilian text alludes to Lucretius' version of the virgin's sacrifice, its close affinity with Vergil's own rendition of Iphigeneia's death in Book 2 and with that in Aeschylus'

---

[38] Cf. Eur., *Hec.* 21–24; *Tro.* 16–17 and 481–83.

*Agamemnon* allows a consideration of the death of Lausus through the issues that preoccupy Vergil's and Aeschylus' texts. Aeneas' responsibility for Lausus' death may thus be said to be comparable to that of Agamemnon. Aeneas' disregard for his role as a father and son in the heat of the battle is analogous to Agamemnon's disregard for his role as a father in his desire for political and military gain. Aeneas' words of consolation to Lausus, that he fell at the hands of a great enemy (himself) (10.829–30), testify to the fact that he places greater emphasis on his role as a warrior even as he realizes Lausus' extraordinary *pietas* as a son. Aeneas' act, then, is implicitly cast in multiple ways as one crime in a long list of repeated perverted sacrifices. It remains to examine the workings of retribution that have the potential to allow ritual correctness to occur.

## 2. Retribution: Pyrrhus and Helen

The problem of violent retribution, a central preoccupation within the poem, is discernible in the case of the death of Pyrrhus, about which the reader is informed in Book 3. When Aeneas arrives at Buthrotum, he meets Andromache pouring libations at the cenotaphs of Hector and Astyanax. The Trojan woman recounts the fate of her late husband Pyrrhus:

> ast illum ereptae magno flammatus amore
> coniugis et scelerum furiis agitatus Orestes
> excipit incautum *patrias*que obtruncat ad *aras*.      (3.330–32)

> But Orestes, incensed by great love for his stolen
> wife and driven by the furies punishing crimes
> caught him unsuspecting and murdered him at his *father's altar*.

Pyrrhus' death at an altar replicates his slaying of King Priam, thus fulfilling the king's dying wish for retribution:

> at tibi pro scelere,' exclamat, 'pro talibus ausis
> di, si qua est caelo pietas quae talia curet,
> persoluant grates dignas et praemia reddant
> debita...'      (2.535–58)

> But, he shouted, "in return for such a crime, for such deeds,
> if there's in heaven any piousness that cares for such things,

may the gods repay you with worthy thanks and return the rewards
that are your due..."

The language of exchange places great emphasis on Pyrrhus' death as
punishment for his atrocity against Priam. The exactness of the retribution is rendered even more explicit in the almost identical repetition of
line 2.663 (*patrem qui obtruncat ad aras*) in 3.332 (*patriasque obtruncat ad
aras*; see also Austin 1964: 250). At the same time, the use of the adjective *incautum* (3.330) evokes Sychaeus' murder at the altar (1.350), which
now stresses the sacrilegious nature of Pyrrhus' murder. The perpetrator
of perverted sacrifice dies like a sacrificial victim, at the altar, in a place
of worship (Delphi).[39] The theme of sacrificial perversion thus continues, and, even as justice appears to have been served, ritual purity is not
restored.

The description of Pyrrhus' death appropriates Euripides' dramatization of the death of Pyrrhus/Neoptolemus in *Andromache*, a play important in *Aeneid* 3. Neoptolemus is the first war criminal; in addition to
Priam's killing, he is credited with a host of other murders, including the hurling of Astyanax over the walls of Troy and the sacrifice of
Polyxena. Euripides' play, however, is silent about Neoptolemus' culpability (Allan 2000: 26). On the contrary, Orestes' involvement with his
death at Delphi and the depiction of his murder as an act of cowardice
seem Euripidean inventions. *Andromache* thus highlights the troubling
aspects of the revenge taken by Apollo, who wanted Neoptolemus' death
because he was offended by Priam's murder at the altar (Allan 2000:
28–30). Neoptolemus is portrayed as an ambushed victim, dying at the
altar like a sacrificial animal.

Vergil mobilizes the intertext of this particular version of Pyrrhus'
death and attributes to Orestes two motives. Of these, Orestes' jealousy
over Pyrrhus' marriage to Hermione is petty; the other, however, is seriously disturbing: Orestes is said to be driven by Furies (*furiis agitatus*), an
image recalling his representation at the famous tragic simile in *Aeneid* 4
linking him explicitly to the matricide (471–73),[40] Aeschylus' *Choephoroi*

---

[39] On the problem of *patrias aras*, see Williams 1962: 125.

[40] Mynors does not capitalize *furiis*. Nor does Williams (1962: 124–25), although
he notes that "the story of the avenging Furies in Aesch. *Eum.* is present as an
overtone."

(1048–1062), and Euripides' *Orestes* (36–38). The text's emphasis on Orestes' state as fresh from the matricide problematizes his killing of Pyrrhus in a manner similar to the *Oresteia*'s dramatization of the quest for retribution and a viable system of justice.[41] In Aeschylus' play, both Agamemnon's guilt and the problematic nature of Orestes' revenge are paramount for the development of the trilogy.[42] Similarly, in the *Aeneid*, both Pyrrhus' atrocity and his punishment are cast as perverted sacrifices and thus amount to further delays on the path toward ritual restoration.

The issue of retribution as a crime-upon-crime first surfaces in Book 2 when Aeneas feels the urge to kill Helen. Had he done so, he would have committed human sacrifice, since the woman, hidden in the temple of Vesta, was sitting at the altar (*abdiderat sese atque aris inuisa sedebat*, [she had hidden herself and was sitting invisible at the altar], 574). Aeneas, though overcome by anger for his fallen city (577–87), appears sane enough to be aware of the sacrilegious nature of the action he contemplates: *exarsere ignes animo; subit ira cadentem / ulcisci patriam et* sceleratas *sumere* **poenas** [fire burned in my heart; anger came over me to avenge my falling city and to exact **punishment** with a crime] (575–76). Aeneas' startling use of the word *sceleratas* reflects his recognition of the problems arising from this type of retribution.[43] The killing of Helen would replicate the murder of Priam (Reckford 1981: 88) and would thus constitute a similar act of sacrificial perversion.

---

[41] The phrase *patrias aras* contains allusion to *Ag.* 1277, where Cassandra refers to her death at her father's altars (βωμοῦ πατρώιου) while she contemplates her impending death and predicts Clytemnestra's own death at the hands of Orestes. Zeitlin (1965: 471) suggests that the words may recall at once the sacrificial killing of Iphigeneia by her father and the tradition of Priam's death at the altar. A similar argument can be made for this instance in the *Aeneid*. Pyrrhus' death thus mobilizes the network of repeated sacrifices in the poem.

[42] It should also be noted that Agamemnon's guilt is directly linked to the atrocities the Greeks committed at Troy (Lebeck 1971: 37–46; Conacher 1987: 7–16, 23–28). So the parallel between him and Pyrrhus is quite exact.

[43] I read *sceleratas* as meaning "sinful, atrocious." *OLD* s.v. 3b gives "app. of punishment inflicted on the guilty." However, the *OLD* offers only the present passage as evidence for the existence of this meaning. C. Day Lewis's translation is in agreement with my reading: "punish her crime by a crime upon her." See also Reckford 1981: 87.

Aeneas' subsequent inner monologue incites him to go through with his impulse, his reasoning proclaiming the punishment just and deserving: *et sumpsisse* merentis / *laudabor* **poenas** [I shall be praised to have exacted deserving **punishment**] (585–86).[44] Aeneas' desire to kill Helen recalls Orestes' plan to kill Helen in Euripides' *Orestes* (Reckford 1981: 90–93). In the play, Orestes' action is presented as a repetition of the killing of his mother (Reckford 1981: 92). Aeneas' association with Orestes exemplifies the problematic nature of violent retribution. Venus' intervention, which alone saves Aeneas from becoming another Pyrrhus, or another Orestes, also serves to reinforce the need for a different way of dispensing justice that promotes rather than undermines ritual purity.

Perverted sacrifices thus constitute delays in the ritual plot's move-ment toward closure, which intensify the expectation for restoration. Each sacrificial repetition is part of a dynamic space of a ritual text, where interconnections of events are illuminated and provide the reader with a compass with which both the narrative and the ritual texts may be navi-gated. The *Aeneid* appropriates and manipulates the tragic pattern of sac-rificial corruption and purity so as to render the eventual restoration of the disrupted religious order even more effective. In other words, on the level of the ritual plot, as in the narrative plot, Aeneas and his Trojans are promised to be hailed as proponents of a new and enlightened system of justice and of a new and enlightened system of governance. Sacrificial corruption is synonymous with the ailments of the previous religious and political order, which Aeneas (and his successor Augustus) will restore to its rightful and deserving place. An examination of the deaths of Dido and Turnus in the following chapter will demonstrate, however, that, at least in the ritual plot, sacrificial perversion persists, sacrifice fails in its mission to guarantee the proper communication between human and divine, and Aeneas' new system of justice proves unable to restore the desired ritual purity.

---

[44] I read *merentis* as accusative plural. On the possibility of *merentis* as genitive sin-gular and the grammatical difficulties involved, see Austin 1964: 227.

# 2 Suicide, *Devotio*, and Ritual Closure

THIS CHAPTER FOCUSES ON THE DEATHS OF DIDO AND TURNUS.
I treat these figures separately because of their paramount importance
for the development of both the narrative and the ritual plot. Moreover,
they share a key ritual link, which rests mainly on their association with
the specifically Roman rite of *devotio*. Dido performs a complicated ritual
that, among other things, includes elements akin to the *devotio*, while
Turnus is the victim of a distorted *devotio*. Dido's suicide may thus be
read as a perverted sacrifice that creates the expectation of ritual purity,
an expectation that Turnus' death promises but eventually fails to fulfill. As a result, the tragic pattern of sacrificial perversion is also at work
in the case of these two heroes but is ultimately transformed because it
does not lead to restoration. The chapter ends with a consideration of the
concept of closure as it pertains to the ritual plot and its impact on the
poem's narrative ending.

## I. DIDO'S RITUAL SLAUGHTER

The rituals that Dido performs in Book 4 occur in a discernible pattern, so that one may speak of a ritual plot existing side by side with
the narrative plot. Unlike the other sacrifices examined, which mostly
consist of sacrificial symbolism or adopt sacrifice as a metaphor, Dido's
sacrifices are part of the fabric of the narrative. As a result, ritual and
narrative plot merge in the scene of the supernatural wedding and in
Dido's death on the pyre. In all other instances, the ritual plot flanks
the movement of the narrative: Dido's decision to pursue a union with

Aeneas is followed by her ritual of extispicy and the long description of the magic ritual leading to her death on the pyre is preceded by the appearance of portents connected with ritual corruption. In addition to the incongruency between actual ritual practice and its representation in the Dido episode, there is a further incongruency at work, since the outcome of the narrative is at odds with the outcome of the ritual plot. In the narrative, Aeneas' departure is divinely inspired and sanctioned. Similarly, Dido's curse and death provide a mythological *aition* for the enmity between Romans and Carthaginians, while the reader knows all along that Rome will eventually triumph over Carthage. On the ritual level, however, Dido's death is cast as a human sacrifice, and the ritual perversion culminating in her slaughter is never restored to ritual correctness. This paradox between the narrative resolution and the lack thereof in ritual prefigures further perversion, conflict, and violence, as is evident from other instances of ritual corruption later in the poem, most significantly, the "sacrifice" of Turnus.

Book 4 begins with Dido's moral conflict over her love for Aeneas and her loyalty to her dead husband, Sychaeus. Anna immediately realizes that a match between Aeneas and her sister is politically expedient. Her speech convincingly demonstrates to both Dido and the reader that the queen's erotic attachment to the Trojan hero is closely interwoven with concerns of public welfare and policy (39–49; Monti 1981: 30). The ceremony she undertakes is motivated by her desire for a marriage but is also consistent with the practice of Roman public figures about to embark on an undertaking of national consequence:[1] Dido, encouraged by Anna, proceeds to perform sacrifice and extispicy, as Roman religious custom prescribed.[2] This ritual practice was part of a proper formal wedding, and as such it triggers the ritual plot:

> principio delubra adeunt pacemque per aras
> exquirunt; mactant lectas de more bidentis
> legiferae Cereri Phoeboque patrique Lyaeo,

---

[1] Monti 1981: 106 n.28. He also notes that the gods invoked by Dido in this sacrifice are especially connected to the prosperity of her city (31). O' Hara (1993: 108 n.23) compares Dido's divination with that of Decius Mus before his *devotio* (Livy 8.9.1).

[2] See Austin 1955: 41; Treggiari 1991: 164.

Iunoni ante omnis, cui uincla iugalia curae.
ipsa tenens dextra pateram pulcherrima Dido
candentis uaccae media inter cornua fundit,
aut ante ora deum pinguis spatiatur ad aras,
instauratque diem donis, pecudumque reclusis
pectoribus inhians spirantia consulit exta.
heu, uatum ignarae mentes! quid uota furentem,
quid delubra iuuant? . . .                                                   (4.56–66)

First they visit the shrines and ask for peace
at every altar: according to custom they sacrifice chosen sheep
to Ceres, giver of laws, to Phoebus, and to father Lyaeus,
to Juno, above all, under whose care are the bonds of marriage.
Dido herself, most beautiful, holding a chalice in her right hand,
pours libations between the horns of a white heifer,
or, with the gods looking on, moves slowly by the rich altars
and daily renews the offerings, and, poring over the victims'
opened bodies, consults the pulsing entrails.
Alas, how ignorant the minds of the prophets! Of what avail are vows
or shrines to one who is frenzied? . . .

Ceremonial attention to detail ensures the correctness of the procedure (*de more*). Yet the passage, instead of conveying the soothing solace of divine accord, generates a feeling of uneasiness and foreboding, as the conclusion to Dido's ceremony contains an authorial comment that casts serious doubt on the efficacy of this carefully executed ritual. The outcome of the extispicy is suppressed and dismissed as irrelevant:[3] Dido has already fallen prey to her consuming passion, eloquently illustrated in the empathetic image of the queen as a wounded doe following the divination scene. Perhaps a reference to the outcome of the ritual is not necessary. The reader knows that the ritual extispicy foretells Dido's own death at the pyre, as the ensuing simile of the wounded doe makes plain. The Roman reader also knows that Dido's participation in the performance of the ceremony would render it abortive, since her decision to

---

[3] O'Hara (1993: 112) argues that the syntactical difficulty of the phrase *uatum ignarae mentes* reflects the difficulty that both Dido and the reader have in interpreting the language of the entrails.

seek the auspices for a second marriage in effect constitutes a violation of her oath to Sychaeus. Her identification as *furens* further betrays her unsuitability for conducting any ritual procedure, since in actual practice it is precisely this kind of problematic element that the *uates*, as the intermediary between human and divine, is supposed to eliminate by keeping the sacred separate from the profane. Dido's inability to interpret the extispicy correctly does not preclude the reader's ability to guess the outcome correctly. The incongruency between Dido's ability to interpret the will of the divine and that of the reader displays the problematic nature of divine and human communication in this instance in the narrative.

The ensuing wedding ceremony between Dido and Aeneas enacted by supernatural forces also imparts an unnerving sentiment despite its ritual correctness (Austin 1955: 69):

> speluncam Dido dux et Troianus eandem
> deueniunt. prima et Tellus et pronuba Iuno
> dant signum; fulsere ignes et conscius aether
> conubiis summoque ulularunt uertice Nymphae.
> ille dies primus leti primusque malorum
> causa fuit; neque enim specie famaue mouetur
> nec iam furtiuum Dido meditatur amorem:
> coniugium uocat, hoc praetexit nomine culpam.                    (4.165–72)

> Now Dido and the Trojan leader arrive in the same
> cave. Primal Earth and Iuno as *pronuba*
> give the signal; fires flashed and sky was the witness
> to the wedding and the Nymphs on the mountaintop cried out.
> That day was the first cause of death and the first of
> evils; for Dido is not moved by appearance or reputation,
> no longer does she contemplate a secret love:
> marriage she calls it, with this name she veils her sin.

Once again, attention to detail is instrumental in generating maximum ritual effect: *Tellus* represents the bread of the marriage rite; the *pronuba* Juno is the matron who presides over the ceremony; the *ignes* stand for the marriage torches; the air is a witness (*conscius*; Austin 1955: 69); *conubium* is the legal term for marriage (Treggiari 1991: 43). The Nymphs' cry corresponds to the wedding song, although the verb employed, *ulu-lare*, ominously suggests a rather different ritual context.[4] The narrator declares that this is a wedding in name only, but a wedding his readers have witnessed nonetheless. The stark incongruity between this fictional representation of a wedding rite and the actual ceremony heightens the paradox of a bond that the gods are shown to abet yet that is doomed to be dissolved by the demanding forces of destiny. Ritual representation is put to work here to underscore the uneasiness imparted by the narrative. Viewed in conjunction with the previous ritual, it confirms what the extispicy merely implied: that this supernatural rite constitutes ritual distortion.

When Dido realizes the inevitability of Aeneas' departure, she turns once again to the divine. As her end draws nearer, anomaly is intimated in the results of the ritual:

> quo magis inceptum peragat lucemque relinquat,
> uidit, turicremis cum dona imponeret aris,
> (horrendum dictu) latices nigrescere sacros
> fusaque in obscenum se uertere uina cruorem;...        (4.452–55)

> And so that she may complete what she has started and leave the light,
> she saw, as she placed gifts on the incense-burning altars,
> (horrible to relate) the holy water turn black
> and the wine she poured change in polluting blood;...

At first glance, the ominous outcome of this divination appears to contrast with the analogous ritual at the opening of the book. Yet a more careful examination reveals that this is a perverted version of Dido's opening ritual: here too the queen herself makes wine (among other) offerings at the altars. The use of the word *inceptum* suggests that the similarity of the two ritual descriptions is too close to be entirely fortuitous. Scholars interpret the word to refer to Dido's resolve to die and explain the following phrase, *lucemque relinquat*, as an amplification of the first (Austin 1955: 452). Rather than explaining away a somewhat compressed phrase by positing a tautology, I would like to suggest that

---

[4] Austin 1955: 69. See also Hardie (1993: 90), who characterizes the wedding as elemental and a demonic parody of the Roman wedding ceremony.

we read *inceptum* as referring to the preliminary extispicy whose outcome was suppressed and, by extention, to the wedding itself. Dido refers to her union with Aeneas as *inceptos hymenaeos* (316). In view of this reading, Dido's proposal to complete what she has begun (i.e., the ritual sacrifices) also suggests that the *telos* of the rites lies beyond the immediate context, in the future, where the sacrificial victim will be the queen herself. At the same time, we can trace the progression of the ritual plot, in which the initial correct ritual, however uneasy, is inverted to become a ritual marked by full corruption. The portents accompanying this description (457–65) also indicate that malevolent forces are at work. The benign and beneficial ritual sacrifice and extispicy fail to forewarn and protect but, now reversed, offer tangible evidence of pollution (*obscenum*).[5]

Dido's subsequent magic rite masks her resolve to end her life, while it also signals a second and final merging of the narrative with the ritual plot in the book. Magic rites of *defixio* conflated with those of customary sacrifice turn rituals familiar to the audience into rituals alien and unsettling. The magic ceremony is itself divided into three parts, with a progressive transformation of the rite from *defixio* to funeral rite to a self-sacrifice comparable to a *devotio*. This fusion of all three rites maximizes the divide between Dido's actions and standard ritual practice and underlines the corrupt nature of all three ritual processes it depicts.

Dido's recourse to magic was taboo for Romans. This act alone would be sufficient to signal ritual corruption and perversion of religious custom and law: magical practices were common in Rome and were taken very seriously when they were thought to involve a sudden and unexplained death. Roman religious authorities since the time of the Twelve Tables condemned such practices, and Augustan legislation renewed the state's sanctions against them (Livy 4.30, 25.1, 39.16; Dio Cassius 49.43, 52.36; see Graf 1997: 46–60). Despite the fact that Dido's magic ceremony is not without literary precedents,[6] Dido's rite

---

[5] On pollution as a sign of sacrificial perversion, see also Chapter 3, pp. 83–90.

[6] Simaitha in Theocritus' *Idyl* 2 and Medea's practices in Apollonius' *Argonautica*, as well as Amaryllis in Vergil's own *Eclogue* 8, are the most obvious models. Of course, both Apollonius and Theocritus, like Vergil, depend on their audience's sense of the impropriety of magic.

is more complex and more ominous, constituting the climax of a carefully prepared ritual plot that aims to underscore the idea of corruption of religious custom.

The opening of the description of Dido's ceremony points to the magic practice of *defixio*. Dido instructs Anna to build a pyre, prescribing that it contain the *monimenta* (498) of her marriage to Aeneas: the weapons (*arma*, 495) and clothes he left in their marriage chamber (*exuuiae*, 496; see Conington 1884, 2: 303) as well as the bed itself (*lectum iugale*, 496). The construction of the pyre inside the palace is appropriate to the obviously private character of the ritual; for now, her objective appears to be to free herself from her marriage bond with Aeneas. Yet in the same passage there are elements that point to a rite that seeks the opposite of what Dido asserts. The *effigies*, an image of Aeneas probably made of wax, along with *exuuiae*, relics of his clothes, are all used by Amaryllis in *Eclogue* 8 (*effigies*, 75; *cera*, 80; *exuuias*, 92) in her successful effort to bind Daphnis to her will, to make him return after he has abandoned her.[7]

Dido's magic, however, is fused with rites peculiar to funerals not only to heighten the pathos for the queen's impending death but also to expose fully her desire to cause Aeneas' destruction, his *funus* (Tupet 1970: 237–58). Scholars have long noted the passage's connection with Misenus' burial later in Book 6 (214–35; see Austin 1955: 151). Aeneas' *exuuiae*, his sword, and his effigy on the pyre (507–508) suggest that we are about to witness his symbolic funeral; Vergil uses the plural *funera* (500) for Dido's rites, a usage that I believe supports this reading. Moreover, the inclusion of elements from ritual sacrifice (the sprinkling of the *mola salsa*) already point beyond the *defixio* to the final transformation of the ceremony: Dido plans Aeneas' symbolic sacrifice. Interestingly, just as happened with the first ritual description, the narrative continues on to other matters, and the rite is forgotten until the final scene of the book.

---

[7] Tupet (1970: 237–38) offers a full discussion of all the ritual elements of this segment of Dido's ceremony. Eitrem (1933: 29–41), after a careful examination of Dido's magic rite, concludes that the ritual described would never have succeeded and that in fact it was never meant to succeed. A useful summary of his argumentation is found in Austin 1955: 149–50 and Tupet 1970: 238.

Dido's last instructions reveal that the true purpose of her activity
was to perform blood sacrifice to the Stygian Jupiter:[8]

> 'Annam, cara mihi nutrix, huc siste sororem:
> dic corpus properet fluuiali spargere lympha,
> et pecudes secum et monstrata piacula ducat.
> sic ueniat, tuque ipsa pia tege tempora uitta.
> sacra Ioui Stygio, quae rite incepta paraui,
> perficere est animus finemque imponere curis
> Dardaniique rogum capitis permittere flammae.'        (4.634–40)

> "Dear nurse, bring my sister, Anna, here:
> tell her to hurry and sprinkle her body with river water,
> and to bring along the victims and the offerings for atonement, as directed;
> Let her come then, and you, cover your brow with the holy headband.
> The rites to Stygian Jupiter, which I have started according to ritual
>    custom,
> I mean to bring to completion and put an end to my cares,
> and entrust to the flames the pyre of that Dardanian."

It is not difficult to discern what is by now a familiar pattern: the emphasis on ritual correctness (the purificatory sprinkling with river water, the
prescribed offerings of atonement, the sacrificial garland) is ironically
undermined by the very anomaly of the choice of a human sacrificial victim. The use of the expression *incepta paraui* serves as a subtle reminder
that it is the same ritual left unfinished when the narrative plot diverged
from the ritual plot.[9] Yet as Dido prepares to take her life, a further
reversal occurs. The queen directs her last words to the objects that symbolically stand for Aeneas. The sword that has hitherto been described as
an offering (*munus*, 647) becomes the slayer.[10] Aeneas thus symbolically
turns from sacrificed to sacrificer: the roles previously outlined in the
magic rite are now completely reversed. Dido's death on the altar (*arae*,
676) thus perverts proper sacrificial procedure.

---

[8] Cf. 4.638–39. See also Heinze 1915: 141–43 (= Harvey 1993: 105).

[9] See also Tupet (1970: 250–51), who argues that the magic rites were preliminary to the main rite, a rite of destruction.

[10] A similar symbolism occurs in Sophocles' *Ajax*, where the sword is referred to
as σφαγεύς, the slayer (815). On Dido and Ajax, see Chapter 6, pp. 182–98.

Intertextual contact with Clytemnestra's killing of her husband in Aeschylus' *Agamemnon* confirms that ritual perversion is at the core of Dido's sacrifice:

παίω δέ νιν δίς, κἀν δυοῖν οἰμωγμάτοιν
μεθῆκεν αὐτοῦ κῶλα· καὶ πεπτωκότι
τρίτην ἐπενδίδωμι, τοῦ κατὰ χθονός
Διὸς νεκρῶν σωτῆρος εὐκταίαν χάριν.           (1384–87)

I hit him twice, and with two groans
he relaxed his limbs; and after he had fallen
I give him yet a third blow, a grace for my prayer
to the infernal Zeus, the savior of the dead.

Clytemnestra describes the death of Agamemnon as a sacrifice to the Zeus of Hades. This is the climactic moment of the play and presents the most horrifying reversal of ritual: a deadly blow is called a gift or service accompanying a prayer. Agamemnon's blood is a libation, and the three strokes evoke the customary rite of pouring three libations after the feast: one to the Olympian gods, one to chthonic gods, and one to Zeus the savior. The inversion is twofold: the libation is of blood instead of wine; Zeus the savior, the benign deity who blesses the feast, is here the Zeus of Hades, the savior (keeper) of the dead (Zeitlin 1965: 472). Dido also purports to sacrifice to the Stygian Jupiter her "husband," that is, the symbolic image of Aeneas.

Yet in turning the blade of the sword toward herself, Dido is also a victim, as the famous tragic simile attests:

aut Agamemnonius scaenis agitatus Orestes,
armatam facibus matrem et **serpentibus** atris
cum fugit ultricesque sedent in limine Dirae.           (4.471–73)

Or as when at the theater Agamemnon's son, Orestes,
hounded, flees his mother armed with firebrands
and black **serpents**, and the avenging Dirae sit at the doorway.[11]

---

[11] Dido's likening to Orestes points to the end of Aesch. *Cho.* (1048–50), where the young man is chased by the Furies after he has committed matricide: σμοιαὶ γυναῖκες αἵδε Γοργόνων δίκην / φαιοχίτωνες καὶ πεπλεκτανημέναι / πυκνοῖς **δράκουσιν** [savage women these, like Gorgons, wearing gray garments and entwined with swarming **snakes**].

The intertext of Aeschylus' *Oresteia* is thus particularly important in the depiction of Dido's torment but also appears central to her portrayal as a dangerous Erinys, as her final words to Aeneas, a formidable curse, attest:

'... spero equidem mediis, si quid pia numina possunt,
supplicia hausurum scopulis et nomine Dido
saepe uocaturum. sequar atris ignibus absens
et, cum frigida mors anima seduxerit artus,
omnibus umbra locis adero. dabis, improbe, poenas.
audiam et haec Manis ueniet mihi fama sub imos.'                    (4.382–87)

"... indeed I hope, if the pious divinities have any power,
that amid the rocks you will drink up the punishment and often call
Dido's name. I shall follow you with black torches, though absent,
and, when cold death has separated my limbs from my soul,
I shall be present everywhere as a shadow. Cruel one, you will be punished.
I shall hear and this story will reach me in the Shades below.

Hardie (1993: 41) argues convincingly that this curse suggests Dido's future existence as a Fury who will make sure that Aeneas will be punished. This image of Dido as an Erinys is akin to Clytemnestra's identification with Ate and Erinys in Aeschylus' *Agamemnon* (Conacher 1987: 51–53; see also Lebeck 1971: 140). Furthermore, Dido's oscillation between priestess and victim, slayer and slain points to her ritual function as an object of *defixio*, whose death will bring destruction to Aeneas and his people. In this respect, her ritual shares important elements with the *devotio*, whereby a Roman general's death brings destruction to the enemy and ensures victory for the Roman side. Tupet (1970: 256) and Hardie (1986: 279–80; 1993: 29) have both recognized elements of *devotio* in Dido's ceremony and point out that she dedicates herself to the powers of the Underworld. Earlier in the narrative, at the moment when the queen falls in love with Aeneas, she is described as "devoted to future destruction" (*pesti deuota futurae*, 1.712).

Dido's depiction as both priestess and victim is most salient in her final curse on Aeneas and his people: the words *exoriare **aliquis nostris** ex ossibus **ultor*** [**another avenger** will rise **from our** bones] (625) and ***moriemur inultae** / sed moriamur* [**we shall die** unavenged / but let us die]) (659–60) mobilize yet another intertextual link with Aeschylus'

*Agamemnon*: the curse of the prophetess Cassandra, Apollo's priestess, who foresees her own killing by Clytemnestra but also prophesies that her death will find retribution: οὐ μὴν ἄτιμοί γ᾽ ἐκ θεῶν τεθνήξομεν· / ἥξει γὰρ ἡμῶν ἄλλος αὖ τιμάορος [but **unavenged** by the gods **we shall** not **die**; for **another avenger of ours** will come in turn] (1279–80).[12] On the ritual level, this curse situates Dido's self-sacrifice in the realm of *devotio*, whereby victory in war is achieved. Vergil's mobilization of this ritual context in this instance announces the most shocking defeats in store for Rome. On the allusive level, however, Dido is cast as Cassandra, the most innocent victim (along with Iphigeneia) of the entire trilogy, who was "sacrificed" by Clytemnestra in the name of revenge. As a result, Dido's death, the blood sacrifice necessary for the completion of her ritual, is cast through her link with Cassandra as terribly corrupt.[13] The tragic pattern or ritual perversion thus calls for purity and restoration.

In conclusion, the ritual plot in Book 4, while it cannot fail to inspire readerly sympathy for Dido, indicates that her death as sacrifice cannot be sanctioned by religious law. Through the use of a ritual plot, the poet is able to articulate in no uncertain terms the violent nature of Aeneas' mission, by putting to work a language his audience could intuitively understand and interpret. At the same time, this ritual plot provides him with a mechanism through which he can offer a resolution of the ritual perversion in the manner of Greek tragedy. Indeed, the poet satisfies readerly expectations for such a resolution on the narrative level by providing Aeneas with divine justification for his actions; as the ritual plot unfolds, however, the cumulative effect of its reversals and perversions, which culminate in Dido's self-sacrifice, is the dismantling of this very resolution. If one of the functions of ritual is to contain violence by transforming it into a structured and controlled force beneficial to society, this it fails to achieve in Book 4. Turnus' death at the end of the epic, rife with elements of *devotio*, constitutes a ritual equivalent to

---

[12] Scholars have long noted the allusion. See, for instance, Pease 1935: 493; Fraenkel 1950: 596.

[13] To be sure, as one of the anonymous readers reminded me, Cassandra in this instance, for all her innocence, also recalls Clytemnestra with the emphasis she places on revenge. At once victim and avenger, Cassandra, like Dido, defies simple classification.

that of Dido. It remains to examine whether this time it will succeed in bringing ritual closure.

## II. TURNUS' *DEVOTIO* AND RITUAL CLOSURE

Closure in recent literary criticism emerges as a concept open to negotiation, amplification, and redefinition (Fowler 1989; 1997). In this section, I would like to address the question of closure and aperture in the *Aeneid* by focusing on ritual representation and symbolism as formal closural devices in the epic. More specifically, I explore the important implications of the presence of ritual symbolism in the killing of Turnus. To be sure, critics have long noted that Aeneas employs the vocabulary of ritual sacrifice in his final words to Turnus.[14] I argue that the use of ritual vocabulary in this instance is part of the larger ritual intertext at work in the poem. Turnus' killing constitutes a perverted sacrifice and, in particular, a perversion of the Roman ritual practice of *devotio*. A consideration of the ending of the *Aeneid* from this perspective reveals that Vergil not only inverts the Homeric closural pattern[15] but also employs the tragic pattern of perversion stripped of the possibility of ritual restoration. As a result, the epic fails to assuage the readerly anxieties that the ritual symbolism has aroused and defies expectations for resolution and closure.

My analysis is divided into three parts. I first outline Vergil's appropriation of vocabulary properly belonging to the realm of *devotio*, which mobilizes a subtext (or intertext) that complicates and enriches the narrative plot line as well as the characterization of Turnus. Within this subtext, sacrificial perversion occurs, thus raising the expectation of ritual restoration. In the second part, a comparison between Livy's *devotio* narrative and that of the *Aeneid* illuminates the reasons behind Vergil's mobilization of this particular ritual intertext. The representation of Turnus as a *devotus* transforms him into a symbol of collective unity as his death appears a restorative act that would ensure the future fusion of Romans and Latins into one people. The section ends with a discussion

---

[14] The bibliography on the scene is vast. On the sacrificial vocabulary, see Putnam 1965: 195–96; Mitchell-Boyask 1991; and Hardie 1993: 21, 28.

[15] See Hardie 1997a and Perkell 2001.

of the poem's ritual intertext as a closural device. I suggest that the pattern of ritual corruption followed by restoration derives from Greek tragedy and therefore distorts the generic integrity of the *Aeneid*.

## 1. The Ritual Intertext of *Devotio*

The specific ritual context of *devotio* is first activated in Book 11, where Turnus, in response to Drances' accusations of cowardice, passionately announces his desire to sacrifice himself to save his people from further bloodshed.[16] As scholars have long recognized, the ritual term *deuoui* (11.442) is emphatically placed at the first metrical *sedes* with enjambment and a pause:[17]

> '... ibo animis contra, uel magnum praestet Achillem
> factaque Volcani manibus paria induat arma

[16] On *devotio*, see Schwenn 1915: 154–64. Burkert (1979: 63–64) classifies the practice as one of the transformations of the pattern of the scapegoat. The leader is seen as an offering to the deities of the Underworld. Aside from the classic example of P. Decius Mus (*Liv.* 8.6.9–16, 8.9.1–13, 8.10.11–14), the second instance of *devotio* in Livy is that of Decius' son in the battle of Sentinum in 295 during the Third Samnite War (10.28.12–17). Burkert (1979: 63) argues that the elder Decius' example "seems to have become a kind of heroic myth itself, obscuring the normal procedure." See in addition Stübler 1941: 173–204; Versnel 1976, 1981; Levene 1993; and Oakley 1997. The practice is also mentioned in Ennius' *Annales* (191–93 Skutsch) and in Cicero's *Sest.* 48. Macrobius (*Sat.* 3.9.9–13) gives a very different account of the same ritual, on which see Versnel 1976: 365–410.

[17] See, for instance, Highet 1972: 63 and Hardie 1993: 28. Conington (1884, 3: 359) notes that this is a kind of "formula of self-devotion, not unlike that given in Liv. 8.9." He also notes that the natural construction would have been *pro uobis*, "the dative being used of the powers to whom the person bound himself over: but Virgil as usual has chosen to vary it, regarding Latinus and the commonwealth as the parties to whom Turnus is thus consigned" (ibid.). Indeed, Decius utters strikingly similar words in *Liv.* 8.9.4: *agedum, pontifex publicus populi Romani, praei uerba quibus me pro legionibus deuoueam* [come, state pontiff of the Roman people, dictate the words that I may devote myself on behalf of the legions] and in 8.9.8: *ita pro re publica <populi Romani> Quiritium exercitu, legionibus, auxiliis populi Romani Quiritium, legiones auxiliaque hostium mecum Deis Manibus Tellurique deuoueo* [in this way on behalf of the state of the Roman people of the Quirites, of the army, the legions, the auxiliaries of the Roman

ille licet. uobis animam hanc soceroque Latino
Turnus ego, haud ulli ueterum uirtute secundus,
*deuoui.* solum Aeneas uocat? et uocet oro;
nec Drances potius, siue est haec ira deorum,
morte *luat*, siue est uirtus et gloria, tollat.'                        (11.438–44)

" ... I'll face him with all my heart, though he may surpass great Achilles
and wear armor to match, wrought by Vulcan's hands.
To you and Latinus, my father-in-law, I, Turnus,
second in courage to none of my ancestors, *have devoted* my life.
Aeneas challenges me alone? I pray that he should challenge me;
and not that Drances rather, if this is the gods' anger, *may atone* it
with his death, nor, if this is honor and glory, that he may win them for
    himself."

Once activated, the intertext of *devotio* is sustained throughout the
narrative of Book 12 and soon merges with the main plot line: Trojans
and Latins agree that the outcome of the war must be decided in a duel
between Aeneas and Turnus. The two hosts ratify this pact in a solemn ceremony described in rich detail (161–221). Toward the end of the
description of the ratification of the treaty, dialogue gives way to narrative: resentment grows on the Rutulian side as the probability of their
leader's death becomes all too apparent. After the animals are sacrificed
(213–15), Turnus approaches the altar in supplication:

At uero Rutulis impar ea pugna uideri
iamdudum et uario misceri pectora motu,
tum magis ut propius cernunt non uiribus aequos.
adiuuat incessu tacito progressus et *aram*
*suppliciter uenerans* demisso lumine Turnus
pubentesque genae et iuuenali in corpore pallor.                        (12.216–21)

people of the Quirites, I devote the legions and the auxiliaries of the enemy
along with myself to the Divine Shades and to the Earth]. See also Renger 1985:
88. Pascal (1990: 252) argues that a close study of the speech of Turnus and
the scene in which it takes place are "enough to rob the fateful word and all its
vehemence of its ritual import." On *devotio* in the *Aeneid*, see further Johnson
1976: 117–19; Schenk 1984: 143; Renger 1985: 87–90; Pascal 1990: 251–68;
Leigh 1993; Hardie 1993: 28–32; and Thomas 1998: 284–85.

> But indeed that battle seemed unfair to the Rutulians
> for a long time and their hearts filled with changing emotions,
> even more now, as they see at closer view the men unequal in strength.
> Turnus fuels this, advancing with silent gait and *worshipping*
> *as a suppliant the altar* with eyes downcast;
> so too his wan cheeks and the paleness in his youthful figure.

I argue that in the Vergilian narrative Turnus' depiction as a sacrificial victim in the impending duel forms an integral part of Turnus' *devotio*, which in turn is linked to the ritual subtext deployed in the final segment of the poem. Scholars have not seen a connection between the ratification of the treaty sanctioning the duel between the two combatants and the ritual vocabulary of *devotio* at work in the representation of Turnus. On the contrary, they interpret the latter as an instance of "self-serving rhetoric" (Pascal 1990: 267), present only in Turnus' own "skewed view of reality" (Hardie 1993: 28), or as a case of "deviant focalization" not related to the final sacrificial moment of the epic (Thomas 1998: 284–85).

The narrator, however, in the description of Turnus' role in the ongoing rites, employs ritual language appropriate for a sacrificial victim (219–21). Turnus' self-representation as a *devotus* is thus followed by the presence of sacrificial symbolism. This is accomplished by a shift in the focus of the narrative, which now zooms in on the Rutulians' feelings as they realize the inequality between the two combatants (*impar ea pugna*) and the inevitability of their leader's death. Turnus appears last in the procession and is depicted as a double of the animals prepared for ritual slaughter: his downcast eyes (*demisso lumine*) contrast with Aeneas' and Latinus' gazes toward heaven as they utter their prayers (Aeneas and his men: *illi ad surgentem conuersi lumina solem*, 172; Latinus: *suspiciens caelum*, 196). As is often the case with sacrificial victims, Turnus' youth is emphasized[18] and his paleness foreshadows his death.[19] The animals

---

[18] The animals usually sacrificed are *bidentes*, i.e., two years old. On the significance of the youth of the victim, see Versnel 1981: 143–45, 163.

[19] Interestingly, the word *pallor* is used only one other time in the entire Vergilian corpus. At *Aen.* 4.499, when Dido tricks her sister into preparing the pyre, the narrator concludes that as Dido finishes her speech, paleness covers her cheeks. Once again, the idea of paleness is connected with death.

just slain also prefigure Turnus' final sacrifice.[20] The narrative thus symbolically transgresses the ritual norm of sacrifice that we have just witnessed (which prescribes the slaughter of animals) and replaces it with the expectation of human slaughter. Turnus' imminent death is signaled as an act of sacrifice for the poem's characters and readers alike.

The ritual intertext is evoked through both the narrator's and Turnus' words. It remains therefore to demonstrate that it can be identified as that of *devotio* in particular. In the following scene, the disguised Juturna intervenes, seeking to inflame the already disturbed Rutulians, renew the fighting, and obstruct ritual procedure.[21] In order to carry her point, Juturna invites the Latins (and the reader) to consider Turnus as sacrificial victim and the treaty itself as a *devotio*:

> 'non pudet, o Rutuli, *pro cunctis talibus unam*
> *obiectare animam*? numerone an uiribus aequi
> non sumus? en, omnes et Troes et Arcades hi sunt,
> fatalisque manus, infensa Etruria Turno:
> uix hostem, alterni si congrediamur, habemus.
> ille quidem ad superos, *quorum se deuouet aris*,
> succedet fama uiuusque per ora feretur;..."        (12.229–35)

> "Are you not ashamed, O Rutulians, *to expose one life*
> *for so many*? Aren't we equal in numbers
> or strength? Look, all of them are here, Trojans and Arcadians,
> and the fate-driven host, Etruria, enemies of Turnus.
> Even if every other man joins the battle, we barely have a foe for each.
> Turnus will indeed rise in fame to the gods, *on whose altars*
> *he devotes his life* and he'll be alive upon the lips of men...."

Although it may be argued that Juturna is using the rhetoric of *devotio* in order to achieve her goal, her opening remarks capitalize on the

---

[20] Putnam (1965: 164) notes that the use of *suppliciter* "leads the reader directly to the final lines of the poem where Turnus is the actual suppliant (*supplex*) before Aeneas." On the connection between the gods Latinus invokes in the ratification of the treaty and those invoked in Decius' *devotio*, see Renger 1985: 88–89.

[21] On this episode as an instance of disruption and chaos, see also Hardie 1993: 21.

Rutulians' feelings, which, as we have seen, are rooted in the expectation shared by both Trojans and Latins that Turnus is going to die. Juturna, by emphasizing Turnus' sacrifice for his people (229–30), draws attention to a constitutive characteristic of the process of sacrifice in general and of *devotio* in particular, the principle of substitution (Versnel 1981: 159–60). A structural parallel emphasizes the link between the themes of sacrifice, the treaty, and the *devotio* in these instances: as noted earlier, sacrificial symbolism describing Turnus' role in the treaty follows Turnus' self-representation as a *devotus*. Similarly, a striking passage brimming with sacrificial perversion follows Juturna's declaration of the treaty as a *devotio*.[22] As violence disrupts the rite, the killings in battle that ensue are cast in terms that evoke ritual slaughter:

> Messapus regem regisque insigne gerentem
> Tyrrhenum Aulesten, avidus *confundere foedus*,
> aduerso proterret equo; ruit ille recedens
> et miser *oppositis* a tergo *inuoluitur aris*
> *in caput inque umeros*. at feruidus aduolat hasta
> Messapus teloque *orantem* multa trabali
> desuper altus equo grauiter ferit atque ita fatur:
> 'hoc habet, *haec melior magnis data uictima diuis*.'          (12.289–96)

> Messapus, eager to *break the treaty* with charging horse
> terrifies Aulestes, the Etruscan king who wore a king's
> insignia; that one stepping back stumbles, and *whirls*,
> poor man, *on the obstructing altar* behind him, falling
> *on head and shoulders*. And Messapus blazing swoops down
> with his spear, high on his horse, and, though the man *begged* for mercy,
> he strikes him hard from above with his beam-like weapon, and
>     speaks thus:
> "He's had it, *this finer victim given to the great gods*."

---

[22] Another ratification of a treaty has occurred earlier in the *ekphrasis* of the shield in *Aen.* 8.635–41: that treaty is between the Romans and the Sabines and includes the sacrifice of a pig at the altar of Jupiter. The solemnity of the event is stressed throughout the description and contrasts sharply with the sacrilege of the broken treaty between Aeneas and Latinus in 12.169–296. See also Gransden 1976: 166–67 and Putnam 1998: 122.

Contrary to proper ritual practice, where animal takes the place of human offering, Messapus' slaying of Aulestes represents a complete reversal of the sacrificial norm of substitution, as a human victim replaces the animal.[23] This kind of reversal at once provokes readerly anxiety over the collapse of the ritual order and raises expectations for ritual correctness and resolution. Turnus' voluntary self-sacrifice, his *devotio*, appears the only means by which the disrupted ritual order may be restored.[24]

The perversion motif generates the expectation of Turnus' self-sacrifice as an act of restoration. In the next scene, Aeneas reinforces this expectation by claiming Turnus' life as a prescribed offering for the broken treaty, through which ritual purity may be attained:

> 'quo ruitis? quaeue ista repens discordia surgit?
> o cohibete iras! ictum iam foedus et omnes
> compositae leges. mihi ius concurrere soli;
> me sinite atque auferte metus. ego foedera faxo
> firma manu; Turnum *debent haec* iam *mihi sacra.*'          (12.313–17)

> "Where are you rushing to? What is this sudden outbreak of discord?
> Curb your anger! A pact has now been struck and all
> the terms have been agreed upon. It is right for me alone to fight;
> let me do so and cast out your fears. With this hand I'll make
> this treaty firm; *these rites have* now *bound* Turnus *to me.*"

The conclusion of Aeneas' speech casts him in the role of sacrificer and Turnus in that of the sacrificed, while its formulaic tone, due to the heavy alliteration of *f* and the presence of the archaic *faxo*, has ritual resonance. Moreover, Aeneas employs the verb *debere* to describe Turnus' death as the only acceptable recompense for the violated rite, thus furthering the delineation of the treaty as a form of *devotio*. Compensation is also one of the distinctive characteristics of the *devotio*, as the verb *debere* is also found in Livy's description of the sacrifice of the *imperator* P. Decius Mus

---

[23] Contrast the correct application of the sacrificial principle of substitution that the reader has witnessed within the controlled ritual context of the games in *Aen.* 5; *hanc tibi, Eryx, meliorem animam pro morte Daretis / persoluo* [to you, Eryx, I vow this finer life as payment for Dares' death] (483–84).

[24] On the voluntary aspect of the *devotio* and of sacrifice in general, see Versnel 1981: 146–47.

to the gods below (8.6.10).[25] Thus Aeneas' vocabulary locates Turnus' sacrifice, the treaty, and the *devotio* within the larger context of sacrificial perversion and imminent restoration.

Despite a series of events that delays the final duel, the ritual subtext of *devotio* remains active alongside the main narrative movement.[26] It resurfaces as Turnus reasserts his intent to meet his death honorably, his voluntary self-sacrifice further bolstering the reader's hopes for ritual restoration. Aeneas proceeds to attack Latinus' city, and the Rutulian hero, realizing that his resistance will only cause further bloodshed, appeals to the gods of the Underworld in terms that suggest self-consecration, yet another constitutive element of the *devotio*:

> terga dabo et Turnum fugientem haec terra uidebit?
> usque adeone mori miserum est? uos o mihi, *Manes*
> este boni, quoniam superis auersa uoluntas.
> *sancta ad uos anima atque istius inscia culpae*
> *descendam* magnorum haud umquam indignus auorum.      (12.645–49)

> Shall I turn my back and will this land know that Turnus is in flight?
> Is it to die so terrible? You, *Shades of the Underworld,*
> be kind to me, since the goodwill of the gods above has turned
>      away from me.
> *As a pure spirit innocent of that crime I shall go down*
> *to you* never unworthy of my great ancestors.

Much like Livy's Decius, Turnus also invokes the *Manes* as he prepares to enter the realm of the dead. In the case of Decius, his self-consecration is reported as part of a ritual ceremony.[27] Turnus, by contrast, does not

---

[25] On *debere* and *devotio*, see Versnel 1981: 161, 169.

[26] On delay as a device related to closure, see Hardie 1997a: 145–46.

[27] See Livy 8.9.8, quoted earlier in note 17. Also compare Livy 10.28.13: *iam ego mecum hostium legiones mactandas Telluri ac Dis Manibus dabo* [now I shall offer the legions of the enemy along with myself to be sacrificed to the Earth and to the Divine Shades]. On the self-consecratory aspect of *devotio*, see Versnel 1981: 150–51, where he also makes a distinction between *consecratio* and animal sacrifice: "it is the gods (of the netherworld) who must take the *consecratus* either through the mediation of the enemy troops or in some other way...and thus accept the offer. Here we have one essential difference with the normal animal-sacrifice where *consecratio* and *mactatio*, though ritually distinguished, are

participate in a ritual act but employs language containing ritual terms
(*sancta anima, inscia culpae, descendam*), asserts the purity of his spirit, and
signals his liminal status as he is destined for the Underworld yet still
resides in the world of the living. This passage too then belongs to the
poem's ritual intertext, proclaims Turnus' suitability as a *devotus*, and
reinforces the connection between the *devotio* and the impending duel.

Finally, Turnus declares that his imminent death constitutes expiation and cleansing for the ritual perversion that has occurred.[28] A few
moments after his self-consecration, Turnus addresses his troops, asks
them to cease the fighting, and readily offers himself as atonement for
the breaking of the treaty.[29]

> 'parcite iam, Rutuli, et uos tela inhibete, Latini.
> quaecumque est fortuna, mea est; me uerius *unum*
> *pro uobis* foedus *luere* et decernere ferro.'                    (12.693–95)

> "Rutulians, stop now, and you, Latins, hold your weapons.
> Whatever the outcome is, it is mine. Better that *I, alone*
> *in your stead, atone* for the treaty and fight it out with the sword."

Turnus' words confirm what the poem's ritual subplot has suggested all
along: his sacrifice will signal the end of the conflict and will allow his
people to live in peace with the Trojans. The use of the formula *unum pro
uobis*, the sacrificial principle of substitution, attests that the ritual subtext is here hard at work. Moreover, the presence of the verb *luere*, which
was also employed in Turnus' declaration of *devotio* in Book 11 and which
conveys the notion of cleansing, links yet again the poem's ritual subtext
with sacrifice and with *devotio* in particular.

---

nevertheless closely connected and, more important, are practically in the same
hands." See in addition Oakley 1997: 482.

[28] Livy 8.9.10: *piaculum omnis deorum irae* [an atonement for all the anger of the
gods]; 8.10.12: *piaculum caedi* [a victim is slain in atonement]; 10.28.13: *luendis
periculis publicis piacula simus* [that we should be sacrificed as atonements for the
nation's perils].

[29] See also Turnus' first declaration of *devotio* at 11.444 (*luat*), where he presents his
death as atonement for the ill repute of the whole of his community. See further
Hardie 1993: 29. Schenk (1984: 184–85) reads this final *devotio* as Turnus' ploy
to regain repute and good standing with the Latins.

Vergil's narrative outlines the constitutive elements of *devotio*: substitution, self-consecration, compensation, and expiation. The accumulation of these elements in the deployment and delineation of the poem's ritual intertext intensifies and reinforces the possibility of release from the anxiety that the disrupted ritual order has generated. At the same time, the repeated promises of closure in the ritual plot contrast notably with the successive delays in the narrative, which postpone the duel between Aeneas and Turnus and which frustrate and obstruct the poem's movement toward its end (see note 26, p. 63). The incongruity between the progression of the two plots underscores the ritual import of the duel.

Confirmation of the growing expectation that Turnus' *devotio* will restore ritual corruption and provide closural relief comes full circle in the scene of Juturna's withdrawal from the action. As she returns to the water, the nymph now signals the end of the ritual crisis she herself has launched by a symbolic sign of acceptance of her brother's *devotio*:

> tantum effata *caput* glauco *contexit* amictu
> multa gemens et se fluuio dea condidit alto.                    (12.885–86)

> So saying, she *covered her head* in a gray mantle
> and with many a moan the goddess plunged into the deep river.

While it evokes practices of mourning and ritual lament,[30] Juturna's gesture also points to the veiling of the head which is specific to Roman sacrificial practice,[31] and which Livy presents as an important component of *devotio*.[32] Since Juturna has instigated ritual corruption, her symbolic acknowledgment of the necessity for ritual purity which her brother's voluntary sacrifice will attain has particular importance for the process of final restoration.

Having established the existence of a ritual subtext in the last book of the *Aeneid*, it remains to explain the reasons behind its mobilization. In order to do so, it is first necessary to chart the characteristics of the

---

[30] On the lament of Juturna, see Barchiesi 1978, 1994 (= 1999); Perkell 1997.

[31] Compare Helenus' directions to Aeneas on sacrificial procedure at *Aeneid* 3.405.

[32] Livy 8.9.5: *Pontifex eum togam praetextam sumere iussit et uelato capite, manu subter togam ad mentum exserta, super telum subiectum pedibus stantem* [The pontiff ordered him to put on the toga praetexta and with his head veiled, his hand thrust out of the toga and on his chin, standing on a spear laid under his feet].

*devotio* rite as they are given by Livy as well as the function of the ritual within the narrative of Book 8 of *Ab urbe condita*. The numerous links between the two texts suggest that *devotio*, although a ritual rarely practiced in real life, was a conceptual framework available to Vergil for fruitful use. At the same time, this discussion will shed further light on the interconnections among ritual, closure, and genre.

## 2. Livy's *Devotio* and the *Aeneid*

The fullest account of the ritual practice of *devotio*, which prescribed that a Roman leader's voluntary sacrifice in battle would ensure victory for the Roman side, is preserved in Livy's narrative of the *devotio* of P. Decius Mus during the Great Latin War of 340 BCE. Livy provides a dramatic account of the *aition* for the ritual:[33]

Ibi in quiete utrique consuli eadem dicitur uisa species uiri maioris quam prohumano habitu augustiorisque, dicentis ex una acie imperatorem, ex altera exercitum *Deis Manibus Matrique Terrae deberi*; utrius exercitus imperator legiones hostium superque eas se *deuouisset*, eius populi partisque uictoriam fore.                                                              (8.6.9–10)

There in the quiet they say that by both consuls an image was seen, of a man of greater size than human and more majestic, saying that the imperator of the one side, and the army of the other is *bound to the Manes and to the Mother Earth*; and that, in whichever army the imperator would *devote* the enemy's legions and himself with them, victory would belong to that people and that side.

The extent to which Livy's description reflects actual Roman ritual is uncertain (Burkert 1979: 63–64; *Skutsch* 355; Feldherr 1998: 85–92). The contours of the ritual, however, can be mapped out: *devotio* is a rite of substitution, compensation, expiation, and self-consecration. In all rites of substitution, a man or beast, as the repository of the collective guilt, ensures the community's salvation from peril. In the particular context of *devotio*, this sacrifice is also viewed as an indemnity, a necessary debt that needs to be paid to the gods (Versnel 1981: 169). In addition, the

---

[33] See, for instance, Conington 1884, 3: 359; Highet 1972: 63; and Hardie 1993: 28.

*devotus* is envisaged as taking upon himself the religious impurities of his people, his death thus constituting an act of expiation and cleansing.[34] Decius' self-sacrifice is an act of self-consecration as well: the rite bestows sacrosanct status on the *devotus*, placing him in a liminal stage between the living and the dead, human and deity, and separating him from the community.[35]

In Livy's narrative of Decius' *devotio*, the superhuman powers of the *imperator* become remarkably visible and transform him into something greater than human. These powers thus testify to his special contact with the divine and at once separate him from the community and bestow upon him the power to confer victory.[36] At the same time, however, Decius' voluntary sacrifice also promotes collective unity: the rite, grounded in religious law, elevates him to the realm of exemplary heroism and transforms him into a symbol that, by inspiring unity among the ranks of an army on the verge of defeat, brings about an overwhelming victory. Turned into an *exemplum* of legendary patriotism, Decius thus serves as an embodiment of the extraordinary power of the Roman state and articulates for Livy's audience a model of Roman national identity (Feldherr 1998: 91–93).

The inclusion of the ritual subtext of *devotio* in the portrait of Turnus, however, invites inquiry into the reasons behind its mobilization. Since the latter half of the *Aeneid* in effect revolves around the problem of civic turmoil, the patriotic resonance of *devotio* within this context is obvious. Certainly, the problem of intracommunal violence is paramount in Livy's

---

[34] Burkert 1979: 64–67; Versnel 1981; Oakley 1997: 482. Feldherr (1998: 88–89) argues that the touching of the chin during the ritual symbolizes the *devotus'* taking upon himself the impurities of his people and spreading them to the enemy.

[35] Versnel (1981: 148–52) discusses the sacrosanct status of the *devotus* and identifies the practice as a rite of separation.

[36] Versnel 1981: 150–51; Feldherr 1998: 90. See also Livy's description of the appearance of the charging *deuotus* at 8.9.10: *conspectus ab utraque acie, aliquanto augustior humano uisu, sicut caelo missus piaculum omnis deorum irae qui pestem ab suis auersam in hostes ferret* [he was seen by each army, a sight somewhat more majestic than human, as if he was an atonement sent from heaven for all the anger of the gods who would carry destruction away from themselves and bring it on to the enemy]. On the role of spectacle in this instance, see Feldherr 1998: 91.

narrative of the Great Latin war as well.[37] Livy's representation of the conflict of 340 BCE between the Latins and the Romans as fratricidal[38] is conspicuously anachronistic and rather reflects events leading to the Social War of 90 BCE (Oakley 1997: 408–409). The rhetoric of the Latin side in the diplomatic exchanges before the outbreak of the war places particular emphasis on the kinship between the two peoples and claims a share in Roman government: *unum populum, unam rem publicam* (8.5.5). The reality of the times, however, was that the Latins, far from taking Roman rule for granted, as Livy's text implies, fiercely resisted Roman expansion.[39]

The common ground between the war of 340 BCE and that described in the second half of the *Aeneid* may appear as justification enough for the mobilization of the ritual subtext of *devotio*. Turnus' adoption, however, of the vocabulary of a ritual most familiar from the self-sacrifice of the Decii presents the readers of the *Aeneid* with a jarring incongruity. Turnus, an enemy of Rome and the personification of *furor* in the poem, is symbolically linked to a legendary hero of the early Republic (Thomas 1998: 284–85). As we have seen, critics usually explain this incongruity by ascribing it to narrative focalization or do not see a link between the

---

[37] The exact relationship between the texts of Vergil and Livy, however, still remains the object of speculation on the part of scholars.

[38] Livy 8.6.15: *Curam acuebat quod aduersus Latinos bellandum erat, lingua, moribus, armorum genere, institutis ante omnia militaribus congruentes: milites militibus, centurionibus centuriones, tribuni tribunis compares collegaeque iisdem <in> praesidiis, saepe iisdem manipulis permixti fuerant. Per haec ne quo errore milites caperentur, edicunt consules ne quis extra ordinem in hostem pugnaret* [It was sharpening their anxiety that they had to fight against the Latins, who shared the same language, customs, type of weapons, and, above all, military institutions; soldiers with soldiers, centurions with centurions, tribunes with tribunes had mixed together as equals and colleagues in the same guards, and often in the same maniples. For these reasons and so that soldiers might not be captured by some mistake, the consuls order that no one fight against the enemy out of rank]; and Livy 8.8.2: *fuit autem ciuili maxime bello pugna similis; adeo nihil apud Latinos dissonum ab Romana re praeter animos erat* [the battle besides was most like a civil war; indeed among the Latins there was nothing different from the Romans except their courage].

[39] See Oakley 1997: 409. Feldherr (1998: 82) also notes the similarity of the compromise offered by the Latins at this juncture and at the end of the *Aeneid*.

duel and Turnus' words, which they dismiss as rhetoric (Pascal 1990). To be sure, a duel and a *devotio* do not appear as related processes because of their different outcomes: the *devotus* is expected to die in battle, while the fighter of a duel is expected to win (Feldherr 1998: 91). Upon closer examination, however, single combat emerges as a practice with roots to ritual: oaths are customarily administered before the actual fighting takes place.[40] At the same time, scholars have posited that the ritual of the dedication of the *spolia opima* could be evidence for a period in early Roman history where a duel decided the outcome of wars (Oakley 1985: 398).

Interestingly, scholars do not usually see a connection between Livy's narrative of the Decian *devotio* and the duel of the younger Torquatus, which is also found in Book 8 of *Ab urbe condita*. Yet in Livy the relation between the stories of Decius and of the younger Torquatus is both thematic and structural. Not only does the young Roman share Decius' willingness to die for his country; his story is also embedded within the larger *devotio* narrative and is central to the overall theme of Book 8: the successful and humane settlement between Romans and Latins through an exploration of the problems inherent in exercising the great powers of *imperium* (Oakley 1997: 113). In an insightful analysis of Livy's passage, Feldherr (1998: 93) observes the similarity of the two practices. He further notes that the difference between the *devotio* and the duel is that in the former the *devotus* plays a double role, at once acting as a scapegoat for the victorious Romans and effecting the enemy's destruction. In the case of the duel, however, victory belongs entirely to the Roman side, while death befalls entirely on the enemy. Moreover, both the *devotio* and single combat constitute practices in which the individual represents the state;[41] and much like *devotio*, single combat can also be seen as a kind of judicial procedure (Fries 1985: 17–18; Feldherr 1998: 98).

---

[40] See *Aen.* 12.197–211; Feldherr 1998: 98.

[41] Oakley 1985: 405. It should be noted that Oakley here refers to the origins of the practice of single combat: "The practice of one man fighting on behalf of the state (the relics of which are to be found in the institution of the *spolia opima*) was abandoned early and instead the theme of the individual bearing the burden of the whole state is found in other institutions." Although the historical details are not important for my purposes here, it is clear that the connections between the representation of *devotio* and the duel between Turnus and Aeneas are very much relevant in this portion of the epic narrative.

In the case of the *Aeneid*, Vergil manipulates the connections between *devotio* and the duel in order to underscore the themes of successful symbiosis, unity, and peace. The *devotio* proper prescribes the death of the *imperator* and the destruction of the enemy's army.[42] Vergil, however, utilizes the ritual framework afforded by the rite of *devotio* to emphasize the ultimate fusion of the two warring sides into one community. The intracommunal nature of the conflict and the prospective unity between Romans and Latins envisaged at the end of the epic render the killing of Turnus at once necessary and problematic. Through the killing of Turnus, Aeneas appears as vanquishing the forces of madness and emerges as the leader of a new order; yet since the conflict is cast as civil war, killing the enemy is no simple matter. The portrayal of the duel as part of a ritual subtext of *devotio* allows Turnus to be a *devotus* whose death ensures "victory" for both sides: his willing self-sacrifice justifies Aeneas' action and accepts Trojan claims to Latium; his association with a legendary Roman general transforms him into a symbol of the future collective unity and shared "national" identity. The ratification of the treaty offers a ritual context within which Turnus' *devotio* can be realized, secures divine sanction, guarantees that further bloodshed will be averted, and legitimates the outcome. These points of contact between the *devotio* and the treaty, as well as the narrative emphasis on the participants and their reactions during the ritual ceremony and after its disruption, testify to the fact that Turnus' declaration of self-sacrifice is firmly situated within the context of a commonly understood and accepted ritual experience.[43]

The voluntary death of Turnus, painstakingly prepared in the course of the deployment of the ritual subplot of Book 12, may not compensate

[42] In a way, this is what happens in the *Aeneid* as well: Turnus' victory will result in the "defeat" of the Trojans, who are envisaged as losing their name and becoming Latins in 12.826–28. See especially Juno's request, *occidit, occideritque sinas cum nomine Troia* [Troy is fallen, let her be fallen along with her name] (12.828).

[43] The references to the audience also point to spectacle in general and gladiatorial games in particular. On *devotio* and gladiators, see Barton 1992: 40–46. Barton argues that the concept of *devotio* in the late Republic and early Augustan period applies both to heroic generals and criminals. I believe that Turnus' *devotio* belongs to the former category. Barton's argument helps explain the peculiar *devotio* in Ovid's *Ibis* (465–66). Watson (1991: 200–213), in her analysis of *defixiones*, discusses the Ovidian passage and refutes the possibility of its representing a *devotio*. Admittedly, *devotio* ritual is a type of *defixio* (on this, see Versnel 1976).

for the atrocities of warfare or for the loss of the Trojan and Italian youth, the most brilliant and precious component of Aeneas' new order. Turnus' death, however, constitutes the only plausible conclusion for the narrative plot, while the ritual subtext of *devotio* attests to the deeper significance of this death as a voluntary and restorative act that ensures victory for the Roman side. At the same time, the casting of Turnus as a Decius, the hero synonymous with *devotio* and a symbol of the heroic Roman past, both promotes the kinship between Trojans and Latins, already articulated in the scene of the divine reconciliation between Jupiter and Juno earlier in Book 12, and transforms Turnus from a personification of *furor* into a symbol of collective unity and peace. This does not mean that the anxiety over the preservation of peace and of the stability of the ritual order is eliminated. Rather, this symbolic sacrifice, as is the case with every ritual act, affirms the importance of preserving the ritual order so that similar crises may be averted.

Vergil's careful representation of Turnus in terms that evoke the *devotio* not only asserts his status as a hero but also sets the backdrop against which ritual closure may be achieved. As this ritual subplot unfolds, the deployment of the motif of ritual perversion intensifies and reinforces the expectation for ritual restoration. Yet the poem fails to satisfy this expectation, because Turnus' *devotio* is soon corrupted and never fully restored. To understand the significance of this flaunting of expectations, we must now consider how Vergil's adaptation of the use of ritual in Greek tragedy affects the problem of closure in the poem.

## 3. Ritual, Tragedy, Closure

The much-contested ending of Vergil's *Aeneid* presents modern students of closure with a fascinating problem. In particular, Philip Hardie has recently demonstrated how closural devices operative within the various segments of the epic promote openness, which in turn is linked to the Augustan ideological discourse that proclaims the endlessness of Roman power.[44] Exploring the problem of closure in the *Aeneid* also raises questions of generic constraints (Quint 1993: 50–96). The poem's generic and

---

[44] Hardie (1997a) discusses the series of closural devices employed in the course of the narrative as well as at the poem's ending. On closure from a psychoanalytic perspective, see Mitchell-Boyask 1996.

intertextual kinship with the Homeric epics invites an assessment of the poem's close in light of those of the *Iliad* and the *Odyssey*. The Homeric epics are marked by openness, whether this is due to their oral and performative pedigree or to the vicissitudes of textual transmission (Fowler 1997: 11; Hardie 1997a: 139). In order to circumvent the uncertainty surrounding the concluding sections of the *Iliad* and the *Odyssey*, critics have turned to the study of other, more formalistic mechanisms of closure: within this framework, the representation of a concluding ritual ceremony at the end of the poem's narrative appears an effective closural device, achieving a resolution of the problems, tensions, and ambiguities that take place in the course of the epic narrative (Redfield 1975: 160– 223). More specifically, in the *Iliad*, the crisis created by Achilles' refusal to participate in the fighting is finally resolved through the ritual ceremony of Hector's burial, a ceremony that effects a reconciliation, albeit a temporary one, between the two enemies, Achilles and Priam (Seaford 1994: 31). Similarly, in the *Odyssey*, as Richard Seaford (1994: 41) has recently argued, the crisis that Odysseus' absence generates for his household is resolved in the domestic sphere with the wedding-like reunion of Odysseus and Penelope, while further violence between Odysseus and his neighbors is eventually averted through a divinely imposed reconciliation. Ritual corruption, though threatened in the course of the epic, is never realized (Redfield 1975: 167–69; Seaford 1989).

Closer to home, Philip Hardie (1997a) has insightfully demonstrated Vergil's self-conscious awareness of the closural problems inherent in his Homeric predecessors and calls attention to Vergil's inversion of the Iliadic ending: the poem concludes with the violent act of the killing of Turnus, while a ritual celebration (in the form of a triumph) is cast as a pledge for the remote future. Hardie goes on to note the absence of formal ritual ceremony at the end of the *Aeneid* but chooses to concentrate on thematic and structural aspects of closure. In his earlier *Epic Successors* (1993: 28), however, he had offered a reading of the poem's ritual vocabulary. Pointing out that sacrifice begins and ends the *Aeneid*, he argues that "the successful sacrifice of Turnus brings to an end the series of misfortunes inaugurated by the failure to sacrifice Sinon."

Nevertheless, as we have seen, a closer look at the ritual representations and the use of vocabulary properly belonging to the ritual intertext in the course of the last book of the epic, far from championing Turnus' death as a "successful" sacrifice, reveals striking instances of ritual perversion: the breaking of the treaty between the enemies is an instance of controlled ritual gone awry; the killings in battle that ensue are now cast as human sacrifices; and in the final scene, the self-designated *devotus* appears no longer willing to submit to a process demanding his life. The incongruity between actual ritual practice and the ritual representations of the narrative is sharpened by the further incongruity between the resolution achieved on the level of plot and the lack thereof on the level of ritual.

In following this tragic pattern of corruption-restoration, the ritual discourse of *devotio* in Book 12 of the *Aeneid* foreshadows a similar mediation of opposites and affirms ritual purity over ritual perversion. The final scene of the poem, however, by defying readerly expectations that the tragic motif of corrupted sacrifice has aroused, robs the reader of the closural relief that ritual restoration provides. In the face of certain death, Turnus asks Aeneas to display the kind of *clementia* expected of a Roman conqueror[45] and grant the poem's final supplication in the manner of Achilles in the *Iliad*. The victim's volition, a constitutive element of *devotio*,[46] as well as of every sacrificial act, is paramount for the successful execution of the ritual and for the restoration of the disrupted ritual order. It does not follow, however, that the subtext of *devotio* is somehow abandoned or no longer operative: *devotio* and ritual perversion are inextricably linked and therefore require restoration and purity in the guise of a successful sacrifice.

Yet the promised successful sacrifice in the form of a *devotio* casts Aeneas as simply the recipient of Turnus' selfless act and effectively deprives him of any active role in the process of restoration and closure. As a result, a new ritual subtext, that of supplication, emerges and places Aeneas at the center of this process.

[45] Compare Anchises' words in 6.851–53, on which see Putnam 1965: 151–201. Of the vast bibliography on this scene, Hardie (1993: 32–35) offers an excellent discussion on the multiplicity of substitutions at work that eventually results in a confusion of the identity of Aeneas himself. See also Thomas 1998.

[46] Compare Livy 8.6.12: *mors voluntaria* [voluntary death], Ennius *Annales* (191–93 *Skutsch*) and especially the use of the word *prudens* (*Skutsch* 356). See also Versnel 1981: 146 and Oakley 1997: 483.

Certainly, Turnus' depiction as a suppliant looks back to the *Iliad* and the exchange between Hector and Achilles (22.306–74); yet there the narrative focuses equally on the two warriors and ends with the death of the one and the certainty of the death of the other. Hector's final words, a curse on his slayer,[47] balance Achilles' rejection of his supplication and affirm that the enmity of the two men will persist even after death. The savagery displayed by Achilles at the moment of Hector's supplication and his disregard for agreements and oaths,[48] however, will eventually be mitigated by his acceptance of Priam's supplication to bury Hector's body at the poem's end. Yet there is a further contrast between the *Iliad* and the *Aeneid* in this final scene. Achilles' rejection is exceptionally cruel because Hector's stance is that of utter submission; nevertheless, the supplication itself is devoid of any of the formal ritual gestures.[49] As a result, in the *Iliad*, the ritual order, though threatened, is never formally corrupted. The pattern of ritual corruption and subsequent restoration appears as a potential problem in Homer but is actualized only in tragedy.

The *Aeneid*, by contrast, presents us with a corrupted *devotio* followed by a corrupted supplication. Unlike Hector, Turnus displays the formal characteristics of supplication: Trojans and Latins (as well as the readers) see him on his knees with his right hand reaching out to Aeneas (*duplicato poplite* [on bent knee], 927; *ille humilis supplex oculos dextramque precantem protendens* [that one, brought low, a suppliant, gazing at him and stretching his right hand], 930).[50] Aeneas rejects the supplication by employing the vocabulary of human sacrifice (*immolat*, 949). As such, his slaying of Turnus is a perversion of the ritual of supplication, which prescribes the granting of the request and prohibits the sacrifice of humans.

At the same time, Turnus' unwillingness to die is also a perversion of the ritual of *devotio*. Turnus' sacrifice bears a striking resemblance

---

[47] On the significance of the absence of this curse in the *Aeneid*, see Johnson 1976: 115–16.

[48] See, for instance, Schein 1984: 152–53 and Thornton 1984: 139.

[49] Thornton 1984: 138; Gould (1973: 75–77) describes these gestures in full.

[50] The narrative poignantly marks the presence of spectators in this final scene of the poem. The emphasis on the spectators of the duel forms a parallel to the spectators of the treaty earlier in the book.

to the earlier instance of sacrificial perversion that took place after the disruption of the treaty. As we have already seen, in that passage we witness a confusion of the boundaries between ritual slaughter and slaughter on the battlefield:

> ... at feruidus[51] *aduolat hasta*
> Messapus teloque orantem multa trabali
> desuper altus equo grauiter ferit atque ita fatur:
> 'hoc habet, haec melior magnis data uictima diuis.'  (12.293–96)

> ... but Messapus blazing, *flies* with his *spear*
> high on his horse, and strikes hard down upon him with his beamlike
>     weapon even as the man begged for mercy and speaks thus:
> "He's had it, this is a better victim given to the great gods."

> ... *uolat* atri turbinis instar
> exitium dirum *hasta* ferens orasque recludit
> loricae et clipei extremos septemplicis orbis;  (12.923–25)

> The *spear flies* like a black whirlwind
> bringing dire death and lays loose the corselet's rim
> and the outermost circles of the sevenfold shield.

Much like Aulestes, who had stumbled on the altar and begged for mercy, Turnus too is making a formal request as a suppliant while simultaneously declaring his unwillingness to undergo the process of self-sacrifice. The last line of the poem, Turnus' life fleeing indignant with a moan to the shades below, looks back to *devotio* by calling attention to the unwillingness of the victim; the reference to the shades below (*sub umbras*, 952) evokes, however indirectly, the victim's dedication to the gods of the Underworld, one of the characteristics of *devotio* proper. All expectations for ritual restoration, repeatedly aroused and reinforced, are thus permanently defied, and formal closure is thwarted with the persistence of ritual perversion.

---

[51] Aeneas is also described as *feruidus* as he gives the final blow to Turnus: *hoc dicens ferrum aduerso sub pectore condit / fervidus* [saying this, blazing, he buries his sword into the breast facing him] (12.950–51).

Turnus' final plea to Aeneas not only corrupts the proper form
of *devotio*, which the ritual plot of the final book had been at pains to
establish, but also disrupts his portrayal as a heroic and unifying force in
the poem. We have seen that Turnus' depiction as a *devotus* renders him
a symbol of the unity between Latins and Trojans. The concept of unity
and incorporation is paramount in supplication as well.[52] The stress on
the power imbalance between supplicated and suppliant emphasizes the
status of the latter as an "outsider" who seeks his incorporation within
the community (Gould 1973: 101). Yet an important distinction needs
to be made. In the case of the *Aeneid*, the ritual intertext of *devotio* has
promised that unity between the warring sides would be accomplished
through the willing self-sacrifice of Turnus. When Turnus refuses to fulfill his role as a scapegoat and becomes a suppliant, he requests his own
incorporation within Aeneas' new order.

Nevertheless, unity, reconciliation, and peace need to be achieved
side by side with the restoration of ritual purity. *Devotio* and supplication
intersect in the final scene of the poem. Turnus, be it as a *devotus* or as
a *supplex*, acts as a symbol of the collective unity that Jupiter and Juno
proclaimed earlier in the poem. However we may choose to interpret
Turnus' request for his own incorporation within this new order, it is
certain that while ritual perversion persists, unity between the warring
sides cannot be realized. Unlike what happens in Greek tragedy, ritual
corruption in the *Aeneid* appears stripped of the possibility of restoration,
and ritual closure is thereby denied.

Within this context, the absence of ritual purity at the end of the
poem poignantly underscores the inefficacy of the final sacrifice of Turnus
while at the same time promoting uncertainty regarding the ability of
Aeneas' new order to establish lasting peace. I have shown the mechanisms through which the vocabulary of the Roman ritual of *devotio* is
deployed in the last portions of the *Aeneid*. This vocabulary indicates the
existence of a ritual intertext of *devotio* in the poem that would be intuitively recognized and understood by the readership of the *Aeneid*. The
ritual plot is subsequently manipulated to raise and sustain expectations

---

[52] Gould 1973: 95. To be sure, Gould's analysis focuses on Greek *hiketeia*. One
should stress, however, that Vergil's Roman audience would have been able to
relate the implications of this Greek ritual practice to their own experience.

for ritual closure. The inclusion of the tragic pattern of ritual corruption intensifies and reinforces readerly expectations for ritual correctness. The poem ends, however, with an act of sacrificial perversion, as Turnus is transformed from willing victim to slain suppliant. The conclusion of the ritual plot thus undermines the closural effect of the narrative plot, sharpening anxiety, resisting completion, and permanently defying expectations for closure.

# SECTION B

# RESTORATION

# 3 The Fragility of Reconciliation: Ritual Restoration and the Divine

IN THE PREVIOUS CHAPTERS WE HAVE EXAMINED THE WAYS IN which the narrative plot of the *Aeneid* mobilizes a ritual intertext consisting of representations of rituals and the use of ritual vocabulary and metaphors. This ritual intertext is inspired by and is akin to Greek tragedy's manipulation of ritual to exhibit the conflict and crisis of the tragic plot. The correct execution of rituals on the part of humans guarantees smooth relations with the gods. In this chapter, I turn to the divine figures of the epic and suggest that they too play an integral part within the epic's ritual intertext. As we have already seen, the poem's narrative opens with Juno's grievances against the Trojans, grievances linked with the ritual practice of sacrifice. In her anger, Juno envisions a future where humans disregard her divinity by forgoing the practice of rituals in her honor. The poem ends with Jupiter's promise of new rituals honoring Juno and his assurance of the people's unequaled piety. The representation of the divine in the *Aeneid*, therefore, goes side by side with the deployment of the poem's ritual intertext.

Since the *Aeneid* is, among other things, a poem about civil war, the ability of the warring parties to come to reconciliation is a central concern. This theme of reconciliation dominates the depiction of the relationships among gods, from the collusion of archenemies Venus and Juno to the final compromise between Jupiter and Juno that ushers in the end of the poem and lends legitimacy to the killing of Turnus. By placing reconciliation on the divine level, the poem proclaims it as lasting and permanent. Nevertheless, divine reconciliation is implicated in the intertext of ritual corruption at work in the poem, thus exposing its inherent fragility.

More specifically, I argue that divine action in the *Aeneid* mirrors the tragic ritual pattern of corruption and thwarted restoration found in the context of other rituals in the poem. Both Juno and her minions instigate ritual corruption or even delight in their participation within the framework of ritual perversion operative in the poem. We witness, as it were, a replication of the pattern of repetition (for the term, see Chapter 1, pp. 14–16) in the depiction of the divine, as different versions of Juno oppose afresh Aeneas and his mission throughout the epic narrative. By the poem's end, however, Juno and these other supernatural forces (whether they are openly in the service of Juno or simply appear to share an opposition to Aeneas) all undergo a transformation that allows them not only to accept but also to support Aeneas' mission and the future of Rome. This divine transformation is analogous to the process of ritual restoration that is expected to occur on the human plane. Nevertheless, just as the poem's ritual intertext is devoid of any ritual restoration, so is the divine sphere: Juno and her entourage resist transformation and retain their original attributes.

Juno, however, is not the only deity who manipulates and perverts the religious order to serve her own agenda. Jupiter and Venus have no qualms about using religious perversion to achieve their own goals, even though they appear to proclaim a new and superior idea of justice on which Aeneas' new state will be founded. The gods' disregard of the religious order is manifested either through their active involvement in ritual perversion (as is the case with Venus' collusion with Juno) or through their marked passivity while Juno's agents run rampant at Aeneas' expense. By the poem's end, after the reconciliation of the opposing deities, Jupiter may be said to have been assimilated to the realm of Juno. As a result, the ideological polarities the deities represent are eventually confused, and the pattern of ritual corruption-restoration is thwarted on the divine level as well, calling into question the effectiveness of the process of reconciliation.

The representation of the divine in the *Aeneid* thus mirrors the ideological (op)positions that the poem explores on the human plane. Gods are as much a part of the epic fiction as the humans, as Lyne and Feeney have shown; they are epic characters, whose depiction is consistent with some of their fundamental divine attributes but also contingent upon narrative demands (Lyne 1987: 61–99; Feeney 1991: 129–87). As both deities and epic characters, it is not surprising that they too are embedded within the pattern of ritual repetition operative in the poem. As a result, an analysis of the gods' actions needs to be included in our examination of the epic's ritual intertext.

Since a great variety of forms of divine representation from state cult and literary practices was available to Vergil for manipulation (Feeney 1998: 92–104), his divinities exhibit traits traditionally associated with their deity. But the poet also appropriates the rich tradition of the divine representations in epic and tragedy. While Vergil's gods display many attributes of their Homeric counterparts, they are unlike the Homeric gods in that they are entrenched in the poem's teleology vis-à-vis the foundation of the Roman state and its future domination and supremacy over others. On both these counts the gods in the *Aeneid* resemble those of Greek tragedy.[1] An analysis of the defining characteristics of divine figures suggests that the overall deployment of the action of the gods in the epic shares important similarities with the representation of the gods in Aeschylus' *Oresteia*. The *Aeneid*, however, has an ending much different from the conclusion of the trilogy: in Aeschylus, the Erinyes, formerly persecuting Orestes, become the protectors of Athens, the city that offered him asylum. By contrast, in the *Aeneid* their transformation is not as complete as it may initially appear, and the triumph of Jupiter's justice remains open to question.

In what follows, I will first examine the deployment of the motif of ritual pollution on the divine level, with Juno and the Furies as its primary agents. I will then show that the supernatural forces of ritual corruption are intimately bound up with the theme of civil war; that the process of *concordia* is jeopardized by divine manipulation of proper rituals; and that the final reconciliation between Jupiter and Juno appropriates and transforms the solutions to the problem of violence propounded in Aeschylus' *Oresteia*.


## I. VERSIONS OF JUNO: FURIES AND RITUAL POLLUTION

Epic tradition prescribes that the hero face and overcome perils of various kinds. As dictated by the epic's literary models (in this case, the *Odyssey*

---

[1] See, for instance, Harrison 1972–73 and Feeney 1991: 132, 143, 153.

and the *Argonautica*), various supernatural creatures hinder Aeneas' journey to Latium as well as facilitate the outbreak of war between Trojans
and Latins. To be sure, the repeated intrusion of these creatures is necessary for the creation of the plot. In the *Aeneid*, however, they are more
than obstacles that the hero must successfully surmount. They constitute
versions of Aeneas' archenemy, the goddess Juno, actual (creatures working on her behalf) or symbolic (creatures that display her characteristics
and/or employ her methods). Moreover, their appearance is accompanied
by a distortion of the proper performance of rituals and thus belongs to
the larger context of the repetition of ritual distortion in the poem.

In the following, I argue that the link between the Furies of the *Aeneid*
and ritual distortion is achieved through the appropriation of a host of
elements characterizing the Erinyes in Aeschylus' *Oresteia*: the confusion
between the Olympic and the chthonic realm; the clash between supernatural creatures associated with the female and the divine order associated with the male; and a proliferation of violence against attempts to
restore peace. As a result, we may speak of a continuous replication of
certain oppositions, which can be outlined as follows:

| | |
|---|---|
| Jupiter | Juno |
| Olympian (Venus, Mercury, Apollo, Neptune, Pallas Minerva) | Chthonic (Dirae, Harpies, Allecto) |
| Male | Female |
| Concordia/peace | Discordia/(civil) war |
| Empire without end | Endless (repetition of civil) war |

Since the importance of the Furies in the epic is paramount, it is necessary to discuss briefly their precise identity. Thought to be a collective
deity in the *Iliad* and in the *Oresteia*, they are given the individual names
Tisiphone, Allecto, and Megaera by subsequent authors. All three names
also appear in the *Aeneid*. Throughout the poem, the Furies are named
with the Greek terms *Erinyes* and *Eumenides*; the Latin terms *Furiae* and
*Dirae* also appear to apply to them interchangeably. Servius remarks that
the Furies live on Earth, the Dirae in Heaven, and the Eumenides in the
Underworld and goes on to note that poets confuse the three names.[2]

---

[2] Servius on *Aen.* 4.609. On the terms *Erinyes* and *Eumenides*, see Brown 1984:
267. Brown argues that the equation of the Eumenides with the Erinyes occurs

Aeneas' encounter with the Harpies in Book 3 is a fine example of the rich array of connections among supernatural creatures, the Furies, and ritual pollution. Hungry after long wanderings in the ocean, the Trojans land on the shores of the Strophades and slaughter some of the cattle roaming freely. As they prepare to feast, the Harpies attack them and defile their food. The link between the Harpies and the Furies/Dirae is meticulously detailed throughout the episode[3] and reaches its impressive climax with the Harpy Celaeno describing herself as *Furiarum maxima* (352) before she utters her horrifying prophecy.[4] This correlation between the Harpies and the Furies is well based on conceptions of the Harpies in Greek thought, where they are associated with the Erinyes as early as Homer.[5] It is also present in the other important text for this episode, Apollonius' *Argonautica*: Phineus calls one of the Harpies attacking his food *Erinys* (2.220).[6]

The theme of ritual distortion and pollution is also central to this episode, as the Harpies attack the Trojans while they prepare a ritual meal.

---

first in Euripides' *Orestes*. He also notes that in using the term *Eumenides* to refer to the Furies (*Aen.* 4.469, 6.250, 280, 375), Vergil perhaps follows Ennius' *Eumenides* (though direct evidence is lacking) and Varro's satire *Eumenides*. Hübner (1970) argues for a distinction between Jupiter's Dirae and the Furies of the Underworld. Edgeworth (1986) believes that the Dirae are different from the Erinyes, yet he recognizes that all the creatures are infernal. Mackie (1992), after examining pictorial evidence from South Italy and Etruria, argues that the Dirae of *Aeneid* 12 are the Furies (Allecto, Tisiphone, and Megaera). Dyson (2001: 128 n.12) believes that Vergil's views on this identification are ambiguous.

[3] See Hübner 1970: 64–70. Note that the word *dira* is used five times in a span of fifty-seven lines, consistently associated with the Harpies: *uox...dira* (228); *dira...gente* (235); *dira...fames* (256); *dirae...uolucres* (262). See also Williams 1962: 106–107.

[4] The same phrase is used at 6.605 of Tisiphone, "one of the Furies who is engaged in the harpy-like activity of preventing Tantalus from touching the food" (Williams 1962: 106).

[5] See *Odyssey* 20.78, where they hand the daughters of Pandareus over to the Erinyes.

[6] Both Homer's episode of the slaughtering of the cattle of Helios and *Argon.* 2.178–310 (especially 262–97) are important for Vergil's rendition of the myth here. Similar links between the Furies and the Harpies are found in Aeschylus' *Eumenides* 50–51, where the Pythia, in her effort to describe the sleeping Erinyes, first likens them to Gorgons, then to Harpies.

In his narrative, Aeneas emphasizes that he and his comrades made sure that Jupiter and the other gods took part in the meal by offering the due portion of the sacrifice to them (*diuos ipsumque uocamus / in partem prae-damque Iouem* [we call the gods and Jupiter himself to share the spoil], 222–23). But the vocabulary describing the slaughter (*inruimus ferro*, 222; *praeda*, 223) belongs to the realm of battle and hunting rather than to that of sacrifice (Vance: 1981: 131). What is more, by killing animals that roam freely (*nullo custode*, 221), they further transgress ritual norms, which prescribe that only a domestic animal may be sacrificed.[7] The Harpies react to the Trojans' transgression by defiling their food. Instead of enjoying the nourishment of the sacrificial meal,[8] the Harpies embody the pollution incurred after its corruption.[9]

Ritual vocabulary describing pollution abounds in the episode, evident in the extensive use of the verb *foedare* to describe the actions of both the Harpies and the Trojans and of the adjective *foedus* (*foedissima uentris / proluuies* [most foul their droppings], 216–17; *contactuque omnia foedant* [they defile everything with their touch], 227; *ferro foedare uolucris* [to wound the birds with their sword], 241; *uestigia foeda relinquunt* [they leave foul traces], 244).[10] One could certainly translate *foedare* here as simply "to soil, stain" (*OLD* s.v. *foedo* 1). In a sacrificial context, however, the word may very well retain its religious connotations. The problem of pollution is compounded by the Trojans' effort to solve the problem of ritual perversion by repeating the ritual, whereupon they provoke yet another onslaught by the Harpies:

> instruimus mensas arisque reponimus ignem;
> rursum ex diuerso caeli caecisque latebris
> turba sonans praedam pedibus circumuolat uncis,
> polluit ore dapes.                                                    (231–34)

> we set up the tables and light again a fire on the altars;
> again from various parts of the sky and dark hiding places

---

[7] Vance 1981: 131; see also Vernant 1989: 166–67 on the slaying of Helios' cattle in *Od.* 12.

[8] Vance (1981: 131) notes that the episode contrasts proper sacrificial food that is life-giving to that which is improper and corrupting.

[9] On the Harpies and pollution, see also Hübner 1970: 71.

[10] See also *polluit ore dapes*, 234.

> the noisy crowd flies about their prey with its hooked talons,
> and pollutes our meal with its mouth.

The repetition of ritual thus results in further pollution, to which the Trojans react with violence, a violence that brings about the horrifying prophecy of the Harpy Celaeno, that the Trojans will eat their own tables upon their arrival in Italy (256–57).[11] Their violent attack on the Harpies is described in terms that connote that the Trojans' act is equally polluting: *ferro foedare uolucris* (241). Although the verb in this instance is usually taken as a very strong word meaning "to wound" (*OLD* s.v. *foedo* 3: "to wound savagely, mangle, hack, mutilate"),[12] it constitutes a verbal repetition of the words hitherto employed to describe the Harpies. Thus the Trojans' improper ritual has caused the attack of the Harpies, which embody the idea of ritual pollution. At the same time, the Trojans' efforts toward ritual restoration result in a proliferation of this pollution.[13]

Repetition is prominent in this episode with the Trojan's twofold attempt at a sacrificial meal and the Harpies' repeated attacks. This repetition, so necessary for the advancement of the episode's action, is also related to the larger theme of ritual distortion at work in the poem. It looks back to the episode of Polydorus, where the hero, in preparation for the performance of a sacrifice, attempts to uproot bleeding branches three times, thus provoking the apparition of the dead Polydorus, who warns of the pollution Aeneas is about to incur. Aeneas has committed an improper act, and ritual perversion is averted as he and his men execute burial rites for their dead compatriot.[14] But repetition is also at

---

[11] On the sacrilegious nature of this action, see Horsfall 2000: 111.

[12] See Williams 1962: 104.

[13] Despite the hideousness of their physical appearance and their violent behavior, the Harpies in the *Aeneid* act defensively rather than aggressively (Putnam 1995: 64). The Trojans attempt to drive the Harpies away from what they consider their territory (*patrio...regno*, 249). Vergil reverses the effect of Apollonius' narrative: the focus in the *Argonautica* is on Phineus' torture. Yet when Phineus asks the Argonauts to help him, Zetes extracts a promise from him that in doing so they would not offend the gods (*Argon.* 2.251–53). No such caution exists in Vergil's narrative when the heroes, themselves subjected to Phineus' notorious torture, engage in a fight with the Harpies.

[14] On the episode of Polydorus and Aeneas' execution of ritual ceremonies, see Dyson 2001: 35–39.

work in the casting of the Harpies as Furies, who thus implicitly constitute agents of Juno. As versions of the goddess, they belong to the larger
framework of repetition of ritual distortion through which the goddess
operates in the epic.

Since the Harpies are cast as Furies, they share their chthonic nature.
It is no surprise, therefore, to find them dwelling in Hades later in the
poem (6.289).[15] In opposing Aeneas and his Trojans, they also oppose
the Olympian order of Jupiter that protects and favors the foundation
of the new city and the creation of the Roman empire. Celaeno, however, confuses this carefully outlined distinction between Olympian and
chthonic, when she proclaims that her prophecy comes straight from the
mouth of Jupiter with Apollo as the go-between:

> accipite ergo animis atque haec mea figite dicta,
> quae Phoebo pater omnipotens, mihi Phoebus Apollo
> praedixit, uobis Furiarum ego maxima pando.            (3.250–52)

> take then these words of mine and fix them to your hearts;
> what the almighty father foretold Phoebus, and Phoebus Apollo
> to me, I, the greatest of the Furies, disclose to you.

The Furies then, if we believe Celaeno, are privy to Olympian knowledge.[16] By the end of the epic, we have been told to expect a triumph of
the Olympian forces over those of Furor. But for the moment, at least,

---

[15] Lines 6.285–89 recall Aeneas' journey: the hero now reacts to the Harpies in
the same way he did in Book 3: once again he grabs his sword and threatens
them. The reference in the same passage in Book 6 to Scylla, a creature not normally associated with Hades (Austin 1977: 122), also points to the connection
between this passage and Aeneas' voyage.

[16] Celaeno's prophecy is unique to Vergil. See Williams 1962: 107. When the
prophecy is fulfilled at *Aen.* 7.109–29, Aeneas (erroneously) recalls that it was
given by Anchises. On Apollonius' influence on this episode, see Nelis 2001:
32–38. Nelis observes that Apollonius' description of the Harpies differs from
Vergil's in that it supports an interpretation of the Harpies as winds (33). He
also notes that Celaeno's prophecy is an inversion of the helpful prophecy of
Phineus after the Harpies have been chased away by the Argonauts (35). In
Apollonius it is Iris, Celaeno's sister (Hesiod, *Th.* 266–67), who speaks as the
Harpies are driven away. Nelis (36) rightly suggests that Celaeno's curse is a
counterpart to Helios' anger at the slaughter of his cattle (*Od.* 12.377–83).

Jupiter appears to be implicated in Juno's plan to persecute the Trojans, as the Harpies emerge to be as much his minions as hers.

The paradox of the close relationship between Celaeno and Apollo is further complicated through an intertextual connection between the Harpy's words and Aeschylus' *Eumenides*: Διὸς προφήτης δ'ἐστὶ Λοξίας πατρός [Loxias is the prophet of his father Zeus] (19).[17] The plot of that play is structured around a similar opposition between Zeus and Apollo on the one hand and the Erinyes on the other, between forces that are explicitly Olympian and chthonic, respectively. The Pythia's description of the Erinyes (ἐπεὶ κακόν / σκότον νέμονται Τάρταρόν θ᾽ ὑπὸ χθονός, / μισήματ᾽ ἀνδρῶν καὶ **θεῶν** Ὀλυμπίων [since they live in evil darkness and in Tartarus beneath the earth, hateful to men and to the Olympian **gods**], 71–74) also shares intertextual contact with the description of the Harpies: *nec saeuior ulla / pestis et* ira **deum** Stygiis *sese extulit undis* [no plague more savage or wrath of the **gods** ever rose from the waves of Styx] (3.214–15).[18] We see therefore that the episode of the Harpies has bearing on the larger tragic pattern at work in the epic, which results from the intersection of the ritual and allusive intertexts.

Pollution is also a theme central both to this episode of the *Aeneid* and to Aeschylus' *Eumenides*. In the play, Orestes claims that he has been ritually purified (*Eum.* 280–83); but the Pythia describes his hands as dripping with blood (*Eum.* 42–43). Apollo's purification is thus negated by the blood-thirsty Erinyes and will be effective only after the Erinyes are transformed to Eumenides. In the *Aeneid*, the pollution incurred from the Harpies is recognized by Aeneas' companions after Celaeno's prophecy. They ask for a reconciliation with offerings and prayers. The ritual import of the request is indicated by the use of a religious formula (*sed uotis precibusque iubent exposcere pacem* [but they bid to ask for peace with offerings and prayers], 261)[19] and confirmed by Anchises himself, the religious authority of the Trojans, who proclaims that sacrifices are due (*meritosque indicit honores*,

---

[17] The connection is found in Macrobius, *Sat.* 5.22.13, who also cites Aeschylus' *Hieriae* (86 *TrGF Radt*) as Vergil's source: στέλλειν ὅπως τάχιστα· ταῦτα γὰρ πατὴρ / Ζεὺς ἐγκαθίει Λοξίαι θεσπίσματα, [send as quickly as possible; for these oracles father Zeus entrusts to Loxias].

[18] The words in bold are common to the two texts, while the words underlined with a dotted line are not exact translations but express similar ideas.

[19] Williams 1962: 109, 131.

264). Ritual vocabulary emerges next when the Trojans reach Actium and perform purification in honor of Jupiter (*lustramurque Ioui uotisque incendi-mus aras* [we perform rites of cleansing to Jupiter and we light the altars with offerings], 279) followed by the celebration of games.[20]

Aeneas' stop at the site of the future single most significant Augustan victory provides a very desirable continuity between past and present, which the games can only intesify. Games were celebrated both in Rome and at Nicopolis, a city founded by Augustus after his victory and located opposite the site of the battle (Lloyd 1954: 296). If the narrative replicates Augustus' games, then the ceremony of purification preceding them requires an explanation. In 28 BCE, the same year that the Actian games were celebrated in Rome, a censorial lustration had also taken place as a symbol of the ending of civil war (Lloyd 1954: 298). Aeneas' purification from the ritual pollution effected by the Harpies is thus linked with the pollution Rome incurred because of the civil strife. Yet it is important to note that Aeneas' purification here is rather unsuccessful as Furies continue to persecute him in Italy and violence is not yet brought to an end. It is time to consider next in what ways civil war determines the depiction of Furies in the epic.

## II. FURIES AS AGENTS OF DISCORDIA

The active role of the Furies in the war narrative of the *Aeneid* is well established. Furies are responsible for or participate in almost every battle scene in the poem. For instance, the Fury Allecto is the sole instigator of the collision between Trojans and Latins that dominates the second half of the epic,[21] while in Aeneas' narrative of Book 2 a Fury is used as a metonymy for the destruction of Troy (*in flammas et in arma feror, quo tristis Erinys, / quo fremitus uocat et sublatus ad aethera clamor* [I am driven between flames and weapons, where grim Erinys, where the roar and the cries rising to the sky call], 337–38).[22] Furthermore, the Furies

---

[20] On the games as part of the purification, see Hübner 1970: 71. See also Lloyd 1954: 296.

[21] On Allecto's relationship with ritual perversion, see Chapter 4, pp. 128–129.

[22] This is the first appearance of the word *Erinys* in the poem. Later on in the same book, Aeneas calls Helen *Troiae et patriae communis Erinys* [Erinys of her fatherland and Troy alike] (573). Commentators have pointed to Aeschylus'

are identified with Discordia, as two important passages in the poem make clear. This identification is linked to their portrayal as chthonic forces that cause ritual distortion. Such forces are typically at work during times of civil unrest. The end of the poem holds the promise of their transformation followed by ritual restoration.

Both Furies and War share infernal attributes: in the description of Hades in Book 6 the Furies' dwelling is located between Bellum and Discordia:

> ... mortiferumque aduerso in limine Bellum,
> ferreique Eumenidum thalami et Discordia demens
> uipereum crinem uittis innexa cruentis.                  (6.279–81)

> ... on the threshold opposite [are] death-dealing War
> and the iron chambers of the Eumenides and raving Discord,
> her snaky hair bound with bloody ribbons.

The topographical placement of these three entities denotes their deep connection, also indicated by the use of the adjective *ferreus* to describe the home of the Furies. Discordia's snaky hair further casts her as a Fury.[23]

The connection between Furies and Discordia is both confirmed and complicated in the *ekphrasis* of Aeneas' shield, which depicts the battle of Actium:

> omnigenumque deum monstra et latrator Anubis
> contra Neptunum et Venerem contraque Mineruam
> tela tenent. saeuit medio in certamine Mauors
> caelatus ferro, tristesque *ex aethere* Dirae,
> et scissa gaudens uadit Discordia palla,
> quam cum sanguineo sequitur Bellona flagello.        (8.698–703)

> monstrous gods of every shape and barking Anubis
> wield weapons against Neptune and Venus

*Agamemnon*: τὰν δορίγαμβρον ἀμφινεικῆ θ' / Ἑλέναν [the bride of the spear who caused death on both sides, Helen] (687–88); also compare νυμφόκλαυτος Ἐρινύς also of Helen [a Fury who brought tears to brides] (749). There is a similar phrase in Euripides' *Orestes* (1387–88), a passage intertextually linked to that of Aeschylus. See Willink 1986: 310.

23 It is important to note that this description of Discordia will be recalled in other appearances of Furies: e.g., Tisiphone later in this book (555), Allecto in Book 7 (cf., for instance, 351), and the Dirae at the battle of Actium (8.702).

and against Minerva. In the middle of the battle Mars rages
embossed in steel and the grim Dirae *from the upper air*;
Discordia marches rejoicing in her torn mantle,
and Bellona follows her with bloody scourge.

The passage at first creates a neat juxtaposition between gods Egyptian
(monstrous gods and Anubis) and Roman (Neptune, Venus, and Minerva).
By contrast, Mars (notably a Roman god), the Dirae, Discordia, and
Bellona all operate on both sides. Once again, we find the Dirae as agents
of civil war, located between War and Discordia. Despite their function as destructive forces, however, they seem to have abandoned their
infernal abode. They no longer occupy the lower end of the divine pole,
but have moved upward and have access to Olympus (*tristesque ex aethere
Dirae*).[24] The realm of *aether* is associated in the epic with Jupiter, as the
god's first appearance attests (1.223; see Feeney 1991: 150). As a result,
it is deeply disturbing to see these creatures aligned with the supreme
deity at the most critical moment of the civil conflict, urging the combatants on to more violence. The location of the Dirae thus suggests a
blurring of the boundaries between Hades and Olympus, order and dis-
order, friend and foe.

Such confusion is typical of narratives of civil war and is frequently
followed by instances of ritual pollution. The reader awaits a restoration
of these distinctions at the end of the poem, where the reconciliation
between Jupiter and Juno takes place. Having examined the identity of
the Dirae as agents of pollution and Discordia, we may now turn to the
process of *concordia* and how it is achieved between opposing deities in
the course of the poem.

## III. VENUS, JUNO, AND THE FRAGILITY OF *CONCORDIA*

Venus' intervention in the action of the poem parallels that of Juno. As
the goddess who protects Aeneas and champions his interests to Jupiter,
she forms a natural polar opposite to the goddess who does everything
in her power to destroy him. Although the two deities have conflicting

---

[24] This representation goes against the traditional belief that the Erinyes are hated
by the gods: for instance, see Aesch. *Eum.* 73, 644.

agendas, their modus operandi is very similar. Much like Juno, Venus often treats ritual acts as opportunities for furthering her goals. Accordingly, she distorts rites in a manner that recalls Juno's manipulation of bacchic ritual (in Book 7) or the rites of a treaty (Book 12). As a locus where the human and the divine meet, ritual acts constitute the means by which deities may communicate their will to humans. Yet Venus, like Juno, is not satisfied simply to convey her will through these appropriate channels but actively interferes in human affairs, often in the context of ritual. An examination of the moments of Venus' active participation in the plot of the poem reveals an utter disregard for correct ritual procedure. By negating ritual correctness, she is complicit in the instigation or perpetuation of ritual disruption and crisis and may thus be read as a version of Juno: she constitutes yet another divine figure who promotes repetition of ritual corruption in the epic. At the same time, since she is aligned with the Olympic realm of Jupiter, she foreshadows the eventual assimilation of the Olympic order into that of Juno.

The kinship between Venus and Juno becomes most salient in *Aeneid* 4, where the two deities collude with an aim of establishing a union between Dido and Aeneas. This is a rare and important moment of *concordia* in the poem, albeit one that is as artificial as it is temporary: both Venus and Juno place emphasis upon the kinship of their divine spheres – namely, *amor* and *conubium*, respectively – in order to reach their common goal. Their *concordia*, however, is predicated upon a distortion of rituals, and specifically those of *hospitium* (by Venus) and marriage (by Juno). The goddesses' utter disrespect for ritual correctness prefigures not only the tragic outcome of the affair between Aeneas and Dido but also the fragility of the process of achieving *concordia*. Furthermore, their pact illuminates the *concordia* achieved in the reconciliation scene between Jupiter and Juno in Book 12.

Juno outlines the terms of this alliance as preserving equality between the two goddesses, whose competition (*certamine*, 98) is at the center of their relationship. She carefully delineates the contours of this equality, aiming at appeasing her rival's pride, and assures her that their interests are best served by their alliance. She proposes lasting peace (*pacem aeternam*, 99) both between themselves and between the two peoples they protect, a peace based upon community (*communem . . . populum*, 102) and equality (*paribusque regamus / auspiciis* [let us rule with equal authority],

102–103). Juno suggests that this peace should be sealed with a marriage (*pacem aeternam pactosque hymenaeos* [lasting peace and an arranged
marriage], 99), a tactical ploy on her part, designed to undermine the
equality she proposes in two ways. First, the institution she supports as
goddess of marriage will now preside over and protect the love that Venus
has instigated. At the same time, although marriage ideally celebrates
the complementary nature of the roles of husband and wife, in reality it
reflects and replicates a patriarchal social structure that prescribes the
submission of wife to husband, as Juno's vocabulary makes plain (*liceat
Phrygio servire marito* [let her serve a Phrygian husband], 103). According
to Juno, Dido and Carthage will be under Aeneas' sway. By casting this
specific marriage as an expansion of Venus' domain (*dotalisque tuae Tyrios
permittere dextrae* [yield her Tyrians to your power as dowry], 104), Juno
attempts to convince her rival that she is getting the better end of the
deal; in actuality, however, not only does Dido's and Aeneas' marriage
fall neatly within Juno's sphere of influence (and therefore Venus' place in
this equation is undermined), but also Aeneas' role as leader of Carthage
ensures that Rome will never be founded. Juno argues that marital *concordia* will generate *concordia* in gods and humans alike, a desirable goal
for both divinities. Nevertheless, she is fully aware, as is Venus, of the
implications of her proposal.

Juno's choice of vocabulary as she presents her arguments to Venus
further highlights the fragility of the reconciliation she proposes. Her
repeated use of the term *pax* and its derivatives (*pactos*, 99) is not lost
on Venus, who responds by using the same type of vocabulary (*foedera iungi*, 112). Their agreement is thus contractual and legalistic, more
appropriate for two warring parties entering a temporary moment of
mutually advantageous ceasefire than a sincere reconciliation. True peace
would have been denoted by the term *concordia*, which, though implied
by Juno's and Venus' rhetoric, is wholly absent in the scene. The two
divinities thus echo Roman writers such as Cicero, who describes *concordia* as an affective state, a genuine sympathy between opponents, and
a marker of true and lasting peace, as opposed to the term *pax*, which
appears to be no longer enough to denote all the attributes of peace that
the Romans thought indispensable (Jal 1961: 212–21).[25] Juno and Venus

---

[25] I owe this point to Neil Coffee.

fully understand and readily exploit the fine nuances of the ideological vocabulary they employ, thus reinforcing the notion that they are not so different from one another.

The two goddesses emerge as equals only in their manipulation and distortion of ritual institutions and in their exploitation of the very ideal of *concordia* they profess to support. Juno, by holding Dido's and Aeneas' wedding ceremony in supernatural terms, renders it ambiguous and destabilizes its meaning. She ensures that all the elements of wedding ritual are present,[26] and she has a role in it herself (*pronuba*, 166); yet this ceremony defies the fundamental nature of ritual, which is to provide a space controlled by humans so that communication with the divine can be achieved. Viewed in this light, the differing interpretations that Dido and Aeneas draw from the events in the cave may be explained as a consequence of the distorted ritual in which they participate.

Venus replicates Juno's pattern of action earlier in Book 1, where she orders Amor to infect Dido with love for Aeneas. Though markedly different from the way in which Juno stirs up chthonic forces in the service of war and destruction, Venus' act, nevertheless, will also result in the death of Dido and will set in motion the course of events that will bring about the Carthaginian wars and the destruction of the city of Carthage. But Venus acts like Juno on another deeper, and in many ways more disturbing, level in that she operates by distorting and manipulating the ritual elements of *hospitium*. The goddess claims that Dido's hospitality may be treacherous (*Iunonia hospitia*, 672) and thus justifies her interference; without hesitation, she uses the context of the banquet, an integral part of the ritual of *hospitium*, to put her plan into effect.

Before I go on to illustrate how Venus manipulates ritual procedure, a few words on the ritualized nature of *hospitium* are in order. Though primarily a social institution, *hospitium* contains ritualized elements, most conspicuously a ceremony of initiation. Greek and Roman epic narratives represent this ceremony as consisting of a series of symbolic gestures enacted in sequence, elaborately described also in *Aeneid* 1: a sacrifice (632–36), gift exchange (647–55), feasting (637–42; 697–722), and a libation to Jupiter *hospitalis* (728–40). As a result, these rites invest

---

[26] On the wedding ceremony in Book 4, see also Chapter 2, pp. 48–49.

the bond of *hospitium* with religious importance and sacrosanctity (*OCD* 612), broken only by means of a formal ceremony. Ritualized friendship thus guaranteed mutual support between parties, which included the exchange of valuable resources (money, troops, etc.), usually designated as gifts, and the performance of important services, such as saving the life of one of the two parties (*OCD* 612). In *Aeneid* 1, while Dido and Aeneas' guest-friendship fulfills all the requirements of an epic topos, it is simultaneously represented in specifically Roman terms: Dido and Aeneas are cast as foreign leaders entering into the bond of *amicitia* that ensures continuing *fides* between them and their communities (Monti 1981: 9–10, 24–25). The presence of the Roman vocabulary of political alliance with a foreign people is not out of place here, since Dido's Carthage is painstakingly cast as a surrogate Rome. It is also regularly employed in other instances of *hospitium* in the *Aeneid* (Monti 1981: 27–28).

Since Romans used the vocabulary of interpersonal relations to describe political relationships, guest-friendship is the alternative to marriage in furthering political interests and forging alliances with foreigners.[27] Intertextual contact between the description of Dido's banquet in the *Aeneid* (1.637–42) and Peleus' and Thetis' wedding feast in Catullus 64 (42–52) mobilizes the ritual context of the wedding and foreshadows the subsequent "wedding" between Aeneas and Dido:

> at domus interior regali splendida luxu
> instruitur, mediisque parant conuiuia tectis:
> arte laboratae uestes ostroque superbo,
> ingens argentum mensis, caelataque in auro
> fortia facta patrum, series longissima rerum
> per tot ducta uiros antiqua ab origine gentis.          (*Aen.* 1.637–42)

> But the glittering house inside is laid out with royal finery,
> and in the midst of the palace they prepare a banquet:
> coverlets adorned with art and majestic purple,
> massive silver on the tables, and the courageous deeds
> of the ancestors wrought in gold, the longest series of feats
> traced through so many men from the ancient beginnings of the race.

---

[27] See, for instance, Finley 1977: 99 on the same concept of marriage and friendship in Homeric epic.

Precious objects, richly embroidered garments, and the commemoration of ancestral feats all constitute the core of the description of Peleus' house as the preparations for the wedding take place:

> ipsius at sedes, quacumque opulenta recessit
> regia, fulgenti splendent auro atque argento.
> candet ebur soliis, collucent pocula mensae,
> tota domus gaudet regali splendida gaza.
> puluinar uero diuae geniale locatur
> sedibus in mediis, Indo quod dente politum
> tincta tegit roseo conchyli purpura fuco.
> haec uestis priscis hominum uariata figuris
> heroum mira uirtutes indicat arte.                    (Catullus 64.42–52)

> But his house [sc. Peleus'], as far as the wealthy
> palace reaches, glows with glittering gold and silver.
> Ivory sparkles on the seats, the cups on the table shine bright,
> the whole house rejoices splendid with regal treasure.
> And the royal marriage bed for the goddess is placed
> in the middle of the palace, polished with Indian tusk
> and covered with purple tinged with the rosy stain of the shell.
> This coverlet adorned with the shapes of men of old
> displays the feats of heroes with wondrous art.

The wedding of Peleus and Thetis is far from a purely joyous occasion. The couple will produce Achilles, who is described as causing war and bloodshed and as taking a wife in death with the sacrifice of the virgin Polyxena at his tomb (338–70). Moreover, the coverlet depicts the story of Theseus and Ariadne, a tale of a breach of *fides* and *pietas*, all of which foreshadows the future of the relationship between Aeneas and Dido. Thus the description of Dido's banquet may also be read as a wedding feast.

In this light, other elements in the narrative acquire new significance. For instance, the scene in which Dido leads Aeneas into her palace where the feast is about to take place may also be compared to the bride's entrance into the groom's house after the wedding ceremony and before the wedding feast can begin (Treggiari 1991: 167–68). Contrary to custom, however, according to which the groom leads the bride into the house, Dido is the one who leads Aeneas into the palace (*Aenean in regia ducit / tecta*, 631–32). Aeneas thus assumes the role of the bride (*ducta*) who enters her new marital abode. This reversal of roles is consistent with the previous representation of the union of Aeneas and Dido as one that ensures continuity and growth for Carthage at the expense of the foundation of Rome.

The sacrifices that Dido performs before the banquet, of which one is in honor of Bacchus (632–36), a god associated with marriage, is yet another instance of the possibility of multiple readings of the episode. Although it is uncertain to which gods sacrifice was made at a wedding,[28] the act itself was never omitted, and if it was, bad luck was expected to follow (Treggiari 1991: 164).[29] Similarly, wedding narratives regularly emphasize the feelings of joy the occasion generates among participants and guests,[30] a theme also repeatedly mentioned during the description of Dido's banquet (*limina laeta*, 707; *laetum . . . diem*, 732; *laetitiae*, 734). Finally, when Venus causes Ascanius to fall asleep so that Cupid may impersonate him, she wraps him in flowers of marjoram (*amaracus*, 693), a plant first mentioned in Catullus' marriage hymn (61.6–7), specifically in the description of the god of marriage, Hymen (*cinge tempora floribus / suaue olentis amaraci* [crown your head with the flowers of fragrant marjoram]; see Fedeli 1983: 24). Ascanius' intertextual connection with Hymen thus intensifies the context of wedding ritual operative in the description of Dido's banquet.

This overlap between wedding and *hospitium* in the ritual elements opens up the episode for new interpretative possibilities and creates fruitful ground for Venus to achieve her goals. The goddess, however, displays her indifference to ritual correctness. Cupid's impersonation of Ascanius as he brings Dido the gifts distorts the process of ritualized gift exchange: far from constituting the expression of trusted friendship, gifts now serve to ensure Dido's falling in love (*iamque ibat dicto parens et dona Cupido / regia portabat Tyriis* [now Cupid went on, obeying her word

---

[28] Tellus and Ceres are often mentioned. See Treggiari 1991: 164.

[29] Dido makes further sacrifices, which are more directly associated with wedding ritual, at the beginning of Book 4. See Treggiari 1991: 164 and Monti 1981: 31–32.

[30] See, for instance, Catullus 64.46, 284.

and carrying royal gifts to the Tyrians], 695–96). This link between the gifts and Dido's love is also asserted later on, where Dido is described as moved equally by the boy and the gifts (*pariter puero donisque mouetur*, 714). As a result, Venus actively compromises the bond of guest-friendship between Dido and Aeneas.

The theme of drinking within the context of the feast also serves to show the greater distortion Venus causes to the ritual of the banquet. Wine libations constitute part of the process of initiation into *hospitium* as symbolic of the new bond between guest and host. Accordingly, Dido as host makes a wine offering. As Roman custom prescribes, a woman may take only a sip of the wine consecrated to the god.[31] The creation of this new bond symbolized by drinking is exploited later in this episode to display Dido's growing love for Aeneas as the result of intoxication (*longumque bibebat amorem* [she drank long draughts of love], 749). Thus drinking is here used as a metaphor for forging Dido's relationship with Aeneas as that of both guest and host and "husband and wife." Venus distorts and confuses the ritual of *hospitium* with that of the wedding, a distortion that prefigures the ultimate failure of both. The casting of Dido's passion for Aeneas as intoxication is further recalled in Book 4, when Dido, angry at the news of Aeneas' intention to leave her, is described as a bacchant (300–303). Similarly, the fusion of the institutions of *hospitium* and marriage in this instance is confirmed when Dido calls Aeneas *hospes* and adds that this alone is left from the name of husband (4.323–24). Thus Venus' interference at this juncture causes a confusion of the two rituals and prefigures their ultimate failure.

In her proposal of a *concordia* Juno manipulates the language of marriage to describe an alliance between herself and Venus, Dido and Aeneas. In doing so, she sets the terms of this alliance in a way that purports to maintain equality and equilibrium between the goddesses but in reality serves Juno's plans. Venus' manipulation of the rituals of *hospitium* and

---

[31] See Servius on *Aen.* 1.737: *et verecundiam reginae ostendit, et morem Romanum. nam apud maiores nostros feminae non utebantur vino, nisi sacrorum causa certis diebus* [shows the reverence of the queen and a Roman custom; for at the time of our ancestors women did not use wine, unless for sacred rites on certain days]. Roman women were forbidden from drinking wine as it was considered synonymous with adultery.

*conubium* in Book 1 recalls Juno's actions throughout the poem, thus signaling a pattern of repeated ritual distortion on the part of the divinities. Juno's and Venus' disingenuous *concordia* also illuminates the reconciliation between Jupiter and Juno in Book 12, to which my discussion will now turn.

## IV. TRANSFORMING JUNO: RITUAL RESTORATION IN *AENEID* 12

Ritual plays a prominent role in the scene of the final divine reconciliation, since Jupiter's persuasion of Juno is cast as an *evocatio*.[32] *Evocatio* is the Roman ritual whereby a deity of an enemy city is persuaded to transfer his or her favor to Rome in exchange for a temple and cult worship. Sources attest to the success of the ritual, the first known example being the transfer of Juno's cult from Veii to Rome in 396 BCE and the building of the temple of Juno Regina on the Aventine.[33] Yet Romans continued to feel anxiety over Juno's loyalty to their city, an anxiety that became most pronounced during the Punic Wars: at the time of the Hannibalic crisis, the Romans paid special attention to the worship of Juno, culminating in a ritual procession to her temple on the Aventine in 207 BCE, while in the course of the third Punic war, an *evocatio* of the Juno of Carthage took place.[34] The ritual of *evocatio* thus appears to be successful but does not eliminate the danger that the deity, especially if that deity is Juno, may not always be on the side of Rome.[35]

In his *evocatio*, Jupiter employs a rather heavy-handed rhetorical strategy: his opening words to Juno assert a divine hierarchy in which his authority reigns supreme, his will identical to the all-powerful *fatum*.

---

[32] Johnson 1976: 123–24. Servius on *Aen.* 12.841 implies that an *evocatio* is operative in this episode. See also note 34 to this chapter.

[33] Livy 5.21.1–7; see also Beard 1998, 1: 1, 35.

[34] See Servius on *Aen.* 12.841: *sed constat bello Punico secundo exoratam Iunonem, tertio vero bello a Scipione sacris quibusdam etiam Romam esse translatam* [but it is agreed that Juno was placated during the second Punic war, but in the third war [waged] by Scipio she was even transferred by means of certain rites to Rome]; see also Palmer 1974: 49 and Beard 1998, 1: 82, 111.

[35] See also Servius on *Aen.* 12.830.

This is not exactly persuasion, but it has the effect of making an important point: Juno has no choice but to comply and indeed will be rewarded for doing so. This *evocatio* is thus immediately signaled as quite different from the entreaties of a Roman general to the tutelary deity of the enemy city, where the power lies entirely with the divinity. Jupiter seeks both to compel and appease Juno when he describes his command as an entreaty (*precibusque inflectere nostris* [yield to my prayers], 800), acknowledging his consort's enormous powers (803–805) while also explicitly ordering her to stop (*ulterius temptare veto* [I forbid you to try any further], 806).[36]

This initial imbalance of power between the two divinities is at once asserted and dismantled in what follows. Juno assures Jupiter that she is in full compliance with his will (even if her arguments are rather weak in the face of the amount of havoc she has caused) and that their interests coincide (*pro Latio obtestor, pro maiestate tuorum* [I beg for the sake of Latium, for the greatness of your kin], 820). Juno's show of respect for Jupiter's authority causes him in turn to acknowledge her as his equal and kin (*es germana Iovis, Saturnique altera proles* [you are Jupiter's sister, the other child of Saturn], 830) and to grant her request that the Trojans be renamed Latins as *victus* and *volens* (833). In other words, Juno yields to Jupiter in order to succeed in eliminating the name of Troy, while Jupiter grants Juno her request believing that his will has prevailed. In this instance too, then, as in the case of the reconciliation between Juno and Venus in Book 4, *concordia* is predicated upon an assumed equality of the two parties, while in reality both of them believe that they have gained the upper hand.[37] Significantly, here too, the word *concordia*, which would denote true kinship of spirit between the two divinities, is absent from their negotiations.

The fragility of such a reconciliation becomes even more poignant if we consider the role that ritual, and wedding in particular, is called to play in this process. Jupiter's gesture of acknowledgment of Juno's divinity is to enumerate her accomplishments in this war:

> uentum ad supremum est. terris agitare uel undis
> Troianos potuisti, infandum accendere bellum,
> deformare domum et luctu miscere hymenaeos:     (12.803–805)

[36] See also Lyne 1987: 96.
[37] On the problems of the reconciliation of Juno, see Johnson 1976: 123–27 and Feeney 1984: 179–94 (= Harrison 1990: 339–62).

> It has come to an end. You were powerful to chase the Trojans
> over land and sea, to kindle an unspeakable war,
> to ruin a home and to merge weddings and mourning:

For Jupiter, Juno's extraordinary powers find expression in the destruction of the home and the perversion of marriage. Jupiter's use of the ritual term for marriage, *hymenaeos*, shows that ritual is key in his (and the reader's) understanding of the concept of marriage. Juno also articulates reconciliation and peace in terms of the restoration of marriage (*cum iam conubiis pacem felicibus (esto) / component, cum iam leges et foedera iungent* [when they now make peace with happy marriage (so be it) / when they now join in laws and treaties], 821–22), while Jupiter seals the pact with the promise of rituals to honor Juno, as in the case of an *evocatio* proper (*morem ritusque sacrorum / adiciam* [I will give them sacred law and rites], 836–37; *nec gens ulla tuos aeque celebrabit honores* [nor will any other people celebrate your sacrifices equally], 840).[38] Both deities are claiming to oversee and protect the proper execution of rituals.

Nevertheless, Juno, despite her (reluctant) assurances to the contrary, continues to display her disregard for the realm of the sacred: in that same speech, in an effort to show her compliance with Jupiter's will, Juno swears the oath of Styx that she never instructed Juturna to take up weapons:

> Iuturnam misero (fateor) succurrere fratri
> suasi et pro uita maiora audere probaui,
> non ut tela tamen, non ut contenderet arcum;
> adiuro Stygii caput implacabile fontis,
> una superstitio superis quae reddita diuis.                              (813–17)

> As for Juturna, I persuaded her (I confess) to help her unfortunate brother
> and for his life's sake approved of still greater deeds;
> but not that she should use the arrow, not that she should shoot the bow;
> I swear by the inexorable fountainhead of Styx,
> the only dreadful oath ordained for the gods above.

[38] On *honores* as sacrifices, see Hardie 1993: 19, and on this particular passage, Dyson 2001: 129. Scholars have posited that perhaps Jupiter's words constitute a reference to Augustus' building a temple to Juno, on which see Conington 1884, 3: 476.

Earlier in the book, however, she had baldly authorized Juturna to use force (*aut tu bella cie conceptumque execute foedus. / auctor ego audendi* [or rouse battle and destroy the treaty that has begun. / It is I who bid you dare], 158–59. Commentators point out the clever rhetoric in Juno's use of the words *fratri* and *pro uita*, as they suggest that Juturna should act to protect only her brother's life (Conington 1884, 3: 474). Juno puts her rhetorical skills to work so as to absolve herself of responsibility for the violation of the treaty. The goddess' manipulation of words is consistent with the practice of oath taking in ancient Rome, which dictated the interpretation of the phrasing of the oath in its most technical and literal sense. Juno may be thus manipulating the language of the oath in order to distance herself from Juturna's actions.

Juno may be said to distort the process of oath taking in other ways as well: Roman oaths were usually followed by the addition of a curse in case of perjury (*OCD* 1056). The goddess, however, does not invoke one in this instance and therefore does not complete the process properly. At the same time, her use of the word *superstitio* to describe the oath may also be seen as problematic: the term usually refers to extreme piety or excessive devotion to ritual and the gods and was viewed as a powerful and dangerous practice that might threaten the stability of *religio* and the state (Beard 1998, 1: 217). Juno's characterization of the oath as *superstitio* may evoke all that is negative vis-à-vis the oath. Once again, the goddess can be shown to manipulate an oath of supreme sacrosanctity, such as that of Styx, to achieve her goals. As a result, her promise of ritual restoration is not entirely credible.

If Juno's practices indeed remain unchanged, then the ramifications for the stability of the reconciliation we have just witnessed are devastating on a number of levels. Jupiter and Juno agree to end a war between Trojans and Latins, out of which a new nation with a prosperous and glorious future will emerge. At the same time, their pact constitutes a promise of a new cosmic order, one that reconciles forces Olympian and chthonic, male and female. Yet Jupiter puts a stop to the war by sending a Dira to instruct Juturna to withdraw from the battle. Throughout the poem, the Dirae have served as Juno's minions. Seeing a Dira execute the will of Jupiter raises questions regarding the nature of this divine reconciliation. In order to appreciate more fully the significance of the Dirae's role in the divine *concordia*, we need to turn briefly to Greek tragedy, and in particular to Aeschylus' conclusion of the *Oresteia*, the *Eumenides*.

## V. CHANGE OF VENUE: THE DIRAE
## AND THE *ORESTEIA*

The resolution of the *Oresteia* is almost as controversial a topic of debate as the end of the *Aeneid*. Orestes' acquittal for his mother's murder by the court of Areopagus and the eventual transformation of the Erinyes, his persecutors, to Eumenides mark a transition from the old justice system of kin killing to the new institution of the court, where justice is now dispensed by nonkin members. The opposing nature of these two systems of justice is articulated throughout the trilogy by linking each of them to opposites: old/new, female/male, chthonic/Olympian. As a result, the old justice system is associated in the plays with the female and the powers of the Underworld, whereas the Areopagus is linked with the male and the Olympian authority of Zeus. The foundation and continuing success of this new system of justice is predicated upon the reconciliation of the deities involved in the conflict, that is, Apollo, Athena, and the Erinyes. Their reconciliation is made possible through the use of Persuasion (Peitho),[39] which allows the deities to reach and accept the court's authority as the earthly representative of Zeus' new concept of Justice (Dike). The Erinyes play a key role in this reconciliation as they are transformed from bloodthirsty creatures to safeguards of the new justice system and guarantors of prosperity for the city of Athens.[40]

More specifically, in the last choral ode of the play (916–1020), the Erinyes deliver blessings upon Athens, namely, prosperity and fertility for the earth, longevity and health for humans, and civic concord. The play ends with a ritual procession, in which Athena and the people of Athens

---

[39] Persuasion itself sustains a transformation at the end of the play: she is no longer a curse but a blessing. See Sommerstein 1989: 255.

[40] At the heart of every reconciliation always lies the risk of an outbreak of violent conflict, and the *Oresteia* is no exception. A case in point is the prologue of the *Eumenides*, which foreshadows the resolution of the end of the play: the Pythia relates the peaceful transition of mantic power at Delphi from the chthonic gods to Apollo's Olympian rule (Conacher 1987: 139; Lebeck 1971: 142). Yet the audience would have been greatly surprised to hear this account, as it explicitly rejects the dominant version of the story, according to which Apollo became the reigning deity of the oracle by force (Sommerstein 1989: 80–81). As a result, not only the outcome of the play but also the problems inherent in this outcome are foreshadowed for the audience early on.

will escort the Erinyes, now transformed to Semnai (the Venerable Ones), to their new home in Athens.[41] Athena stresses that these blessings are conditional only, and that the Erinyes are equally capable of good and ill (see Sommerstein 1989: 260–62, 275–78). I argue that the Erinyes and the Dirae share characteristics that warrant a comparison of the two. Their juxtaposition will help answer questions regarding the quality of divine reconciliation in the *Aeneid*.

Though the Dirae are hardly unknown entities in the poem, their habitat and role are redefined at the moment of Jupiter's decision to employ them:

> dicuntur geminae pestes cognomine Dirae,
> quas et Tartaream Nox intempesta Megaeram
> uno eodem tulit partu, paribusque reuinxit
> serpentum spiris uentosasque addidit alas.
> hae Iouis ad solium *saeuique* in limine regis
> apparent *acuuntque metum mortalibus* aegris,
> si quando *letum horrificum morbosque* deum rex
> molitur, *meritas* aut *bello territat urbes.*                  (12.845–52)

> men tell of twin pestilences, named the Furies,
> whom untimely Night bore in one and the same birth
> with hellish Megaera, wreathing them alike
> with snaky coils and giving them wings of wind.
> These attend on the throne of Jupiter and on the threshold
> of the savage ruler, and *rouse the fears of* ailing *mortals,*
> whenever the king of gods is wreaking *hideous death*
> and *diseases,* or *terrifies guilty cities with war.*

The Dirae's lineage is associated with the chthonic powers of the Underworld: their mother is Night and their sister "infernal Megaera." Earlier in the poem, their abode is the *limen* of Hades (6.279). Here, however, we are reminded that, as we have seen, they actually dwell in the *limen* of Jupiter. Olympus thus appears to have permanently appropriated the topography of Hades.

---

[41] On the particular ritual that the procession is meant to evoke, see Bowie 1993: 27–29.

Fear constitutes a fundamental aspect of the Furies in the *Oresteia* as well. For instance, one of the trilogy's most poignant and memorable moments is Orestes' terror at the sight of the blood-dripping Erinyes persecuting him at the end of *Choephoroi* (1048–50; 1057–58). The opening of *Eumenides* shows that this theme will continue to be important: when the Pythia catches sight of the Furies, she exclaims in terror: ἦ δεινὰ λέξαι, δεινὰ δ᾽ ὀφθαλμοῖς δρακεῖν [indeed terrible things to tell, terrible things for my eyes to see], 34). Fear has a chief role in the play's articulation of the new system of justice and is progressively viewed, like the Furies themselves, as a necessary bulwark of justice (517–25; 698–702) and a guarantee of prosperity (990–91; Sommerstein 1989: 87). In the *Aeneid*, by contrast, we see none of these positive attributes of fear, only Jupiter's use of it as a means to punish humanity for unspecified crimes.

Fear, however, is not the only characteristic shared by the Dirae of the *Aeneid* and the Erinyes of Aeschylus' *Eumenides*. Both oversee death, disease, and warfare.[42] And in both cases they lend their services to Jupiter and Zeus, respectively.[43] Nevertheless, the two works present these deities in markedly different ways. As we have seen, in the final choral ode of the Greek play, the Furies deliver blessings upon Athens. These take the specific form of protection of the crops from disease (μηδ᾽ ἄκαρπος αἰανὴς ἐφερπέτω νόσος [may no deadly disease draw near to kill the fruit], 942), untimely death (ἀνδροκμῆτας δ᾽ ἀώρους ἀπεννέπω τύχας [I ban deadly and untimely death for men], 956), and civil strife (976–83).[44]

In the epic, however, there is no guarantee of protection from these evils; the Dirae appear to exist not in order to ensure that justice prevails (as in *Eum.* 690–92) but rather as minions of Jupiter when he chooses to inflict harm upon mortals and cities. The positive affirmation of fertility, longevity, and peace, which cements the reconciliation of opposing

---

[42] To be sure, the Dirae themselves bring pestilence to humans, as is the case in Verg. *G.* (3.551–53). The motif of disease is familiar to the reader from earlier parts of Book 12. On the "illness" of Turnus, see Putnam 1965: 194–95.

[43] See Sommerstein 1989: 267, where he notes that in *Eum.* (976–87) the Erinyes appropriate blessings that are usually associated with Athena and Zeus.

[44] This passage bears close affinities to the blessings that the Danaids bestow upon Argos in Aesch. *Supp.* (625–709). On the importance of the myth of the Danaids in the *Aeneid*, see Putnam 1994: 171–89.

divine forces in the Greek play, is remarkably absent in the description of the Vergilian Dirae. Yet it is precisely this benevolence toward humans that is essential to the new system of justice propounded in the play, and that unites all under the aegis of Zeus. In the *Aeneid*, by contrast, it seems that Jupiter, instead of converting the Dirae, is himself transformed into a version of Juno.[45]

Thus the Dirae remain embodiments of violent internal conflict. As we have seen, throughout the epic, their chthonic, warlike nature is expressed through their affinity with snakes. This Dira is no exception. As Jupiter dispatches her to terrify Turnus and remove Juturna from the action, the Fury is likened to a poisonous arrow in a description that also evokes her serpentine nature:

> non secus ac neruo per nubem impulsa sagitta,
> armatam saeui Parthus quam felle ueneni,
> Parthus siue Cydon, telum immedicabile, torsit,
> stridens et celeris incognita transilit umbras: ...          (12.856–59)

> Like an arrow, shot from the bow-string through a cloud,
> armed with the gall of fell poison which a Parthian,
> a Parthian or a Cydonian has launched, a shaft beyond all cure;
> hissing, it leaps unseen through the swift shadows: ...

The arrow/Dira is deadly (*immedicabile*); its poison is *saeuum*, the same adjective used of Jupiter a few lines earlier (849) and of Juno and the Furies in many instances throughout the poem (Knox 1997: 227–28); the verb used to describe the shooting of the arrow is the same as the one usually depicting the winding of a snake (*torsit*); and lastly, the arrow/ Dira attacks unseen by its victim, just as snakes often catch their victim unaware. The passage has much in common with the following lines from *Eumenides*, where Apollo's arrow is likened to a snake:

> μὴ καὶ λαβοῦσα πτηνὸν ἀργηστὴν ὄφιν
> χρυσηλάτου θώμιγγος ἐξορμώμενον

[45] See Servius on *Aen.* 12.845 on the Dira's habitat: *et dictae 'dirae', quod non nisi ante iratum Iovem videntur, ut <849> saevique in limine regis apparent* [and they are called 'dirae,' because they do not appear unless Jupiter is angry, as they stand as attendants on the threshold of the savage king].

ἀνῇς ὑπ' ἄλγους μέλανα πλευμόνων ἀφρόν,
ἐμοῦσα θρόμβους οὓς ἀφείλκυσας φόνου.                      (*Eum.* 181–84)

lest you might be even smitten by a winged glistening snake
shot forth from a bow-string wrought of gold
and disgorge in pain black foam from your lungs,
vomiting the clotted blood you have drained.

These lines come from the first encounter between Apollo and the
Erinyes. The likening of Apollo's arrow to a winged glistening snake
recalls the image of the snake in the *Choephoroi*: Orestes was turned into a
snake (ἐκδρακοντωθείς, *Cho.* 549) in order to be able to murder his mother,
and now the god's snake-weapon protects him against the dreaded drag-
onness (δεινῆς δρακαίνης, *Eum.* 128), whose ghost pursues him (Goldhill
1984: 218). At this early stage in the play, both sides, Apollo and Orestes
on the one hand, and Clytemnestra and the Erinyes on the other, while in
conflict, share similar snakelike attributes. That Jupiter's ultimate intervention in the poem looks back to the beginning of *Eumenides*, where
the new system of justice has not yet been established, is of great significance. Much like Juno throughout the epic, Jupiter utilizes the serpentine, chthonic, warmongering qualities of the Dira in order to implement
his divine plan. Viewed in this light, his repeated promises of prosperity,
justice, and a new order demand an explanation.

In the following scene, that of the duel between Aeneas and Turnus,
the reader witnesses the outcome of the divine settlement. When Aeneas
chooses to disregard the supplication of Turnus and proceeds to kill him,
he may be said to act within the framework of a system of justice in
which the shedding of blood is the only way to achieve retribution. No
higher authority settles the dispute, however; no ritual ceremony ends the
epic. The contrast with the ending of the *Oresteia* is stark and poignant.

Supplication and justice are also key problems in Aeschylus' *Eumenides*.
The integrity of the act of supplication is particularly at stake: the
Erinyes twice try to prevent the suppliant Orestes from getting asylum
(Sommerstein 1989: 11 n.39); what is more, supplication proves insuffi-
cient to save him. At the end of the play, however, it is the court that
decides the fate of Orestes, while the functions assigned to the reformed
Erinyes include those of the Semnai Theai in Athenian cult, who are pro-
tectors of suppliants (Brown 1984: 262). As a result, the suppliant drama

ends successfully for the suppliant, even though, contrary to customary practice, he must leave Athens, whereas his prosecutors remain. The Erinyes lose some of their traditional prerogatives but retain their importance for society, transformed to benevolent forces guaranteeing prosperity and justice. The Vergilian Dira's jurisdiction, however, remains akin to that of the Erinyes *before* their transformation to Eumenides. She does not offer any protection to the suppliant Turnus; on the contrary, she serves as a guarantor of his demise. In the *Aeneid*, the suppliant is killed and the Dirae, instead of departing for Hades, keep their place on the threshold of Olympus.

The role of the Dira in this instance in the *Aeneid* and its close relationship with Aeschylus' *Oresteia* may be further illuminated through a brief consideration of the presence of another female deity, Pallas Athena.

## VI. THE MEDIATION OF PALLAS

In an insightful article, Sarah Spence notes that the Dira of *Aeneid* 12 is portrayed as an owl-like bird, the signature bird of Pallas Minerva (*quae quondam in bustis aut culminibus desertis / nocte sedens serum canit importuna per umbras* [which sits sometimes on tombs or deserted rooftops and sings ill-omened things late at night in the shadows], 863–64). Spence suggests that this implicit reference to the goddess casts the Dira as a representative of the feminine aspect of Jupiter and points to the similar role of Athena in the *Oresteia*. For Spence, the connection between the *Aeneid* and the trilogy renders Pallas a figure of peace and inclusion that ensures that violence will come to an end (Spence 1999: 157–58).[46] In the following, I argue that Pallas in the *Aeneid* is yet another Olympian deity whose powers are appropriated by the realm of Juno.

A closer look into the different roles Pallas is called on to play in the poem will bring into sharper focus the themes at work at this particular juncture. Critics of the *Aeneid* have long noted Minerva's association with the demands of fate and the will of Jupiter (Wilhelm 1992: 75). She is a

[46] Spence's larger argument is that the variety of roles that Pallas is called on to play throughout the *Aeneid* emphasizes the liminality of the poem's ending (159).

warrior goddess, initially on the side of the Greeks in the conflict with Troy but eventually a protector of Rome (8.699). In Roman religious life, the goddess occupied a prominent place: she was part of the Capitoline triad, worshipped on the Capitoline hill along with Jupiter and Juno. Compared to her Capitoline counterparts, however, Minerva's appearance in the *Aeneid* is brief. Nevertheless, the moments in which she appears are highly memorable: she is shown as terrible in exacting vengeance from those who wrong her (1.39–45) and as rejecting the women's pleas for help both at Troy (1.479–82) and in Latium (11.477–85).

Although a goddess of great intellectual power, Pallas also displays chthonic attributes (Henry 1989: 91–92). Prominent among these is her kinship with serpents. In one of the most frightening scenes of Book 2, she sends twin snakes to devour Laocoon and his sons (225–27), while snakes also resurface at the scene of Troy's pillaging, which Minerva oversees along with Juno:

> . . . hic Iuno Scaeas saeuissima portas
> prima tenet sociumque furens a nauibus agmen
> ferro accincta uocat.
> iam summas arces Tritonia, respice, Pallas
> insedit nimbo effulgens et Gorgone saeua.                    (2.612–16)

> here most savage Juno first holds the Scaean gates
> and girded with steel furiously calls from the ships
> her allied army.
> Now look, Tritonia Pallas occupies the top of the citadel
> shining with her cloud and the savage Gorgon.

The collusion of Juno and Pallas is marked by their resemblance,[47] with both goddesses cast as Fury-like creatures: Juno's attire links her with Tisiphone, who later in the poem is depicted as leaping upon her victims girded with a whip (*accincta flagello*, 6.570). Pallas' shield, on the other hand, depicts the Gorgon Medusa, a creature famous for its serpentine hair.[48] The similarity of the two goddesses is further reinforced through

---

[47] On other important connections between Pallas and Juno in the poem, see Spence 1999: 152. The image of Pallas rejecting the Trojan women's prayers is in one of the paintings in Juno's temple in Carthage (1.479–82).

[48] Note that Discordia is also presented as having serpentine hair (6.280–81).

the use of *saeua* to describe each of them, an adjective often employed, as we have seen, to emphasize forces hostile to Aeneas and Rome.[49]

Yet snakes are inseparable from Pallas even as she operates on the Roman side. The Pallas/Gorgon motif recurs in Book 8, where the Cyclopes carve the image of the Gorgon on the goddess's shield:[50]

> aegidaque horriferam, turbatae Palladis arma,
> certatim squamis serpentum auroque polibant
> conexosque anguis ipsamque in pectore diuae
> Gorgona desecto uertentem lumina collo.                          (8.435–38)

> they were polishing eagerly the fearsome shield,
> the weapons of angry Pallas, with the scales of serpents and gold,
> and the entwined snakes, and on the goddess' breast
> the Gorgon herself, rolling her eyes in her severed head.

Pallas is here presented in all her frightening destructive power (see also Henry 1989: 99–100). Anger (*turbata*) is her main characteristic, reflected in the image of the Gorgon decorating her shield. This shield, able to turn into stone the goddess' enemies, is a reminder of the intensity of her wrath, the same wrath that had sent the twin snakes to devour Laocoon and his sons at Troy.

The images of Pallas as a deity of war associated with the powers of Hades form a sharp contrast to her role in Aeschylus' *Eumenides* as a rational, calm divinity who supports the justice of Zeus that puts an end to the cycle of violence. In the *Aeneid*, Pallas' linkage with the Dira emphasizes the notion that the divinities of Olympus are being taken over by the forces of anger and irrationality that dominate Hades. Pallas does not

---

[49] The adjective is widely used of the Furies: of the Harpy Celaeno (3.214–15), of Tisiphone's sisters (6.572), and of Allecto (7.329 and 511). On the use of *saeuus* in the *Aeneid*, see Knox 1997.

[50] Furies and Gorgons had been perceived as kindred entities since the time of Aeschylus. In the prologue of *Eumenides*, the Pythia mistakes the Furies for Gorgons (48–52). At the end of *Choephoroi* (1048–50), Orestes makes the same comparison. Sommerstein (1989: 90) proposes that the impetus for the analogy comes from the fact that the Erinyes too, much like the Gorgons, were believed to have hideous faces and snakes for hair. In the *Aeneid*, Allecto is described as *Gorgoneis ... infecta uenenis* (7.341).

help to put an end to violence through the creation of a new institution, as she does in the *Oresteia*. The Dira embodies the angry, violent, and vengeful aspects of the goddess, which cause her to adopt and employ the tactics of Juno. We may thus say that the mobilization of a host of associations with Pallas at this moment both confirms that the *Oresteia* is an important backdrop against which we may read this episode and suggests that Jupiter himself is being transformed into a version of Juno.

## VII. RITUAL AND EMPIRE

Pallas' role in the Capitoline triad and Palladium is one of the many connections operative here between the endlessness of civil war and the endlessness of the Roman Empire promised by Jupiter in Book 1. The emplotment of the divine within the context of ritual pollution and the ultimate appropriation of Jupiter's realm by that of Juno suggest that ritual pollution persists and that restoration is denied. Ritual restoration, however, is synonymous with peace and empire, while ritual pollution is a direct result of (civil) war. As the divinities of Olympus fall prey to the agents of Discordia, the endlessness of the Roman Empire is seriously undermined by the endlessness of violence, the repetition of civil war.

The association of the divine forces with ritual distortion is of tremendous importance in view of Augustus' religious reform and his zealous promotion and establishment of cults (Feeney 1991: 179). The realm of religious worship provided confirmation and support for Augustus' ideological claims. At the same time, however, it affords a space within which the articulation of dissent is possible (see Goff 2004: 10–11; Bell 1992: 197–223). The representation of the divine in the *Aeneid* explores precisely this space and thus plays out the polarities that make up the ideological fabric of the poem.

# WOMEN'S RITUALS

# 4  Maenad Brides and the Destruction of the City

EPIC IS A GENRE THAT DEALS PRIMARILY WITH MEN'S DEEDS. Yet powerful female characters form the very fabric of both Greek and Latin epic, even if their presence is largely dictated by the needs of narratives driven forward by men. Some of the most memorable scenes in the *Iliad* and the *Odyssey* revolve around women. It is in Greek tragedy, however, that women truly occupy center stage. The prominence of women in tragedy has attracted the interest of feminist scholars, who have done much to demonstrate that gender conflict is placed at the heart of the tragic plot. In Latin literature, however, only Roman elegy can claim a similar share of feminist scrutiny. Women in epic have been studied less, often, usually seen as vehicles of opposition to male authority, an opposition eventually overcome by and assimilated to the demands of epic and empire. Yet women's role in epic (as in other genres) deserves a reevaluation in view of more recent work, which has invited scholars to move beyond examining gender categories or women's place within the social hierarchy.[1] Rather, a more fruitful avenue is the study of the different ways in which women become visible and powerful in the social and political arena.

In Greece and in Rome, women are largely absent from the historical record. Nevertheless, women in literature are represented as capable of playing critical roles in public life. In Greek tragedy, women serve as vehicles for the exploration of issues of civic ideology and identity.[2] Drama itself is part of an institution that is both religious and civic, which aims

---

[1] See, most recently, Cole 2004 and Goff 2004.
[2] See, for instance, Zeitlin 1996 and Foley 2001.

at raising civic consciousness and celebrating Athens' growing hegemony in the Greek world. The central role of women in such a context is all the more striking given the limited access that Athenian women had to many aspects of public life. Similarly, in the *Aeneid*, a national epic hailing the dawning of a new era for Rome, women play a pivotal role in the plot and contribute to the articulation of a new Roman national ideology and identity.

Ritual, both public and private, is a sphere where women are indispensable and powerful. Women's ritual activity is closely connected with their social status and sexual role and constitutes a means by which they can exert power: they occupy center stage in marriage ceremonies, lamentations, and burials. Much work has been done to demonstrate the importance of ritual in Greek tragedy as a domain that, though not exclusively female, was a means of participating in and contributing to the life of the *polis*. Aside from female-only rituals, such as the Thesmophoria, women had a central role in other major civic festivals such as the Panathenaia. Similarly, in ancient Rome, women's participation in rituals formed an important part of their lives, although scholars of Roman religion argue that the role of women was peripheral to that of the men (Scheid 1992; Beard et al. 1998: 296–300). Yet there is ample evidence that women participated in public rituals in important ways: their role was prominent in the festival of the Parentalia; the Salian virgins officiated in processions marking the opening and closing of the military campaign season (Scheid 1992: 385); the wives of priests executed important religious tasks, such as sacrifices (Sheid 1992: 384). Moreover, scholarly opinion tends to underestimate the centrality of some female priesthoods and cults in Roman consciousness and their importance for the Roman state, as the priesthood of the Vestal Virgins, the cults of Ceres and of Fortuna muliebris, and the rites of the Matronalia and Matralia attest.[3]

The representations of women's rituals in the *Aeneid*, as well as in Roman epic in general, tell a story different from that suggested by other historical records: women's rituals are potent enough to shape events

---

[3] On the Vestal Virgins, see Beard 1980, 1995 and Scheid 1992: 381–84. On the cult of Ceres, see Spaeth 1996; on the Matronalia and Matralia, see Scheid 1992: 385–87. See also Schultz 2006.

affecting the whole community. Women as performers of religious activity become visible agents and articulate a different point of view. The literary evidence thus reflects and refracts social realities, tensions, and anxieties about women's ritual activity in Roman public and private life.

A close look at women's rituals in the *Aeneid* reveals the remarkable fact that there is no single female figure in the poem that is not associated with ritual, in actual or metaphorical terms. Aeneas meets Andromache as she pours libations to Hector's cenotaph; Dido performs sacrifices to find out whether the gods favor a union with Aeneas; Lavinia is sacrificing at an altar; and Amata conducts a bacchic revel. Further examination shows that in almost all cases women are involved in the worship of Bacchus and bacchic rituals, actual or metaphorical. Ritual correctness, however, does not accompany the execution of ritual acts. This distortion of correct ritual procedure results in situations where women appear to resist male authority and thus transgress gender boundaries, confuse sexual hierarchies, and pose a threat to the hero and his mission. As a result, they emerge as empowered representatives of a point of view that is opposed to the one that champions victory and empire. As we have seen in previous chapters, the use of the motif of corrupted or perverted ritual to articulate cultural and political crises is one of the characteristics of Greek tragedy. The ritual perversion developed over the course of the play is eventually replaced by a restoration of the disrupted religious order through the correct performance of ritual or the institution of a new cult. The placement of the women of the *Aeneid* at the heart of the epic conflict shares many elements with the representation of women in Greek tragedy.

In the *Aeneid*, women often instigate war and violence around them, especially in the poem's second half. Nevertheless, they appear to suffer the consequences of war more keenly than their male counterparts. Furthermore, the death of a woman is frequently necessary so that Aeneas' mission can continue. Through this double role as aggressors and victims, women present a threat to the completion of the goals of Rome, while they also embody and therefore underscore the cost of victory and empire. Many of the women in the *Aeneid* represent moral and social values and ideals important to the welfare of Rome, ideals dismantled through their death. As a result, women both pose a threat to male action and appear capable of articulating alternative points of view, which, though doomed to failure, nevertheless call into question the very processes that cause their destruction. Ritual activity is instrumental in the deployment of this double portrayal of women in the epic.

In what follows, I examine the ways in which women's rituals illuminate the role of women in the epic. The prominence of bacchic ritual in their representation, however, requires first a brief discussion on Bacchus in Greece and Rome, and on the function of the bacchic element in Greek tragedy.

## I. BACCHUS IN GREECE AND ROME

Dionysus is an Olympian god, but he also possesses chthonic qualities (Henrichs 1979: 2–3; Segal 1997: 10). He crosses the boundaries between god and beast; his appearance displays characteristics appropriate to both males and females; he is both Greek and Asian; and he transcends social hierarchies, offering the gift of wine and ecstasy to all, men and women, rich and poor. The god's ambiguous identity can be a source of creative energy but also a source of destruction.[4] It is precisely because of the god's ambiguous nature that the Greeks were never quite at ease with Dionysus (Henrichs 1979: 3).

In Dionysiac cult, fusion replaces the demarcation of individuality, primarily by means of intoxication, an element apparently shared by all festivals honoring the god.[5] Dionysiac worship was celebrated in state festivals as well as in smaller group festivals, the *orgia*, which took place every other year. Secret cults and mysteries also developed at an early date (Burkert

---

[4] Segal 1997: 13. I largely follow Segal's exposition of the god's attributes in worship and ritual. Burkert (1985: 164) also notes that the myths concerning the discovery of wine contain dark and ominous elements. On Dionysiac ambiguity, see also Vernant 1988b.

[5] Burkert 1985: 163. Dodds (1960: xiii), however, argues that the maenadic ritual does not seem to be a wine festival, since the time to celebrate would be the time of the new wine, the spring. But he does not offer an explanation of how the maenads achieved their ecstatic union with the god, a state often described as insanity. The problem of the relationship between the rites described in literary texts and actual cultic practice is a vexed one. For a recent discussion of the issues and relevant bibliography, see Goff 2004: 214–17; 271–79.

1985: 163). Men and women expressed their worship in different ways: men celebrated him as the god of wine in festivals, while women held biennial rites that took place in midwinter and on mountain tops (Henrichs 1979: 2). Maenadism, however, is mainly associated with women (Des Bouvrie 1997: 84–88). In particular, it brings together married and unmarried women, thus temporarily subverting societal restrictions that confine them to the household. In the ritualized state of maenadism, the *polis* defines "a controlled period in which female susceptibility to Dionysiac frenzy may be both expressed and contained" (Seaford 1994: 258).

In Rome, the ancient local deities Liber-Libera were initially associated with Ceres and had a general jurisdiction over fertility. It seems that as early as the sixth century Liber Pater was assimilated with Dionysus and over time became a synonym for wine (Bruhl 1953: 23–29; Dumézil 1970: 377–78, 516). Roman authors of the republic and the Augustan age often refer to Bacchus; yet it is difficult to discern which elements derive from Roman religious life and belief and which are modeled on Greek, or more precisely Alexandrian, influence.[6] Catullus, Vergil, and Ovid, however, describe maenadic rites that, though they owe a great deal to poetic imagination, display a vividness of detail that has led scholars to suggest that they also represent actual cultic practice.[7]

Such a ritual is attested to by Augustine (*De ciuitate dei* 7.21), who relates that in certain Italian cities the cult in honor of Liber-Libera took the following form: a phallus, carried in a chariot into the country, was brought back to the city in triumph; at Lavinium a whole month was consecrated to Liber, during which everyone indulged in obscene words until the moment when the phallus, after being carried through the Forum, was restored to its resting place; the most virtuous matron had the duty of crowning it with wreaths in public, thus driving away the *fascinatio*, or enchantment, from the fields and assuring a prosperous harvest. Thus it appears that certain kinds of indigenous bacchic rites took place around the deities of Liber-Libera.[8]

---

[6] Bruhl (1953: 133–44) presents a survey of the use of Bacchus in Latin literature through the time of Augustus.

[7] Catullus 64.251–64; Ovid, *Met.* 6.587–600.

[8] Bruhl (1953: 27) suggests that Amata's bacchic orgy in *Aeneid* 7 may be modeled upon Euripides' *Bacchae* but that its inclusion in Vergil's text indicates that it reflects a certain Roman reality. See also Pichon 1913: 164.

The ancient Liber Pater, however, had never been involved in anything that might have disturbed the Senate, and in 186 BCE he was regarded as having no connection with the scandalous Bacchanalian affair (Dumézil 1970: 516). There appears to be a tension in Roman thought between those aspects of the god that are beneficial and those that can be threatening for the community. Livy's account of the affair (39.8–19) and the preserved *Senatus Consultum de Bacchanalibus* inform us of the official stance of the Roman state. The authorities treated the scandal as a prime example of pernicious Greek influence,[9] but their reluctance to extirpate the cult reveals the profound attachment of the Italian and Roman people to the god. The *senatus consultum* restricted access to the cult almost exclusively to women; a male citizen had to ask permission to become a bacchanal. (Dumézil 1970: 521). Livy's account emphasizes the devastating consequences for the morality and masculinity of the men who participate in what was considered a female cult: male initiates to the bacchic mysteries are said to undergo a feminization that affects their ability to be suitable Roman soldiers.[10]

This summary exposition of the major aspects of Dionysiac worship and cult demonstrate the close connection between the Greek and

---

[9] Bruhl 1953: 114–16; Dumézil 1970: 516; Beard et al. 1998, 1: 95–96. See also Gruen (1990: 34–78), who argues that the Bacchanalian affair supplied the Roman state with a means to curb individual inclinations toward Hellenism.

[10] See Liv. 39.15.9–10, where the consul explains to the Roman people the evils of the bacchic mysteries: *Primum igitur mulierum magna pars est, et is fons mali huiusce fuit; deinde simillimi feminis mares, stuprati et constupratores fanatici, uigiliis, uino strepitibus clamoribusque nocturnis attoniti* [First, then, the great majority are women and this was the source of this evil; then the males become very much like women, committing and submitting to the most obscene sexual acts, frenzied by staying up late, by wine, the uproar and shouts of the night]. In 39.15.13–14, the consul explicitly discusses these young men's fitness to serve in the military and represent the community of Romans: *Hoc sacramento initiatos iuuenes milites faciendos censetis, Quirites? His ex obsceno sacrario eductis arma committenda? Hi cooperti stupris suis alienisque pro pudicitia coniugum ac liberorum uestrorum ferro decernerent?* [Do you think, Quirites, that those young men who are initiated in this cult ought to become soldiers? That weapons ought to be entrusted to those brought up in that shrine of obscenity? That those who have been buried in their own debauchery and that of others would distinguish themselves in war defending the chastity of your wives and children?]

Roman ritual practices, a connection that allowed Vergil to use bacchic ritual elements to enrich and complicate the epic narrative and plot. The representation of maenadism in the *Aeneid* has often been dismissed as a metaphor for insanity. Yet a close reading of the poem does not allow for unilateral interpretation. In the following pages, I argue that the bacchic element as seen in Greek tragedy has a profound significance for an understanding of women's rituals and their role in the *Aeneid*. A brief sketch of maenadism in Greek tragedy is in order, however, before we can engage with the women of the Vergilian epic.

## II. TRAGIC MAENADS

The connection of Dionysus with tragedy is as famous as it is mysterious. In Athens, tragic performances were an integral part of the celebration of Dionysiac festivals, yet the more precise connection of Dionysiac worship with the representations of the god Dionysus as well as the role of Dionysiac elements in the plays is the object of heated debate. In the most recent treatment of the Dionysiac element in Greek tragedy, Richard Seaford has argued that most Greek tragedies center around the destruction of the household (*oikos*).[11] The annihilation of the *oikos* is usually divinely inspired and eventually brings salvation to the *polis* in the form of cult (Seaford 1994: 354). Maenadism, whether it is represented as ritual enactment or used as a metaphor, is closely linked with this theme. While in ritual practice maenadism is a benign communal negation of female adherence to the household, in tragedy it is represented as uncontrollable, causing the collapse of the structures that preserve the integrity of the *oikos* (ibid.: 352).

---

[11] Seaford (1994: 235–80) has provided the most important (and controversial) discussion of this issue. He argues that the Dionysiac element is absent in Homer because the god is identified with the democratic *polis*. As a result, all tragedies are essentially Dionysiac in that they depict the triumph of the *polis* over the aristocratic household. Dionysus appears in Homer, however: we are told of his persecution of the Thracian king Lycurgus in *Il.* 6.130–40, the longest episode concerning the god; Andromache is twice compared to a maenad (*Il.* 6.389, 22.460); and references to Dionysus can also be found in *Il.* 14.325 and *Od.* 11.325 and 24.74.

Though tragic maenadism is brought about by divinely inspired frenzy, frenzy is never the sole reason behind maenadic behavior. It is occasioned by other features such as resistance to the male (ibid. 357). Indeed, the theme of female transgression into the male sphere is a pivotal component of the thematic structure of most tragedies. This transgression may take the form of negation of the bridal transition, which often results in the destruction of the *oikos*. Women who participate in this negation are frequently portrayed as maenads, actual or metaphorical. Thus, in tragedy, according to Seaford, the image of bacchic frenzy followed by the maenadic departure from home is associated with the negation of marriage ritual and the destruction of the household (355–57).

Renate Schlesier presents a few further characteristics in her typology of tragic maenads, which complement those outlined by Seaford. Maenads in tragedy may be said to fall into three categories: maenadic activity is often accompanied by the killing of the maenad's offspring or mate; women may be attracted to maenadism as a result of a violent and painful love, which may not necessarily lead to murder but which may include it; and maenadism can characterize a warrior's excitement on the battlefield (Schlesier 1993: 97–99).[12]

Euripides' *Bacchae* provides us with the most detailed examples of female bacchic behavior and amply illustrates that women's engagement with bacchic ritual is a source of empowerment. Although the play offers a positive view of women's maenadism in the image of the Lydian worshippers, it quickly focuses on the uncontrollable rites of the Theban

[12] Instances of the first category include Agave, who, under the influence of Dionysus, kills her son Pentheus; Euripides' Heracles, who, in a bacchic frenzy inflicted by Hera, slays his sons and wife; and the Erinyes, the divine agents of the slain Clytemnestra in Aeschylus' *Eum.* (500), who, while threatening to kill her son Orestes, call themselves maenads. In the second category, we encounter in Euripides' *Hippolytus* the figure of Phaedra, whose unrequited love for her stepson is cast in terms of maenadic frenzy and ultimately causes the young man's demise, and in Sophocles' *Trachiniae* that of Deianira, whose disillusioned passion for Heracles also brings about the hero's death. Schlesier finds instances of the third type, the warrior's frenzy on the battlefield, in the description of Hippomedon in Aeschylus' *Seven against Thebes* (498) and in the reference to the anonymous warrior in the parodos of Sophocles' *Antigone* (136).

maenads, which culminate in a perversion of the ritual act of sacrifice.[13] The Theban women's empowerment turns them against male authority and results in the dismemberment of Pentheus, the destruction of the Theban royal *oikos*, and perhaps of the *polis* itself; the lost ending of the play makes it impossible to know if any restoration of the corrupt bacchic ritual ever took place.[14] What we can see, however, is that once the women return from their maenadic exit to the *polis*, they are directed to the appropriate channels of women's ritual involvement, namely, weddings and funerals (Goff 2004: 352).

As in tragedy, so in the *Aeneid* instances of bacchic madness range from accounts of ritual enactment to the use of maenadism as metaphorical imagery. Vergil thus also explores issues peculiar to tragedy, such as the destruction of the powerful household, the blurring of gender distinctions, and the collapse of the structures that guarantee the integrity of the civic and religious order.

## III. MAENAD BRIDES

The tragic themes just outlined, resistance to male authority, negation of the bridal transition, and destruction of the household, are central in several episodes of the *Aeneid*, and they are closely linked with women's engagement in bacchic ritual activity. Amata, Dido, the Sibyl, and Helen are all presented as maenads, actual or metaphorical. Through their bacchic activity, the women become powerful agents who enter the public sphere of politics and war, their agency articulating a point of view opposed to that of the men. In addition, the ritual they conduct is a perversion of marriage ritual. This perversion is linked with the outburst of violence between Latins and Trojans, a conflict that is cast as civil. The departure from standard ritual procedure of the women's bacchic activity appropriates that of the Theban maenads in Euripides' *Bacchae*,

---

[13] On the killing of Pentheus as sacrifice, see Foley 1985; Seaford 1994; and Segal 1997.

[14] On this debate, see Seaford 1994: 402–405; Segal 1997: 380–93; and, more recently, Goff 2004: 350–52.

which emphasizes the catastrophic rather than the beneficial aspects of
the god, resulting in the dismemberment and death of Pentheus and the
destruction of Cadmus' household. The destructive nature of the god is
opposed to the benign deity that is equated with Augustus in Book 6
(804–805) and that is commensurate with the triumph of the forces of
civilization.[15]

I will begin my analysis with Amata, as she displays the most extensive maenadic behavior in the poem, and then will continue with the
other female figures in the order in which they appear in the narrative.

## 1. Amata

The outbreak of violence in *Aeneid* 7 is closely linked to the theme of
marriage. Aeneas is to marry Lavinia, the daughter of King Latinus and
Queen Amata. Through this marriage the union between Latins and
Trojans will be achieved, and the two peoples will eventually produce
the Roman nation. In Roman myth, as in history, marriage often averts
or puts an end to war. The Sabine women are the most celebrated example. Though seized by force from their fathers, the women soon become
assimilated into the Roman state and eventually mediate between their
husbands and fathers. In this instance, women act as guarantors of social
stability as they and their children embody the connective links between
the warring sides and succeed in cementing the peace.[16] By offering to
take the blame for conflict upon themselves, the Sabine women's bodies
function as the site on which appropriate male homosocial bonds may be
forged. In the *Aeneid*, by contrast, Amata, by not allowing Lavinia's body
to serve as space that would defuse hostility, ends up unleashing it on a
grand scale.

Amata's resistance to the unifying wedding of Lavinia and Aeneas
destabilizes social as well as sexual relations and serves to promote war.
The theme of resistance to marriage is ubiquitous in Greek and Roman

---

[15] The passage names the god with his Roman name, Liber, thus stressing his
native Roman/Italian character. He is depicted as controlling the forces of the
wild and, along with Heracles, champions order and civilization. On Aeneas as
Dionysus, see Weber 2002.

[16] Liv. 1.9–13.8. On the Sabine women episode in Livy and women's association
with civic values, see Miles 1995: 179–219.

literature. Reluctance on the part of the bride as well as on the part of her natal family is one of the standard features of wedding narratives.[17] This resistance reflects the pain at the prospect of separation and loss that a bride and her family suffer and may take various forms: the young girl is compared to a delicate flower refusing the male's touch, a city that is sacked by the enemy, or a wild animal resisting domestication.[18] Eventually, however, everyone eagerly anticipates the girl's new life as a wife and mother.

Bacchic ritual is often used as a means to express resistance to marriage in Greek tragedy, and the same theme is at work in the *Aeneid*. The Latin queen Amata exemplifies this type of resistance. She passionately wishes for Turnus to marry her daughter, Lavinia. Juno, eager to help anyone who opposes Aeneas, sends the Fury Allecto, who infuses the queen with madness and pushes her to conduct a bacchic revel. The operation of the Fury on the queen gradually escalates into uncontrollable bacchic frenzy. Amata's bacchic activity provides the blueprint for all the themes associated with maenadism throughout the poem: the dangers associated with female sexuality, resistance to marriage, the killing of kin, and ultimately the destruction of the city.

Allecto's attack on the Latin queen foreshadows her eventual maenadic state and displays the link between female sexuality and bacchic activity as dangerous forces for the community.[19] Critics have duly noted the erotic implications of the vocabulary of fire in these lines, which depicts Amata as a woman of fiery passion, harboring feelings for Turnus

[17] See, for instance, the wedding poems of Catullus: 61.82; 62.59–66; 64.118–19.

[18] See Catullus 62.39–47 for woman as flower; 62.25 for marriage as the sacking of a city. The likening of the bride to a wild animal is a topos in Greek and Roman literature, on which see, e.g., Burkert 1983: 58–72 and Seaford 1994: 301–11.

[19] Furies themselves are often depicted as maenads in Greek tragedy: Aesch. *Eum.* 500; Eur *Or.* 339, 411, 835; Seaford 1994: 348. Allecto's serpentine nature is another link between the Furies and Dionysus. The god's association with snakes points to the chthonic aspects of his nature. Serpents are particularly prominent in *Bacchae*: Pentheus' father is Echion, whose name is the masculine of the snake-monster Echidna. The story of his savage death suggests that Pentheus shares in his father's monstrous and chthonic character, to which Dionysus' divine and Olympian nature will be opposed. On Pentheus and the snakes, see Segal 1978–79: 128–36 and Dodds 1960: 144.

that may be considered inappropriate.[20] The snake's motion on Amata displays a physicality that borders on the erotic: *ille inter uestis et leuia pectora lapsus* [that one glides between her clothes and smooth breasts] (349); *fit tortile collo/ aurum ingens coluber, fit longae taenia uittae / innectitque comas et membris lubricus errat* [the huge serpent becomes her necklace of twisted gold, becomes the band of her long fillet and entwines itself into her hair and, slippery, it slides over her limbs] (351–53). In Euripides' *Bacchae*, snakes exhibit a similar behavior as they are said to lick the chins of the maenads (698), while after the bloodbath of Pentheus' *sparagmos* the snakes lick the blood from their cheeks (767–68). In the *Aeneid*, the serpent's motion also indicates Amata's conversion into a bacchant: it becomes her golden necklace and the headband that holds her hair. Amata thus resembles the Theban bacchants in Euripides' play (*Ba.* 101–104). By transforming into the queen's accoutrements, the snake displaces the emblems of her status as a queen and threatens the stability of her social identity within civilized society.

Female sexuality is therefore perceived as opposed to civilization, finding release in bacchic activity, as is the case in *Bacchae*: Pentheus, when informed of the Theban women's maenadic departure from their homes, assumes that maenadism is an excuse for sex:

ἄλλην δ' ἄλλοσ' εἰς ἐρημίαν
πτώσσουσαν εὐναῖς ἀρσένων ὑπηρετεῖν,
πρόφασιν μὲν ὡς δὴ μαινάδας θυοσκόους,
τὴν δ' Ἀφροδίτην πρόσθ' ἄγειν τοῦ Βακχίου.         (222–25)

In hiding spots one by one the women
serve the beds of men
under the pretext that they are maenads
but they put Aphrodite before Bacchus.

The charge that maenadism is a pretext for illicit sexual activity is congruent with common views concerning new mystery cults at Athens in Euripides' time (Dodds 1960: 97–98). These views were shared by the Romans, as seen in Livy's narrative of the Bacchanalian scandal of

---

[20] See Lyne 1987: 13–19 and Zarker 1969: 7–8. On the scene, see also Feeney 1991: 165–68.

186 BCE (see note 10 to this chapter). Amata's first reaction to the snake's attack is said to reflect her rights as a mother while she attempts to dissuade Latinus from agreeing to a political alliance with Aeneas (*solito matrum de more locuta est* [she spoke in the usual way of mothers], 357). But Latinus remains unmoved by her arguments, and the snake attacks a second time, causing an explosion of maenadic behavior:

> His ubi nequiquam dictis experta Latinum
> contra stare uidet, penitusque in uiscera lapsum
> serpentis furiale malum totamque pererrat,
> tum uero infelix ingentibus excita monstris
> immensam *sine more* furit lymphata per urbem. (373–77)

> After trying with these words in vain,
> she sees Latinus opposing and the snake's maddening evil
> glides deep in her heart and slithers through her whole body.
> Then indeed the unlucky queen, goaded by enormous monsters,
> *improperly* rages through the huge city drunk.

Amata's activity is now described as *sine more*: she goes against proper decorum befitting her station. By roaming through the city in an intoxicated state (*lymphata*),[21] Amata confuses the spatial differentiation between male and female and abandons the socially acceptable activities of a female and a queen. What is more, her maenadism is an instance of perverted ritual, one that negates the benign nature of bacchic rites, as is also implied by the word *more*, which in ritual indicates that due procedure is followed. Once again, maenadic behavior merges with the erotic in the use of the word *infelix*, which evokes Dido's frenzied state, the result of love gone awry. Amata, a queen strong-willed and empowered like Dido, will pose a similar threat to Aeneas and his mission.[22]

---

[21] Fordyce (1977: 132) points out that the word *lymphata* is used by Pacuvius in the context of bacchic frenzy: compare 392–93 D' Anna 1967 (of Hesione) *tamquam lymphata aut Bacchi sacris / commota* [as drunk or in ecstasy by the rites of Bacchus]. See also König 1970: 152. The term was also used by Catullus (64.254): *quae tum alacres passim lymphata mente furebant* [these, then, were raging here and there in ecstasy with their mind drunk].

[22] The kinship between the two queens has long been noted by a number of scholars. See, for example, Putnam 1965: 160–62, 177–78, and LaPenna 1967.

Finally, the scene also signals that Amata's future bacchic activity will be disastrous not only for her own household and city but also for her offspring. In *Bacchae*, Agave's madness results in the dismemberment of her son. In Euripides' *Heracles*, Lyssa, a figure whose affinity to Allecto has long been noted,[23] infects the hero with bacchic madness[24] and causes him to murder his family. As a result, Amata's impending activity reinforces the notion that her madness is going to turn her against her own. Amata pushes Lavinia to the background and often appears as having assumed the role of the bride for herself. Amata's actions, however, result in the death of her would-be son-in-law, Turnus.

Maenadic resistance to male authority is also linked with the theme of female resistance to marriage. Allecto's mission is specifically to put a stop to Lavinia's marriage to Aeneas (*neu conubiis ambire Latinum / Aeneadae possint* [that the sons of Aeneas may not be able to sweet-talk Latinus with a wedding], 333–34) and to destroy Latinus' household (*odiis uersare domos* [destroy households with hatred], 336). Both purposes are achieved when the women engage in bacchic ritual. The use of maenadism as a means to indicate resistance to marriage is often found in Greek tragedy: in Euripides' *Troades*, for instance, Cassandra, seeking to avoid an unwanted and shameful marriage with a foreigner and an enemy (Agamemnon), resorts to bacchic frenzy, singing her own wedding song.[25] Amata employs a stratagem similar to that of her tragic counterparts: she hides her daughter in the woods and proclaims her a maenad (*te lustrare choro, sacrum tibi pascere crinem* [it is you she honors with

---

[23] König 1970: 123–36. See *contra* Horsfall 2000: 238.

[24] 889–97, 966, 1086, 1119, 1122, 1142. On similarities between *Bacchae* and *Heracles*, see Seaford 1994: 353–54.

[25] Heinze 1915: 187, n.16 (= 1993: 184). See also Seaford 1994: 356. Another such instance seems to have occurred in Euripides' lost play *Protesilaus*, where Laodameia falsely claimed that she was dedicated to Bacchus in order to avoid marriage. See König 1970: 153. The summary of the play provided by Hyginus (*Fabulae* 104) reports that she had constructed an effigy of her husband, Protesilaus, not one of Bacchus (*Kannicht*: 634). Statius' *Silv.* 2.7, however, reveals that there was also a version of the myth according to which Laodameia practiced a fake cult of Bacchus (*Silv.* 2.7.124–25: *haec te non thiasis procax dolosis / falsi numinis induit figura* [not shameless in deceitful dances does she clothe you in the shape of a false deity]). See Heinze 1915: 186 (= 1993: 151).

the dance, for you she grows her sacred tresses], 391). The peculiarity of
Amata's hiding of her daughter rests on the fact that the negation of
marriage is initiated by the mother of the bride, whereas in parallel cases
in tragedy, it is always initiated by the bride herself. The union that the
queen envisions between Lavinia and the god precludes not only a union
with Aeneas but also, surprisingly, a union with Turnus. It appears that
Amata, by dedicating Lavinia to Bacchus, denies her daughter's bridal
transition altogether as she relegates her to the status of a maenad forever
under the god's control. The mother's natural resistance to the separation
from her daughter, which is expressed in maenadic terms, turns here
into a perverse negation of Lavinia's right to marriage.

The description of Amata's ritual employs elements peculiar to
both bacchic and marriage rituals: she brandishes a blazing torch
(*flagrantem...pinum*, 397), which evokes the torches held at the marriage
ceremony and the pine thyrsus customarily held by maenads. The wedding song that she sings on behalf of Lavinia and Turnus (*natae Turnique
canit hymenaeos*, 398) stands in contrast to Lavinia's previous dedication to
Bacchus and Amata's assertions that Lavinia is also a maenad. In addition, Amata insists on her role and rights as a wronged mother (*si iuris
materni cura remordet* [if care of a mother's right stings your heart], 402).
At the same time, despite the narrator's claim that we are witnessing a
fake bacchic revel, Amata's behavior as a possessed maenad is unmistakably genuine: she is frenzied (*feruida*, 397); her eyes are bloodshot,
her gaze wandering (*sanguineam torquens aciem*, 399);[26] she screams savagely (*toruumque.../ clamat*, 399–400); and the Fury's control over her is
explicitly labeled as bacchic (*reginam Allecto stimulis agit undique Bacchi*
[Allecto drives the queen far and wide with the goad of Bacchus], 405).

Marriage and bacchic ritual elements are thus combined to create
a bizarre and disturbing effect. To be sure, the narrator had hinted at
this by calling the rite fake. This charge appropriates a famous passage
from the *Bacchae*, where Pentheus accuses the women of Thebes of faking

---

[26] Compare Agave's gaze at the moment she is about to tear Pentheus to pieces:
ἡ δ᾽ ἀφρὸν ἐξιεῖσα καὶ διαστρόφους / κόρας ἑλίσσουσ᾽, οὐ φρονοῦσ᾽ ἃ χρὴ φρονεῖν
[foaming at the mouth and *rolling her eyes* all around, not thinking what she
ought] (1122–23). West (1969: 49) finds a parallel between the rolling of
Amata's eyes and the rolling of the top in the simile at *Aen.* 7.381–82.

bacchic possession in order to have illicit sex:

> γυναῖκας ἡμῖν δώματ᾽ ἐκλελοιπέναι
> πλασταῖσι βακχείαισιν, ἐν δὲ δασκίοις
> ὄρεσι θοάζειν τὸν νεωστὶ δαίμονα
> Διόνυσον, ὅστις ἔστι, τιμώσας χοροῖς...                          (217–20)

Our women have left their homes
for *fake bacchic rites*, and in the shady
mountains they sit honoring with dances
the new god, Dionysos, whoever he is...

Pentheus' words display the link between bacchic activity and uncontrollable female sexuality, which jeopardizes the stability of social roles: the women have abandoned their homes and roam far from the city in the wild. Vergil's similar charge against Amata and the Latin mothers maligns the power women can exert through their ritual activity and demonstrates the dangers of their interference in the affairs of men. The same slur is used to describe the rite Helen performs during the sack of Troy in *Aeneid* 6.512–29: she faked a bacchic revel in order to help the Greeks (on which see section 3). Amata, however, very much like the women of the Thebes, is genuinely possessed by divine forces.[27] This important distinction is testimony to the extraordinary powers associated with the performance of ritual. Amata may have begun her rite as a fake bacchic revel; by the end of the description, however, a benign return to norms is impossible: the entire community is infected, and the effects of this pollution are pernicious for Latins and Trojans alike.

Amata's perversion of marriage and bacchic rituals in order to resist her daughter's marriage turns into a women's collective movement that succeeds in reversing social norms: Amata's maenadism transgresses her role as a wife and queen and causes others to do the same. Not only has she left her home and taken refuge in the wild, she has also crossed

---

[27] The narrator is revealed, then, to be just as mistaken as Pentheus and just as hostile toward the women's activities. Moreover, as the maenads caused the dismemberment of Pentheus' body, so the maenads of the *Aeneid* cause the destruction of the main narrative (that of the narrator) and offer their own version of events, an alternative "narrative." The women's maenadism thus articulates the ideological stance of resistance to male social and political authority.

the threshold of silence that Lavinia observes throughout the poem. As the ritual unfolds, the queen raises her voice progressively higher (*locuta*, 357; *uociferans*, 390; *canit*, 398; *clamat*, 400), as bacchic action renders female speech successful where it had failed before (*his ubi nequiquam dictis experta* [after trying in vain with these words], 373). Amata's voice was unsuccessful when she spoke in a way that was socially prescribed (*de more*, 357). In her maenadism (*sine more*), however, Amata's voice has the power to stir the Latin mothers to bacchic frenzy, and they too collectively abandon their homes and run to the woods:[28]

> fama uolat, *furiis*que accensas pectore matres
> idem omnis simul ardor agit noua quaerere tecta.
> deseruere *domos*, uentis dant colla comasque;
> ast aliae tremulis ululatibus aethera complent
> pampineasque gerunt *incinctae pellibus* hastas. (392–96)

> Rumor flies about and the mothers, their breast fired by *madness*,
> are all driven at once by the same passion to seek new abodes.
> They abandoned their *homes*, baring to the wind their necks and hair;
> and some filled the air with quavering cries
> and *dressed* in *fawnskins* bear vine-covered wand spears.

As on other occasions throughout the *Aeneid*, *fama*, the personified voice/rumor, is the agent of this escalation, converting private passion to public response.[29] Amata and the Latin mothers are transformed from civilized beings and respected pillars of the community into maenads. Their shedding of their social status as Latin women is evident in their change of dress: they let their hair loose (394) and wear fawnskins (396).

---

[28] See the intertextual kinship between the maenadic exit of the Theban women in the Bacchae and that of the Latin *matres* (the words italics in indicate words almost identical in Greek and Latin, the dotted underline words that are very close semantically): πρώτας δὲ Θήβας τάσδε γῆς Ἑλληνίδος / ἀνωλόλυξα, νεβρίδ' ἐξάψας χροός / θύρσον τε δοὺς ἐς χεῖρα, κίσσινον βέλος [Out of this land of Hellas, I have first stirred Thebes / to my cry, *fitting* a *fawnskin* to my body / and taking a thyrsus in my hand, an arrow of ivy] (23–25); τοιγὰρ νιν αὐτὰς ἐκ δόμων ὤιστρησ' ἐγὼ / μανίαις [and I have driven them (sc. the women) *with madness* away from their *homes*] (32–33).

[29] On *Fama* as spreading bacchic frenzy, see *Aen.* 4.173–97 and my discussion of that passage on pp. 137–38.

As a result, the movement of the maenads into the wild not only suggests the collapse of the spatial differentiation between human and animal, civilization and the wild, but also dissolves gender and social hierarchies. The women's bacchic ritual, in turn, interferes with warfare, triggering violence among men:

> tum quorum attonitae Baccho nemora auia matres
> insultant thiasis (neque enim leue nomen Amatae)
> undique collecti coeunt Martemque fatigant.                    (580–82)

> The kin, then, of those mothers who in ecstasy danced for Bacchus
> in the wilderness (Amata's name no light encouragement)
> came in from everywhere with cries for Mars.

Women's power to instigate war becomes directly related to their role as mothers (*matres*) as well as to their bacchic ritual activity. Under Amata's ritual lead,[30] women have lost their individuality and act collectively. At the same time, the bacchic rite may render mothers dangerous to their sons, as the example of Agave in Euripides' *Bacchae* poignantly attests. In the *Aeneid* too, the women's frenzy affects their sons: the mothers' bacchic rage is indirectly transferred onto their male offspring as they gather to prepare for battle.

This perverted blend of bacchic and marriage ritual is so potent that it overcomes the authority of men. The women's actions result in stripping King Latinus of his power: soon after he announces his withdrawal from the public sphere, Latinus is confined within the house (*saepsit se tectis*, 600), secluded and silenced, withdrawn from action and speech (*neque plura locutus*, 599). As we have seen, through their bacchic activity, women take on the exteriority associated with men, thus endangering the integrity of the *domus*, which stands to be destroyed in the absence of the women who normally secure its welfare. At the same time, Latinus' resignation from the action suggests that the entire state is in peril as a result of the women's ritual action (*rerumque reliquit habenas* [he dropped the reins of state affairs], 600). The violence that the women's bacchic rituals generates not only threatens social stability but also jeopardizes

---

[30] The name Amata could perhaps indicate a ritual title, as it was a name attributed to Vestals (Aulus Gellius, *Noctes Atticae* 1.12.14). See also Beard 1980: 14–15.

altogether the success of Aeneas' mission, the creation of the Roman state. Women's interference initiates the war that ends in the death of Turnus, thus permanently transforming Amata's "wedding" ritual into a funeral.

## 2. Dido

As we have seen, Dido performs a number of complex and important ritual acts in Book 4. Yet the theme of maenadism figures prominently in the portrayal of her anguish. In this section, I argue that Dido's association with maenadism is not a mere metaphor for madness but is closely related to the tragic model of bacchic frenzy. In tragedy, as Schlesier has shown, maenadism is often linked to the excitement of a violent and painful love, a state of mind that may lead to murder. Dido, unlike other maenads who experience violent emotions, such as Deianeira and Phaedra, does not cause the death of her mate. Yet both her curse to Aeneas and her performance of a magic ceremony that aims at his death indicate that she desires his destruction. As in tragedy, then, in this instance maenadism is paired with aggression against the male generated by the frustration of erotic desire. Furthermore, maenadism's contagious nature turns private madness into public frenzy.

The frustration of Dido's erotic desire triggers the onset of the queen's association with maenadism, as her reaction to the news of Aeneas' departure from Carthage is compared to a bacchant's orgy:

> saeuit inops animi totamque incensa per urbem
> *bacchatur*, qualis commotis excita sacris
> Thyias, ubi audito stimulant *trieterica* Baccho
> orgia *nocturnus*que uocat clamore Cithaeron.[31]          (300–303)

[31] The rite described closely appropriates elements of the various rites represented in Euripides' *Bacchae*: it is biennial (ἐς δὲ χορεύματα / συνῆψαν τριετηρίδων, / αἷς χαίρει Διόνυσος [and they joined (sc. the rites of the mother goddess) to the dances of the *biennial festivals*, in which Dionysus rejoices], 132–34), produces a contagious frenzy (πᾶν δὲ συνεβάκχευ᾽ ὄρος [the entire mountain *reveled along* with them], 726), and is performed at night (τὰ δ᾽ ἱερὰ νύκτωρ ἢ μεθ᾽ ἡμέραν τελεῖς; / νύκτωρ τὰ πολλὰ· σεμνότητ᾽ ἔχει σκότος [do you perform the rites by night or by day? / mostly *by night*. Darkness brings awe], 485–86).

> In her helplessness she goes wild and throughout the city
> *rages* ablaze *like a maenad*, like a Thyias stirred by the shaken
> emblems when she has heard the cry of Bacchus; the *biennial*
> revels excite her and *at night* Cithaeron calls her with its din.

Dido's likening to a maenad illustrates the intensity of her emotional turmoil. Unable to fulfill her erotic desire, Dido experiences a violent anger, which finds expression in the aggression that maenadism affords and which is directed against her mate and his kin, as is the case with Deianeira in Sophocles' *Trachiniae* and Phaedra in Euripides' *Hippolytus*.[32] Dido contemplates dismembering Aeneas (*non potui abreptum diuellere corpus* [could I not have seized him and tear his body apart], 600) and killing his son (*non ipsum absumere ferro / Ascanium patriisque epulandum ponere mensis?* [kill Ascanius himself with the sword / and serve him as a meal on his father's table?], 601–602). She puts this thought into action in her magic rite, which, as we have seen, is really a *defixio* aiming at Aeneas' destruction.[33] Although she does not ultimately succeed, she still poses a threat to Aeneas and his people even after her death, as Carthage will continue to challenge Roman superiority in the coming centuries.

Dido's frustrated desire turns into maenadic intoxication, which is at the root of her self-destruction. Her maenadic state is expressed in her dreams, where she sees herself as Pentheus pursued by Furies:

> Eumenidum ueluti demens *uidet* agmina Pentheus
> et *solem geminum* et *duplices* se ostendere *Thebas*.                    (469–70)

> as maddened Pentheus *sees* bands of Furies
> and *two suns* and *two Thebes* are revealed.

This is perhaps the most famous instance of Vergilian allusion to *Bacchae*. In the play, Pentheus, dressed as a maenad and in ecstasy, declares:

> καὶ μὴν ὁρᾶν μοι δύο μὲν ἡλίους δοκῶ,
> δισσὰς δὲ Θήβας καὶ πόλισμ' ἑπτάστομον.                    (918–19)

---

[32] See Oliensis 2001: 51, where Dido's dreams express her desire to commit infanticide and incest and therefore indicate that Aeneas also stands in the place of a son. On Dido and Euripides' Phaedra, see Hardie 1997b: 322. On Hippolytus in the *Aeneid*, see Dyson 2001: 147–57.

[33] See my discussion in Chapter 2, pp. 51–52.

> I think I *see two suns*
> and *two Thebes* and the sevenmouth city.

The lines indicate Pentheus' maenadic state, the complete victory of the
god over him, and signal his eventual destruction at the hands of his
own mother. The simile thus illustrates the intensity of Dido's madness
and foreshadows her (self) destruction. Dido's maenadism is emblematic
of her passion for Aeneas, a passion that destroys her life; the doubleness
of her vision suggests the rift that Aeneas' presence has caused within
her own identity. While she previously identified with her city and her
people, she now sees herself as separate from them (hence in this dream
she sees herself alone and deserted by the Tyrians, 466–68). This split
in Dido's own identity and her failure to unite with Aeneas result in
suicide.

The simile thus illustrates that maenadic behavior is closely linked
with the shifting of identities: women who resort to maenadic activity
by defying the spatial differentiation between male and female also defy
traditional gender roles, and thus blur gender distinctions. Dido, however, a woman and the leader of her country, had always defied the sexual
categorization imposed by social norms: in the beginning of the epic
narrative she emerges as a woman engrossed by the duties of leadership,
occupying a traditionally male domain. Paradoxically, this does not present a problem for Dido or her city. Her contact with Aeneas arouses the
erotic passion associated with the female and causes a split in her identity. Although Dido's dangerous femininity is emphasized through her
maenadism, she is compared exclusively to male tragic figures (Pentheus,
Orestes). Both these young men, however, share with Dido an identity
crisis, as they have trouble making the transition from adolescence to
adulthood.[34] Similarly, Dido is unable to make the transition from her
androgynous state to full femininity as a wife and mother. Maenadism
thus expresses in ritual terms the problematic and conflicting elements
of Dido's self.

Although Dido's maenadism indicates the potentiality of female
aggression against the male, the simile portrays just the opposite:

---

[34] On Orestes' depiction as a youth on the verge of adulthood, see Zeitlin 1984:
170–71 and Bierl 1994: 85–96. On Pentheus' similarly problematic transition,
see, for instance, Segal 1978–79.

Pentheus' pursuit by the Furies casts Dido in the role of the pursued and Aeneas in the role of the Furies. In the Greek play, Pentheus is not pursued by Furies. Nevertheless, as we have seen, both in tragedy and in the *Aeneid*, Furies are often presented as exhibiting bacchic behavior (see note 19 to this chapter). Dido herself is earlier portrayed as a Fury (4.384–87; Hardie 1993: 41). The fury of maenadism and the *furor* inflicted by Furies and other such creatures are thus closely linked. Dido's frustrated erotic desire when she first learns of Aeneas' plan to abandon her presents the potentiality of recourse to bacchic behavior. As this initial desire continues to be thwarted, further maenadic symptoms are generated, a progression that corresponds to Amata's two consecutive assaults by the serpent. The association of Furies with maenadism at this juncture also foreshadows the pernicious outcome of maenadic behavior in the second half of the epic.

Just as in the case of Amata, so in the case of Dido, maenadism causes a movement from the private realm of womanhood to the public domain of war and destruction. Most tragic heroines, such as Deianeira, Phaedra, Alcestis, as well as the Latin queen Amata in the *Aeneid*, die in their *thalamoi*. Their death thus confirms their connection with marriage and maternity.[35] Dido too chooses to end her life in the innermost recesses of her house (the pyre is erected *tecto interiore*, 494, and *penetrali in sede*, 504). She utters her final words weeping on her marital bed (645–50). Yet unlike the other heroines, Dido's speech is a kind of *res gestae* and reconnects her with her city and her former identity as androgynous leader:

> uixi et quem dederat cursum Fortuna peregi,
> et nunc magna mei sub terras ibit imago.
> urbem praeclaram statui, mea moenia uidi,
> ulta uirum poenas inimico a fratre recepi...                    (653–56)

> I have lived and finished the course that fortune had given me
> and now a great image of what I was will go to the earth below.
> I have founded a glorious city, I have seen my own walls,
> I have taken revenge for my husband from my brother who is my foe.

---

[35] Loraux 1987: 23–24. Dido's mode of suicide mimics the sexual act and reveals that sexuality was the reason behind her demise. See also Goff 1990: 38 n.17.

Dido's *comites* witness the queen's death, and their lamentation resounds through the palace walls out to the whole city. The women's collective voice of lamentation is identified with Fama:

> ...it clamor ad alta
> atria: concussam bacchatur Fama per urbem.
> lamentis gemituque et femineo ululatu
> tecta fremunt, resonat magnis plangoribus aether,
> non aliter quam si immissis ruat hostibus omnis
> Karthago aut antiqua Tyros, flammaeque furentes
> culmina perque hominum uoluantur perque deorum.                    (665–71)

> ...The cries rise to the high
> roof: Rumor rages like a bacchant in the stricken city.
> The palace roars with the moanings of lamentation
> and the women's wailings, the air resounds with the great beatings,
> as though all of Carthage or ancient Tyre were
> collapsing as the enemy rushes in, and raging flames
> roll over the roofs of men's houses and god's temples.

Fama's movement is cast in maenadic terms: by spreading the word about Dido's death, it also spreads the lamentation of the Carthaginian women, which is thus connected with Dido's earlier maenadic behavior.[36] Dido's madness, therefore, emerges as comparable to that of the women's lament. The disruptive and dangerous nature of female lamentation is further illustrated in the simile that compares the women's lament to the falling of a city. The simile, then, does not simply equate the fall of Dido with the fall of Carthage but also suggests the dangers that female lamentation may pose to the integrity of the state.[37] The fury of the flames burning the city in the simile corresponds to the fury of Fama and, of course, to that of the dying Dido. The link between Fama, maenadism, and the eruption of violence occurs again in Book 7, where

---

[36] Note also that the women's wailing is described as *ululatus*, a word etymologically linked with the Greek term for the bacchic cry, ὀλολυγή.

[37] The lamentation over Dido's death fuels the perpetuation of Carthage's hatred for Rome. This hatred may be seen as causing the rise of Hannibal, which will result in the ultimate destruction of Carthage. On the major theme of female lamentation and the dangers it poses for the state, see Chapter 5, this volume.

Fama instigates the maenadic exit of the Latin *matres* (7.392–96). As we have seen, the women's maenadic activity also jeopardizes the stability of Latinus' household.

Fama's effect on the women of Carthage is thus very much like that of Allecto on Amata in Book 7. A combination of Fury-like and maenadic attributes accompanying the description of Fama (4.173–95) renders this supernatural creature yet another agent of female destructive empowerment. The passage skillfully includes the ancient etymology of the word *Dira* (*ira...deorum*, 178) as a means to identify this monstrous bird. Fama's pedigree (178–79) also reveals her chthonic nature. In addition, intertextual contact with Homer's description of Eris (*Il.* 4.442–43 and *Aen.* 4.175–76) fits neatly in the poem's overall depiction of the Furies and Discordia as partners in crime (see Chapter 3, pp. 90–92). Fama's avian nature and habitat will eventually echo in the description of the Dira portending the death of Turnus in *Aeneid* 12.[38]

Dido's maenadism is therefore organically linked with the central issues of the book and of the epic as a whole. It symbolically enacts the queen's movement from public figure to a woman in love and back to her former self, rooted in the public sphere as a leader of Carthage. This movement, highly sexualized in ritual terms, leads to the destruction of Dido's household and city and presents an important threat to the Roman state in both narrative and historical terms. Dido's death may be a requirement for the foundation of Roman cultural order (Keith 2000: 115); nevertheless, as we shall see (Chapter 6, pp. 182–98), her maenadism does not detract from her moral excellence and successful leadership, which constitute both a model for imitation on the part of Aeneas and a reminder of the losses that his order dictates.

## 3. The Sibyl and Helen

The figures of the Sibyl and Helen in Book 6 anticipate the themes of female resistance to marriage and the destruction of the household.

---

[38] Compare 4.186–88: *luce **sedet** custos aut summi **culmine** tecti / turribus aut altis* [by day she sits as a guardian on a high rooftop / or on lofty towers] and 12.863–64: *quae quondam in bustis aut **culminibus** desertis / nocte **sedens*** [which, sitting often by night on graves or on deserted rooftops]. On Fama and the Dira in *Aeneid* 12, see Putnam 1965: 195.

These themes are here associated with ritual maenadism and will receive full treatment in the later parts of the poem. The description of the Sibyl's divinely inspired prophecy is rife with bacchic attributes, while Helen is shown to enact a maenadic rite during the sack of Troy. Each of these two figures exemplifies the power that ritual affords women and the dangers it may present to society and the state.

More specifically, the depiction of the prophetess Sibyl as a maenad embodies the problem of female resistance to sexual initiation and the bridal transition. The link between bacchic frenzy and prophetic ecstasy in Greek and Roman thought and literature[39] offered Vergil fertile ground upon which the Sibyl's maenadic portrait could be deployed. Even before the prophetess is designated as a raving bacchant, the description of her possession by Phoebus contains elements that point to maenadism: contortion of facial features (47), loosening of the hair (48),[40] general excitement and signs of trance (48–49). The Sibyl's maenadic state, however, is rendered explicit when the god takes full possession of her body:[41]

> At Phoebi nondum patiens immanis in antro
> bacchatur uates, magnum si pectore possit
> excussisse deum; tanto magis ille fatigat
> os rabidum, fera corda domans, fingitque premendo.          (77–80)

> But the prophetess, no longer enduring Phoebus, raves wildly
> like a bacchant in the cave, if she could shake off the mighty god
> from her breast; so much more he tires
> her raving mouth, tames her wild heart, and molds her by pressing.

The Sibyl's frenzy is represented as a struggle against the god: vocabulary borrowed from descriptions of horse taming emphasizes the theme of resistance, while it also demonstrates the god's eventual mastery over the maiden (*fera corda domans*).[42] Similar motifs in Greek literature

---

[39] See Plato's *Ion* 533a–534a, where Socrates relates poetry to bacchic possession.

[40] According to custom, however, the prophetess' hair should be unbound, as the sacrifice had been made: see Conington 1884, 2: 432.

[41] Lucan presents his Sibyl in similar terms (5.169–224).

[42] The sexual implications of the description were noted by Norden (1926: 144–46), but dismissed by Austin (1977: 66–67). Ovid's account of the Sibyl

describe female sexual initiation as the "taming" of a maiden by her husband.[43] This portrait of the Sibyl is thus consistent with her usual depiction as the god's bride (Burkert 1985: 117). Horse-taming vocabulary is also used in the description of Amata's maenadic state (*reginam Allecto stimulis agit undique Bacchi* [Allecto drives the queen far and wide with the goad of Bacchus], 7.405). Maenadism is thus important in the representation of the Sibyl's resistance to the god and connects her with the larger theme of female negation of sexual initiation.

In maenadism, female resistance to the male also represents resistance to the bridal transition. The Sibyl's prophecy confirms that this issue is important here as well, since it announces a future wedding:

> causa mali tanti coniunx iterum hospita Teucris
> externique iterum thalami.                                                    (93–94)

> the cause of such great evil for the Trojans is once again a foreign bride
> and once again a foreign marriage.

This wedding, however, instead of bringing alliance and peace, will produce a second Trojan war, and the bride will prove to be a second Helen. The Sibyl's description of a wedding buried in bloodshed, an inversion of marriage to an interminable funeral, illuminates her earlier portrayal as a maenad resisting the god. Her maenadic demeanor is appropriate given the distorted nature of the marriage she is about to prophesy. In this light, the Sibyl's maenadism follows the pattern of maenadic behavior in the epic as indicative of female resistance to marriage. The Sibyl's emphasis on the evils of this new union points to the perverted nature

(*Met.* 14.129–53) exposes Vergil's intimations of sexual invasion and attributes to her Cassandra-like features (see the following note); Ovid, however, does not appropriate the maenadic aspects of Vergil's Sibyl.

[43] First found in Anacreon (*PMG* 417). Subsequent poets further elaborated the image of yoking as a metaphor for sexual initiation. The same connotations are found in the Latin terms *iungere*, *coniunx*, etc. The vocabulary of the taming of a horse employed in the description of the Sibyl's frenzy replicates the portrayal of Cassandra in Aeschylus' *Ag.* 1064–67. Moreover, Cassandra's famous rejection of Apollo's sexual advances also supports the argument that the Sibyl's resistance to Phoebus is linked with the theme of female resistance to sexual initiation.

of this wedding and thus detracts from the benefits that will eventually arise from it, namely, the Roman state and empire.

The Sibyl's maenadism is thus linked with the larger question of the role of women in the formation of the new state. The prophetess's importance in this respect is stressed through her ritual role. It is precisely that role that makes her Aeneas' guide as he is about to perform a katabasis, one that is directly linked with his own transition into a new role as a Roman leader. Although Anchises eventually takes over as Aeneas' guide to the Roman future, the Sibyl, a woman in ritual garb, is an enabling intermediary. As a result, a female ritual role is cast side by side with fatherly guidance as a necessary element for Aeneas' assumption of his new identity.

Maenadism as linked with the negation of marriage and the destruction of the household emerges fully in Deiphobus' narrative of the sack of Troy as engineered by Helen. Deiphobus recounts to Aeneas Helen's maenadic ritual that orchestrated both the fall of his household and that of their city:[44]

> illa chorum simulans euhantis orgia circum
> ducebat Phrygias; flammam media ipsa tenebat
> ingentem et summa Danaos ex arce uocabat.
> tum me confectum curis somnoque grauatum
> infelix habuit thalamus, pressitque iacentem
> dulcis et alta quies placidaeque simillima morti.
> egregia interea coniunx arma omnia tectis
> emouet, et fidum capiti subduxerat ensem:
> intra tecta uocat Menelaum et limina pandit,
> scilicet id magnum sperans fore munus amanti,
> et famam exstingui ueterum sic posse malorum.
> quid moror? inrumpunt thalamo...                    (517–28)

That one, faking a dance, led around the Phrygian women in orgiastic rites singing 'euhoe'; she herself was holding a huge torch
in the middle and was calling the Danaans from the topmost citadel.

---

[44] This story is also told in *Od.* 4.271–89: Helen signals to the Achaeans inside the wooden horse, Deiphobus running behind her (276). Vergil's version, however, recasts a Homeric scene by using the tragic function of maenadism.

> At that time my ill-starred bridal chamber held me worn from cares
> and heavy with slumber, and, as I lay, sleep, sweet and deep,
> very much like peaceful death, was weighing on me.
> Meanwhile, my illustrious wife takes all the weapons from the house
> and even drew my trusty sword from under my head:
> she calls Menelaus inside the house and opens the door,
> hoping, no doubt, that this would be a great gift for her lover,
> and thus the fame of her old misdeeds would be erased.
> Why say more? They break into the bridal chamber...

Helen's rite is identical to that of Amata in Book 7: they are both said to conduct a fake rite, stand in the middle of the chorus (6.517 and 7.389), and rouse the Phrygian women into maenadic frenzy (6.518 and 7.397–98). Once again, we witness a reversal of the usual distinction between male and female spaces: Helen revels outside, throughout the city and on the citadel, while Deiphobus rests in the marital chamber. What is more, Helen is described as taking up arms and disarming her sleeping mate, opening the *limen* of her household to outside aggressors, and offering her husband's life as a gift to her lover. Helen's rites result in the destruction of both Deiphobus' household (*inrumpunt thalamo*) and Troy.[45]

At the same time, however, there is poignant irony in this narrative as told by Deiphobus, who presents the situation with obvious bias: he describes Menelaus as *amans*, the adulterer, while he assumes the role of the lawful husband (Suzuki 1989: 100–101). Yet Deiphobus' mutilated body tells a different tale, as it evokes the punishment a Roman adulterer would incur (Anderson 1969: 60). Similarly, in the case of Amata's fake rite, the queen's maenadism attests to the authority of ritual over the narrator's version of events and promotes the articulation of an alternative point of view.

The episode of the Sibyl reveals a similar problem in identifying the narrative voice. Since the possessed prophetess is a vehicle for the god, the Sibyl's prophecy is an instance of ventriloquism, the real voice of the Sibyl elided. Aeneas' request, however, to hear the prophetess' voice

---

[45] A further link between the two bacchic instances in this book is the coincidence of the Sibyl's name, Deiphobe, with that of the narrator, Deiphobus.

(*ipsa canas oro* [I request that you yourself sing], 76) is no idle statement. The prophecy's focus on the issues surrounding maenadic resistance to marriage betrays a female perspective. Ritual thus in this instance also emerges as powerful enough to help women articulate the loss and perversion that the men's war brings.

Deiphobus' narrative therefore exposes a more general perversion of marriage at work, generated by both men and women, one that has disastrous consequences for both the royal house and the city.[46] Helen's episode, following the Sibyl's prophecy of a second Helen and a second Trojan War, serves to emphasize that this perversion of marriage persists even as Aeneas is about to found a new settlement.

Vergilian maenads thus closely adhere to the pattern of tragic maenadism as outlined by Seaford and Schlesier. Recourse to bacchic behavior in Vergil springs from female resistance to the male: Dido refuses to comply with Aeneas' decision; the Sibyl resists Apollo's invasion; Helen turns against Deiphobus, Amata against Latinus. Like their tragic counterparts, these women appear as both aggressors and victims, at once responsible and blameless for their actions: Venus in large measure causes Dido's demise; Apollo seeks to dominate the Sibyl; Venus absolves Helen of all responsibility for the sack of Troy (2.601–602); and the Fury Allecto brutally invades Amata.

Moreover, as in Greek tragedy, maenadic resistance to the male enables the articulation of female resistance to social and political constraints. The women's negation of marriage and sexual initiation is intimately bound up with the function of marriage in ancient Rome as a homosocial bond, one that ensures the forging of political alliances that will eventually lead to the Roman Empire. Ritual, and maenadism in particular, empowers the women to oppose the role of subordination and mediation that the men require of them. This resistance launches fresh bouts of violence that threaten to destroy the social and political fabric. Nevertheless, the representation of these women as victims makes a compelling case for their point of view, rendering it an alternative ideological

---

[46] Helen's maenadic behavior exemplifies the dangers that Dido poses to Aeneas (Suzuki 1989: 101). Helen's bacchic rite therefore serves to confirm that Dido's maenadic state is not simply a metaphor to denote her madness but linked to the episode's major themes.

position to that of male authority and empire. To be sure, this position is ultimately untenable. Maenadism, however, enables it to be registered most poignantly on the poem's ideological map.

Maenadism's importance in the *Aeneid* is not restricted to the women's bacchic activity. It resurfaces in the act of female lamentation. In the next chapter, we shall see the ways in which ritual mourning, maenadism, and the formation of state identity intersect through the involvement of women.

# 5 Mourning Glory: Ritual Lament and Roman Civic Identity

IN GREECE AND ROME, WOMEN SERVE AS ARBITRATORS OF DEATH rituals, responsible for burying and lamenting the dead. Yet in both societies the state takes pains to regulate and control these female practices, as they can potentially harm the interests of the larger community. In the *Aeneid*, in particular, women's excessive display of grief on such occasions serves as a foil to Aeneas' role as a leader and the responsibilities he has to ensure the progress of his mission. Two episodes where women practice rituals associated with death display complementary notions of the dangers that excessive passion brings to the state. At one end of the spectrum is Andromache, whose grief seals her identity as wife of Hector, perpetuates the loss of Troy, and does not allow her to adjust to new circumstances and assume a new identity. Andromache is portrayed as a double for Aeneas and thus represents an attitude toward the past that presents obvious obstacles to the success of his mission. A second aspect of the problem of grief is explored in the episode of the Trojan women in Book 5. This time, the women's excessive passion over the losses they have suffered transforms into action that turns against their community. The women's rage is linked to funeral ritual, since their decision to act, though divinely inspired, occurs during the ritual act of lamentation. That the women's ritual acts have implications for public life is underscored both in the case of Andromache and in that of the Trojan women. As a result, women's death rituals often transgress the norms prescribed by ritual custom and thus threaten the progress of Aeneas' mission.

## I. LESSONS IN RITUAL MOURNING

### 1. Andromache

The episode of Aeneas' stay at Buthrotum in Book 3 displays the necessity for the hero to move beyond his Trojan past on to his Roman future.[1] Of all the prominent figures in the episode, the tension between past and future, loss and empire finds its best expression in the figure of Andromache. As is the case with most women in the *Aeneid*, ritual serves as a vehicle through which these problems come into sharp focus.

Andromache is the first person Aeneas encounters as he enters Buthrotum. He finds her deep in mourning, conducting a funeral in the cenotaphs of Hector and Astyanax:

> progredior portu classis et litora linquens,
> sollemnis cum forte dapes et tristia dona
> ante urbem in luco falsi Simoentis ad undam
> libabat cineri Andromache manisque uocabat
> Hectoreum ad tumulum, uiridi quem caespite inanem
> et geminas, causam lacrimis, sacrauerat aras.                    (300–305)

> I set forth from the harbor, leaving ships and shore,
> just when, as it happened, in a grove outside the city,
> by the waters of a false Simois, Andromache was performing
> the solemn feast and gifts of mourning to the shades,
> and offering wine to the ashes and calling the ghost
> to Hector's tomb, the empty mound of green turf
> and twin altars she had consecrated, the cause for her tears.

Andromache's rites transgress the spatial and temporal limits of death ritual. She is performing libations at a cenotaph, long after Hector and her son have died. Despite the fact that cenotaphs were not unusual in ancient death ritual practice[2] and that regular commemoration of the dead is important for the affirmation of life, the excess and futility of

---

[1] See Grimm 1967; Storey 1989; West 1983; and Quint 1993: 53–65.

[2] Toynbee (1971: 54) notes that cenotaphs were used when the body was not available for burial, whether the person had drowned or died in battle. References to cenotaphs in literature emphasize the idea of futility. For examples, see Williams 1962: 119.

Andromache's actions permeates the passage: she offers libations to the ashes, yet there are no ashes in the tomb; the surrounding landscape and the tomb itself are described with the adjectives *falsus* [fake] and *inanis* [empty], thus poignantly underscoring the ironic contrast between the individual's desire to dwell in the past and the harsh necessity of adjusting to the future.

Andromache's funeral rites to her lost husband and child express her choice to live in the world of her dead loved ones. While mourning is a transitional period for the survivors, marked by withdrawal from society and ending with a ritually articulated return (Van Gennep 1960: 147; Seaford 1994: 86), Andromache clearly has not undergone the process of reintegration: a perpetual mourner, she longs to be united with her dead husband and child but is forced to exist in the world of the living. The narrative highlights her special connection with the dead in her reaction when she sees Aeneas:

> ut me conspexit uenientem et Troia circum
> arma *amens* uidit, magnis *exterrita* monstris
> *deriguit* uisu in medio, *calor ossa reliquit,*
> labitur et longo uix tandem tempore fatur:                           (306–10)

> When she caught sight of me coming, and saw, *beside herself,*
> the arms of Troy around, *distraught* by these great marvels
> she *stiffened* as she was looking, and the *warmth left her limbs.*
> She collapses and hardly at last she speaks:

The description of her demeanor underscores her affinity with the dead, as she progressively grows stiff and her limbs become cold. It is not a surprise, therefore, that when she finally musters the strength to address Aeneas (*uix tandem* [hardly at last]), we see her more prepared to assume that he is a ghost, a more vivid projection of her world (Grimm 1967: 155), than willing to accept that what she sees is real. At the same time, the excessive nature of her grief is evident in her deep emotional turmoil (*amens* [beside herself]), which jeopardizes her judgment, compromises her rationality, and has the potential to lead her to actions that can be dangerous for herself and others.

Andromache's liminal existence between the living and the dead is also eloquently displayed in her response to Aeneas' questions about her fortunes after the fall of Troy, an account she begins with a wish to have shared Polyxena's fate. For Andromache, death is far preferable to a state of permanent mourning:

> 'o felix una ante alias Priameia uirgo,
> hostilem ad tumulum Troiae sub moenibus altis
> iussa mori, quae sortitus non pertulit ullos
> nec uictoris heri tetigit captiua cubile! ...'                    (321–24)

> 'O happy beyond all others, maiden daughter of Priam,
> bidden to die at an enemy's tomb, beneath
> the lofty walls of Troy, who never bore the drawing of lot,
> nor as a captive touched the conquering master's bed! ...'

By introducing the example of Polyxena, Andromache expresses a longing for the permanence of real death, which will put an end to the perpetual deathlike liminality of her mourning and will bring about the desired unity between her as a mourner and the mourned, Hector and Astyanax.[3] Unlike Andromache, Polyxena, who died as a sacrificial offering at Achilles' burial, was never forced to leave Troy, incur the humiliation of slavery, or suffer the indignity of living as an enemy's wife. Polyxena's permanent virginity in death contrasts sharply with Andromache's changing identities, from Trojan wife and queen to various stages of slavery.[4]

In Euripides' *Hecuba*, Polyxena's sacrifice as a burial offering at the tomb of Achilles is one of the play's focal points.[5] Although Polyxena does not earn more than a passing reference in Vergil, her fate is nevertheless related to some of the episode's most important themes: Andromache's liminal position between the living and the dead; her inability to negotiate her changing identity from princess to slave and the transition from

---

[3] See, similarly, Seaford 1994: 167 on Achilles as a mourner of the dead Patroclus in the *Iliad*.

[4] On Andromache's self-definition as a Trojan and wife of Hector, see Grimm 1967 and West 1983. In Euripides' *Troades*, Andromache compares herself to Polyxena three times (630–31, 641–42, 677–80), and each time she finds the latter more fortunate than herself.

[5] Catullus' rendition of the sacrifice of Polyxena in 64.366–74 is testimony to the power of Euripides' scene.

past to future; the theme of corrupted rituals, and of sacrifice in particular; and the problematic nature of excessive grief, which can lead to revenge and destruction.

In Vergil's passage the main point of comparison between Andromache and Polyxena is that the latter never became a slave. This is also central in Polyxena's speech in *Hecuba* where she eloquently declares (342–79) that to die as a free princess is preferable to slavery in the hands of her foes. Unable to bear life in different terms (357–68), she chooses death. At the same time, this choice renders her a permanent virgin. Polyxena laments her fate as deprived of marriage (ἄνυμφος ἀνυμέναιος ὤν μ' ἐχρῆν τυχεῖν [without the bridegroom and wedding I should have had], 416). Her sacrifice symbolically enacts her wedding, as she is married to Hades (368; 482–83), a fact that her mother confirms after her sacrifice: Hecuba describes her daughter as a bride who is no bride, a virgin who is no virgin (νύμφην τ' ἄνυμφον, παρθένον τ' ἀπάρθενον, 612; Loraux 1987: 39).

The theme of marriage and sacrifice – indeed of marriage as sacrifice – is a pervasive motif in Greek tragedy. Scholars have repeatedly pointed out that Euripides appropriates the scene of the sacrifice of Iphigeneia in Aeschylus' *Agamemnon* as part of a larger allusive schema linking *Hecuba* with *Oresteia*. The erotic aspects of Polyxena's sacrifice have been amply noted by critics,[6] while the brutality of her death constitutes an instance of perverted sacrifice, despite the fact that she offers herself willingly. At the same time, Polyxena's death is closely linked with the theme of burial, which is paramount in the play (Mitchell-Boyask 1993: 122). The sacrifice of Polyxena and the death of Polydorus, the two dead children of Hecuba, act as catalysts for the unleashing of her powerful vengeance. The figure of Polydorus constitutes yet another connection between the Vergilian narrative and Euripides' play: just as *Hecuba* opens with the appearance of the ghost of Polydorus requesting burial (47–50), so Book 3 of the *Aeneid* begins with Aeneas violating the tomb of Polydorus. The episode ends with Aeneas and his comrades honoring their fellow Trojan with complete funeral rites and erection of a burial mound (62–68).

The themes of marriage[7] and perverted sacrifice, so prominent in the tragic versions of the myth, are also manipulated in this episode of the

[6] Segal 1990: 112; Zeitlin 1996: 172–216; and Loraux 1987: 36–39.
[7] On the theme of marriage in Euripides' *Andromache*, see Storey 1989.

*Aeneid*, alongside the theme of revenge and retribution. As Andromache tells Aeneas about her fate, she recounts the death of Neoptolemus:

> ast illum ereptae magno flammatus amore
> coniugis et scelerum furiis agitatus Orestes
> excipit incautum patriasque *obtruncat ad aras*.                      (330–32)

> But Orestes, burning with great love for his raped
> wife and driven by the Furies for his crimes,
> catches him unawares and *slays him at* his father's *altar*.

Neoptolemus' death at the hands of Orestes at the altar in Delphi is enacted in Euripides' *Andromache*. The scene portrays Neoptolemus' death in terms of perverted sacrifice: the hero goes to the oracle unarmed (1119) to ask for forgiveness and perform expiation; while still a suppliant, Orestes kills him at the altar.[8] Neoptolemus' perverted "sacrifice" is directly linked with the problem of revenge in the play, since Orestes kills him as punishment for the loss of his betrothed, Hermione. The notion of revenge is therefore rendered problematic, since it is exacted by means of a "sacrificial" death. The ritual order, however, though disrupted by the perverted "sacrifice" of Neoptolemus, will eventually be restored, since the play ends with an appearance by Thetis, who promises burial for the slain hero. Yet Thetis also proclaims that his tomb will serve as a reminder of the sacrilegiousness of his death (1240–42). Furthermore, Neoptolemus' perverted "sacrifice" is a symbolic extension of the general disruption and crisis of marriage and *oikos* in the play. All marriages depicted in the drama are measured against the ideal marriage of Andromache to Hector, a standard they fail to attain (Storey 1989: 18). The restoration Thetis seems to provide is only in terms of Peleus' *oikos* (she promises burial for Neoptolemus and immortality for Peleus), while Andromache is still identified as a captive wife (γυναῖκα αἰχμάλωτον, 1243), and her eventual union with Helenus underscores her unbreakable link with her Trojan past.

The issue of the captive woman's fate in slavery is central to Andromache's concerns in the *Aeneid*, as well as in Euripides' *Hecuba*,

---

[8] Orestes' sacrilegious behavior toward Neoptolemus would have been even more poignant for the Athenian audience if this sympathetic portrayal of Achilles' son is an innovation of Euripides. On Euripides' innovations regarding the character of Neoptolemus, see Stevens 1971: 5–6, 14–15.

*Troades*, and *Andromache*. The close link between Andromache's social identity as a captive and a slave and her status as a mourner is also evident in the way she describes her fate after Troy: she was a captive of Pyrrhus (*captiua*, 324); she was his slave when she bore him a child (*seruitio enixae*, 327); and her marriage to Helenus was a transferral of one slave to another (*me famulo famulamque Heleno transmisit habendam*, 329; West 1983: 260–61). The mirroring of Aeneas' and Andromache's attitudes toward the past becomes evident when Aeneas addresses her as *Hectoris* [wife of Hector] (319),[9] while Andromache's own last word in her response is *Hector* (343; see also Grimm 1967: 158).

The problem of Andromache's new identity after the fall of Troy is central in Euripides' *Troades* and *Andromache*. In the former play, Andromache considers Polyxena as more fortunate than herself. Polyxena's permanent virginity attests to her loyalty to her natal family, whereas Andromache is the wife whose loyalty to her husband is complete (Scodel 1998: 148). Her new status as a slave in the household of her husband's murderer is stressed poignantly in *Troades* 660, where δάμαρ, the term for the legitimate wife, is followed by δουλεύσω, a word denoting slavery (Scodel 1998: 148). Hecuba goes on to advise Andromache to adjust to her new situation because this is ultimately what will serve the interests of her earlier family, although the play dashes these hopes as Talthybios' entrance announces the Greeks' decision to murder Astyanax. Euripides' *Andromache* can be seen as presenting Andromache's future from the perspective of *Troades* (Scodel 1998: 149). The play opens with the heroine recounting her past and present, but, as her narrative progresses, the audience becomes increasingly aware that her present situation echoes her past: once again she is besieged by Greeks; a Greek woman (Hermione) is the source of her troubles; and her son (Molossus) is in danger (Sorum 1995: 377). Yet by the end of the play, Andromache has proven successful in adapting to new circumstances: she has caused disaster in the victor's family, and in marrying Helenus she returns to her first family (Scodel 1998: 150). The problem of transcending the past is a primary theme in *Andromache*; ironically, in that play, Andromache is the only character who proves capable of adjusting to the demands of her new situation, as her new son pulls her toward the future (Kyriakou 1997: 24).

[9] See Grimm 1967: 156. On Aeneas and Andromache as mirror images, see West 1983: 259 and the discussion following here.

In the *Aeneid*, by contrast, Andromache's perpetual status as a mourner extends beyond her private tragic fate to the entire community. Just as Andromache cannot live her life as other than Hector's wife and Astyanax' mother, so the whole city of Buthrotum is described as a sad replica of Troy, a symbolic burial ground for Andromache's dead kin:

> procedo et parvam Troiam simulataque magnis
> Pergama et arentem Xanthi cognomine riuum
> agnosco, Scaeaeque amplector limina portae.             (349–51)

> I go on, and recognize a little Troy, with a copy of great
> Pergamus and a dry brook named from Xanthus,
> and embrace the portals of a Scaean gate.

For the people at Buthrotum, remembrance of the lost Troy points to their common past and affirms their bonds of kinship and identity as Trojans. Regular commemoration of the dead is critical for every community because it is a very effective means of affirming social solidarity and collective identity. The beneficial effects of commemoration are evident in the practice of public funerals and hero-cult, as well as in the establishment of festivals and games. Yet such commemoration is also necessarily removed from the intense emotions that accompany the processes of mourning (Loraux 1998: 83–109).

Commemoration therefore goes hand in hand with the need for a gradual alleviation of pain that allows the reintegration of the mourners into the world of the living and enables the community to overcome the blow that has been inflicted upon it by death. This kind of necessary oblivion cannot easily be imposed upon the grieving, particularly upon mothers who have lost their children. That is why we see the state in both Greece and Rome at pains to establish rules and regulations that will control the excesses of mourning (Loraux 1998: 9–34). Yet in the case of Helenus and his people, as in the case of Andromache, the community does not seem able to overcome the loss incurred by the destruction of Troy. Aeneas' description of Buthrotum repeatedly makes mention of its small size, which contrasts sharply with the grandeur of the old city: a reminder that the past cannot be recreated, that memory will always fall short of the real thing.[10]

---

[10] On the size of Troy and memory, see Saylor 1970: 26–27.

The dangers that the passions stirred by memory and mourning can present for others are evident in Andromache's excessive display of grief, which affects Aeneas profoundly:

> ...dixit lacrimasque effundit et *omnem*
> *impleuit clamore locum.* uix pauca *furenti*
> subicio et raris *turbatus* uocibus *hisco*...                       (312–14)

> ...She spoke, and shedding a flood of tears *filled*
> *the entire place with her cries.* To her *in frenzy* I can scarcely
> make a brief reply, and *disturbed* I *gasp* with broken words...

Andromache's previous distraught state (*amens*, 307) is now transformed into uncontrollable frenzy. Aeneas' reaction all but mirrors that of Andromache: he is disturbed to the point that he can barely speak, just as Andromache earlier was rendered speechless upon seeing him. This mirroring of Aeneas and Andromache symbolizes the contagious power of grief, with its potential to spill over into the larger social and political spheres. Aeneas' status as a leader is important as he becomes a living example of the dangerous contagiousness of Andromache's excessive mourning. What is more, the entire community, which is captive in the same state of mourning, embraces death. The numerous and striking katabasis elements present in the episode[11] attest to the problems inherent in Andromache's passion and Helenus' inability or unwillingness as a statesman to control it.

Excessive grief leads to rage, and rage can lead to fresh acts of violence that may threaten the entire community. The episode at Buthrotum showcases with subtlety the problems inherent in this situation: the heroine's account of the death of her captor husband, Neoptolemus, occurs at an altar, which constitutes a replication of his slaying of King Priam. Euripides' *Andromache* also dramatizes this particular instance with great emphasis on the inappropriate locale for such a killing (1156). Killing someone at the altar is an act of pollution. As such, it cannot constitute an acceptable means of retribution. When Helenus thus offers the armor of Neoptolemus (3.469) among parting gifts to Aeneas and Ascanius, he gives them a symbol of that particular line of justice, its inefficiency

---

[11] See Quint 1993: 58–60 and Paschalis 1997: 131–33.

marked by the presence of pollution as a symbol of this community's inability to extricate itself from the realm of the dead.[12]

Andromache's state as a perpetual mourner thus demonstrates the inability of funeral ritual to bring relief. Through the repetition of the act of burial and lamentation, Andromache seeks to find comfort for her loss, but all her efforts are doomed to failure. This ineffectiveness of ritual is due to the fact that the rites Andromache practices transgress social norms, since they deprive the mourner of a return to the world of the living.[13] The point of the episode, therefore, is that Aeneas must learn from the negative example of Andromache the appropriate ways of mourning, which allow the living to look toward the future. That he should have to learn this at this juncture in the poem is rather surprising, given that Creusa, his lost wife, had taught him this very lesson earlier in Book 2.

## 2. Creusa

The pairing of memory and mourning so poignantly demonstrated in the episode just examined and the central role of women in this process also figure prominently in the episode of the disappearance of Creusa in *Aeneid* 2. In this instance, Aeneas is taught the correct attitude vis-à-vis loss and mourning. Significantly, this instruction is provided by his lost wife, Creusa. She advocates the need for selective memory as the only means by which a devastating loss can be borne and eventually overcome. Yet the lesson that Aeneas appears to learn so successfully in Book 2 is soon forgotten when he meets Andromache in Book 3. The poem thus offers a standard by which one can evaluate the processes of mourning as they unfold over the course of the poem.

[12] Hardie (1993: 17) notes that Aeneas realizes the constraints imposed upon the citizens of Buthrotum, doomed to live in the past, when his words to Helenus and his people (*uiuite felices* [live happy], 493) combine the language of farewell with the language of funerary epitaph. On the significance of the theme of retribution in this scene, see my discussion in Chapter 1, pp. 41–43.

[13] Indeed, the tenuousness of the boundaries between proper and perverted ritual is a pivotal theme in this episode: the death of Polyxena as a funeral offering at the tomb of Achilles and the killing of Pyrrhus at the altar by Orestes both transgress correct ritual practice (*Aen.* 3.330–33).

Although ritual mourning is a practice usually ascribed to women, the lines describing Aeneas' reaction once he realizes that his wife is lost cast him as a mourner:

> quem non incusaui *amens* hominumque deorumque,
> aut quid in euersa uidi crudelius urbe?                              (745–46)

> What man or god did I not blame *in my frenzy*?
> what sight more cruel did I see in the overthrown city?

Much as in the case of Andromache, so in this instance the overwhelming power of grief takes over the mourner's senses: he is *amens*, just as Andromache is *amens* when she sees Aeneas (3.307). The series of questions that Aeneas utters evokes the mourner's initial anxiety that he may fail to express his grief adequately: a series of questions to this effect usually begin a formal lament (Alexiou 2002: 161). Aeneas, however, expresses the opposite of this convention: in reproaching men and gods for taking his wife away and in equating the loss of Creusa with the loss of the city, he is anxious to establish the propriety of the contours of his lamentation. Aeneas concludes by rushing to look for his lost wife; as his search proves vain, he resumes his mourning:

> ausus quin etiam uoces iactare per umbram
> *impleui clamore* uias, maestusque Creusam
> nequiquam ingeminans iterumque iterumque uocaui.
> quaerenti et tectis urbis sine fine ruenti ...                       (768–71)

> I even dared to cast my cries in the night;
> *I filled* the streets *with shouts* and in my misery
> repeatedly called Creusa again and again in vain.
> As I rushed and sought [her] endlessly among the buildings of the city ...

Aeneas' lamentation here again resembles Andromache's in Book 3 (*impleuit clamore locum* [filled the place with her cries], 313), while the vanity of his efforts is closely akin to Andromache's futile preoccupation with death and mourning. The emphasis in Aeneas' language on triple repetition, marked by the use of *iterum* and *ingeminans*, displays the hero's agony and grief as well as the repetitive endlessness of the act of lamentation. It also points to the funeral practice of calling the name of the dead three times (*Aen.* 6.506). At the same time, Aeneas' violent movement in search of his wife is an indication of the violence and fury of the grief he suffers. The emotional turmoil associated with grief is only one step away from wrath and rage. This association may also be seen in the alternative reading *furenti* provided by M. The good authority of this manuscript adds force to the reading, especially since the fury of the mourner is one of the standard features of lamentation, also seen in Andromache's case of frenzied grief (3.312–14). Aeneas' actions can thus equally be describing a mourner.

Creusa's phantom also instructs Aeneas as to the appropriate forms of lamentation.[14] When she reproaches him '*quid tantum insano iuuat indulgere dolori*...' ["why does it please you to indulge so much in frenzied grief..."] (776), she acknowledges the manic state that pain inflicts upon the mourner and calls attention to the problem of excessive grief, which can be particularly destructive. Her words point to the paradoxical phenomenon of the mourner finding pleasure in the process of mourning, while the close semantic connection of grief and anger in the word *dolor* suggests the complexities of a state that may otherwise appear as harmless. Yet the special link between the mourner and the mourned established through lamentation renders the former eager to prolong that state as long as possible. Creusa here identifies a well-attested fascination with lament, an obsessive component of mourning, because it keeps the memory of the lost one alive and immortalizes the past in the present (Loraux 1998: 100). This, however, is precisely the state that does not allow the reintegration of the mourner into the world of the living, as is the case with Andromache and the people of Buthrotum. As such, it can also prove dangerous because it may excite wrath and a desire for revenge that will lead to a continuation of the cycle of death and suffering, as is so often the case in Greek tragedy.

Female mourners are dangerous, often depicted as "indulging" in grief, while men attempt to control and regulate the women's potential excesses. In this instance, however, Aeneas assumes the feminine characteristics of the mourner, while Creusa recognizes the dangers of dwelling in grief and the past. Her words to Aeneas look forward to his future; she

---

[14] Interestingly, Aeneas' reaction upon seeing Creusa is almost identical to his reaction upon seeing Andromache (3.313–14). This link between Creusa and Andromache once more confirms Andromache's depiction as a living dead.

prophesies the long wanderings awaiting him but also points to the happier days ahead and orders Aeneas to put an end to his mourning: *'illic res laetae regnumque et regia coniunx / parta tibi; lacrimas dilectae pelle Creusae...'* [happy events await you there, a kingdom and a royal wife; banish the tears for your beloved Creusa...] (783–84). Nevertheless, in acknowledging that her husband loves her, she also calls attention to the paradox of her request: how can a bereaved husband desist from mourning the loss of a dear wife? Creusa's strategy is therefore not in keeping with the usual feminine behavior in mourning, which encompasses all that is excessive and dangerous. On the contrary, in depicting her disappearance as part of a larger, divinely sanctioned scheme, she asserts the precedence of Aeneas' mission over the integrity of their family. This contrasts with her earlier attempt to convince Aeneas to defend their (Trojan) household (675–79), a plea whose potential success is implied in the narrative by the subsequent appearance of an omen affirming the decision to flee.[15] As a result, Creusa's disappearance suppresses an otherwise clear dichotomy between the interests of Aeneas' mission and those of their household.

Creusa's association with the interests of Aeneas' greater mission is also underscored by her association with the goddess Cybele: *'sed me magna deum genetrix his detinet oris. / iamque uale et nati serua communis amorem'* [but the great mother of the gods keeps me to these shores. Now fare well and guard the love of the son we had together] (788–89). Throughout the *Aeneid*, Cybele is consistently depicted as protecting Aeneas' mission. In *Aeneid* 6.781–87, in particular, we encounter the striking comparison of the city of Rome and the vast expanse of its empire to the Great Mother embracing her divine offspring. The city thus appropriates the very qualities of fertility and motherhood that the goddess represents. Creusa's contributions to the new city are also associated with her role as wife and mother. Her last words to Aeneas are about their child, whose significance for the future of Rome hardly needs mention. Yet Cybele is also associated with excess and barbarism, emasculation and effeminacy.[16] Aeneas' assumption of the role of a mourner consumed by

---

[15] Perkell (1981: 360–61) notes the contrast between Creusa's priorities and those of Aeneas.

[16] On the different attributes of Cybele and Roman attitudes toward the goddess, see Beard 1994.

grief and Creusa's concerns with the interests of the new state both indicate the kind of reversal of gender roles attested in Cybele's relationship
with her priests.

Creusa's voice thus appears assimilated to the voice of the state, and
as such she advocates oblivion as a means to dissolve Aeneas' mourning.
She does not suggest that Aeneas forget her completely; her memory will
live through the love for their son. She thus proposes a kind of selective
memory, one that allows for both a link with the past and the necessity
to look forward to the future. The "disappearance" of Creusa is thus a
literal expression of the need for selective memory. But her final words
to Aeneas leave no doubt that her loss is as permanent as that incurred
by death: the phrase *iamque uale* is also found in a very similar scene in
Book 5 (738) where Anchises' ghost in the Underworld has just finished
giving Aeneas instructions.[17]

As Creusa's phantom disappears, Aeneas' lament continues:

> haec ubi dicta dedit, lacrimantem et multa uolentem
> dicere deseruit, tenuisque recessit in auras.
> ter conatus ibi collo dare bracchia circum;
> ter frustra comprensa manus effugit imago,
> par leuibus uentis uolucrique simillima somno.
> sic demum socios consumpta nocte reuiso.                     (790–95)

> After she spoke these words, she abandoned me weeping and wishing
> to tell her much, and drew back into thin air.
> Three times there I tried to throw my arms about her neck;
> three times the image, clasped in vain, fled from my hands,
> equal to the light winds, and most like a winged dream.
> Thus at last, when night is spent, I revisit my companions.

The use of the present participles (*lacrimantem, uolentem*) reveals the continuous nature of Aeneas' grief, his desire to prolong their contact as
long as possible. His efforts to embrace her, repeated three times, point
to funeral ritual practices and are symbolic of the mourner's need to be
connected with the lost one, while Creusa's lack of corporeality and her

---

[17] See also 11.827, Camilla's final words before she dies. A similar phrase is found
in Catullus' farewell at his dead brother's tomb (*aue atque uale*, 101.10, a poem
that is part of or a substitute for burial rites).

comparison to a dream signals her permanent separation from the world of the living. The narrative dwells on Aeneas' acts of mourning, which take place in the night, the symbolic realm of the dead. Yet Aeneas' return to his comrades in the morning presents his return to the world of the living, ready to face his future. He thus appears to have completed the various stages of mourning successfully. Although Aeneas reunites with his companions, the narrative is strikingly silent about the process of return. And when he meets Andromache, we see that he still has much to learn about putting the past behind him. Creusa has provided him with the standard that will allow him to control the intensity and excess of grief, but he is far from having internalized this lesson.

Aeneas with his rescued Trojans gather at the mound of Ceres when the hero remembers that his wife was not with them (741–43). The goddess, a mother who lost her daughter, exemplifies the dangers of excessive mourning. The story, however, concludes with the reunion of mother and daugher as symbolic of life triumphing over death. The mound of Ceres thus stands as a reminder of insufferable loss, and as such it triggers Aeneas' memory. Moreover, the figure of Ceres embodies the most important themes of the episode: death and mourning, on the one hand, and the successful control of grief, which eventually benefits humanity, on the other.

Having explored the problems of passive grieving, the poem continues to explore the theme of mourning in Book 5, where the transition "from sorrow to wrath, from wrath to secession" (Loraux 1998: 43) becomes tangible. Women's engagement with funeral ritual, with memory and loss, will provide Aeneas with the final lesson in mourning.

## II. RITUAL LAMENT AND CIVIC IDENTITY

In *Aeneid* 5, the theme of the dangers of funeral lamentation reaches its climax. Women in their ritual role as mourners work up a rage that leads them to invade public space and turn against their own community. Women rebel at Juno's instigation; yet her intervention is effective precisely because it capitalizes on the emotions of grief and rage at work during the ritual ceremony. Women's rites are both embedded within the larger framework of Anchises' commemorative celebration and juxtaposed to those performed by the men. Male and female rites are thus portrayed differently: female mourning is depicted as divisive and potentially destructive, whereas the men's celebration of Anchises' funeral promotes social solidarity and the formation of a new civic identity for Aeneas and his Trojans. This is achieved through a transformation of the tragic pattern of ritual corruption-restoration: while in many Greek tragedies violent conflict is ultimately settled through the foundation of hero-cult, in *Aeneid* 5 the reverse is the case. Hero-cult elements abound in the description of the commemoration of Anchises' burial and the games that follow. But unlike what happens in Greek tragedy, in Vergil we first witness the positive function of hero-cult that benefits the community; then the renewed unity and hope that the community establishes through the ritual celebration of the games is threatened by the women's performance of corrupt rituals that endanger and destabilize the entire mission.

## 1. Anchises' Funeral and Hero-Cult

Death and commemoration are central concerns in Book 5. It opens with the flames of the funeral pyre of Dido and ends with the drowning of Palinurus, a "sacrifice" to Neptune for the successful completion of Aeneas' journey to the Underworld. As they arrive in Sicily, Aeneas, as befits the son of the deceased, presides over the ceremonies commemorating his father's death. Yet we are immediately aware that this is not a private funeral but a public celebration. Although the obvious model for this episode is the funeral games for Patroclus in *Iliad* 23, in this description we witness an amalgam of Greek and Roman ritual elements: the Roman *ludi funebres*, games held after the death of important citizens (Williams 1960: 48), and the ritual of *parentatio*, which serves here as a foundation myth for the ritual of *Parentalia* (Bailey 1935: 291; Williams 1960: 53).[18] These funeral rites and games are cast as public events that help establish a new identity as a new nation for Aeneas and

---

[18] Beard and colleagues (1998: 31) suggest that the *Parentalia* is similar to the cult of heroes in Greece, though not as individuals but as a generalized group under the title *di Manes* or *diui parentes*. They argue (1998: 50) that the *Parentalia* were "essentially domestic festivals focused on family ancestors, though there was also a public element when, on the first day of the *parentalia*, a Vestal Virgin performed the rituals for the dead." On the *parentalia*, see also Wissowa

his comrades. Although the games in honor of the dead Patroclus in the *Iliad* extend to the entire community and represent the integrative virtues of public funeral over the disruptive power of death ritual (Seaford 1994: 187), they do not aim at creating a new identity for the Greeks fighting at Troy. In the *Aeneid*, however, the funeral rites in honor of Anchises and the games enacted within their framework help create a new sense of belonging among Aeneas' comrades, who are in the process of making the transition from Trojans to Romans. In this respect, the function of the funeral tributes to Anchises resembles the use of hero-cult in Greek tragedy, where it also serves to cement Athenian civic identity by transferring loyalty from individual households to the city. Before I go on to discuss in detail how the text highlights issues of unity and collective identity, a few words on hero-cult and its role in Greece, and in Greek tragedy in particular, are in order.

In the Greek world, hero-cult is defined as worship performed at the hero's grave or what is imagined to be his grave. The tomb is in a special precinct, set apart from other burials. Sacrifices and other gifts are offered, and occasionally a special grave monument is erected (Burkert 1985: 203). It appears that the spread of hero-cult is linked with the formation of the city-state (Burkert 1985: 204; Seaford 1994: 110). Hero-cult in the polis replaces the extravagant funeral games for noble lords with institutionalized *agones* of the sanctuaries, honoring a hero. As a form of death ritual, hero-cult eliminates the potential divisiveness of private funeral. The importance of an individual family gives way to events that involve the entire community. Hero-cult thus promotes among nonkin members or the whole citizen body the same type of unity that funerary ritual confers upon kin members. This unity is expressed by the belief in a common descent from the hero (Seaford 1994: 109, 111).[19] In the collective celebration of the hero's death, all distinctions, individual and familial, social and economic, are abolished (Seaford 1994: 107). Other benefits arising from the worship of the hero are more obvious: he may

---

1912: 232–33. Toynbee (1971: 63–64) notes that the last day, the *Feralia*, was a public celebration.

[19] A prime example of funeral ritual used as a means to enhance communal belonging is Pericles' funeral oration in Thucydides (34–46), where praise of the dead fallen in battle serves as a manifesto of Athenian civic identity (Seaford 1994: 106).

be a model for emulation, and morale may be heightened by a belief in his active presence (Seaford 1994: 120).

In hero-cult, the dead receive blood offerings and are imagined as sharing feasts with the living, while laments are sung for the heroes as for the ordinary dead (Burkert 1985: 204–5; Seaford 1994: 114). Three elements expressing the social significance of hero-cult are the centrality of the tomb within the city, the participation of nonkin, and the perpetuation of observance (Seaford 1994: 117). Hero-cult also much encouraged the participation of *epheboi*, the new generation, thus connecting it with the world of the dead and the traditions it represented (Burkert 1985: 208). Contests were also part of these celebrations, but by the time of the formation of the polis they had dropped out of funerary practice. They were, however, still held for the war dead or for an exceptional individual honored by the entire community (Seaford 1994: 120–21). Just as in the funeral proper, the institution of contests provides a controlled outlet for aggressive anger at the death of an important individual. By the same token, when contests are held at regular intervals, in the cult of a hero or god, they can be socially integrative, especially where the dead man was a king or had been killed fighting for the whole community (Seaford 1994: 122–23). Richard Seaford argues that in Greek tragedy the integrative powers of hero-cult can be seen in full force. Hero-cult in tragedy appears able to transform the destructive reciprocal violence that drives the plot into benefit for the whole *polis*. In other words, in tragedy, death ritual is an instrument for the proliferation of reciprocal violence, while hero-cult is an instrument for the promotion of communal solidarity (Seaford 1994: 138).[20]

The main elements of hero-cult operative in the description of Anchises' funeral in *Aeneid* 5 were noted by Bailey: Aeneas addresses his father as *sancte parens* [holy father] (80), a term repeated at the end of the celebration of the games (630), thus pointing to Anchises' status not as a divinity proper but rather as a hero.[21] The altars of his tomb are named

---

[20] Vergil's contemporaries would have been able to relate the author's appropriations of the function of hero-cult in Greek tragedy to instances from their own experience, as hero-cult practices continued in the Hellenistic world. Romans might have been able to relate especially to various cult practices surrounding Homeric heroes, which seem to have enjoyed a resurgence in the Hellenistic era. On this resurgence and its significance, see Alcock 1997.

[21] Compare the earlier *diuinique ossa parentis* [bones of my divine father] (47).

*altaria* (54, 93), a word used, according to Servius, only of the altars to the *di superi* [gods of the upper world].[22] Among Aeneas' offerings to his father are milk and wine, which are normally offered to the dead. He also makes blood offerings, however, which are more appropriate to a divinity.[23] Similar offerings (i.e., blood sacrifices, food, and libations) are part of hero worship (Burkert 1985: 205). We also witness weeping and lamentation for the dead Anchises, but only later on, when the narrative turns to the actions of the women (613–14). The main event of hero-cult, the communal feasting in the company of the hero, is also observed here, albeit implicitly: we are only told that the Trojans light a fire and roast the meat (102–103).

The elements that help construct the public nature of Anchises' funeral are signaled from the very opening of the episode, when Aeneas speaks to his fellow Trojans from a mound (5.44), in the manner of Roman generals addressing their troops (Williams 1960: 49). The first part of the speech (44–54) focuses on Aeneas as a son eager to perform his duty toward his father. Feelings of loss and grief are prominent (*maestasque…aras* [altars of grief], 48; *iamque dies…adest, quem semper acerbum, / semper honoratum…habebo* [the day is here, which I shall consider, always a day of grief, / always a day of honor], 49–50). Yet as the speech continues (55–71), we witness a pronounced shift from private duty to public tribute, initiated by Aeneas' invitation to his companions to participate in the funeral rites and engage in supplication:

> ergo agite et *laetum cuncti* celebremus *honorem*;
> poscamus *uentos*, atque *haec* me *sacra quotannis*
> urbe uelit *posita templis sibi* ferre *dicatis*.                    (58–60)

> Come then, *one and all*, and let us solemnize *the sacrifice with joy*;
> *let us pray for winds* and may he grant that *year by year*
> *when my city is founded* I may offer *these rites in temples consecrated to him*.

---

[22] Servius on *Ecl.* 5.66 and *Aen.* 5.54; Bailey 1935: 293.

[23] Offerings are made twice because the rites were interrupted by the appearance of the snake. Two oxen are sacrificed for every ship, while Aeneas bids his comrades to bring their *penates* and those of Acestes (61–63). The second time he slays two sheep, two swine, and two black heifers (96–97), a sacrifice described as *honores* to his father (94), a term normally used for a sacrifice to a divinity (cf. 1.49). See also Bailey 1935: 294.

The suggestion that Anchises may provide help for all Trojans evokes a belief, crucial to hero-cult, that the hero has the power to benefit the community. Aeneas' words further imply that the whole community has an interest in honoring Anchises. Propitiation of the "hero" directly aids in achieving the communal goal, since the ghost of Anchises is envisaged as capable of ensuring favorable winds for the continuation of Aeneas' journey. At the same time, the act of paying tribute to Anchises unites the Trojans (*cuncti*). In appropriating Anchises as one of their own, the Trojans rejoice in the celebration, while the perpetuation of the observance, proclaimed by Aeneas once the new city is founded, guarantees their continuing solidarity. The placement of Anchises' temple within the new city points to hero-cult, since the hero's sanctuary was centrally located, while the yearly observance affirms the hope that Anchises will continue to bestow his favor upon the community (see also Bailey 1935: 294).[24] Moreover, the feelings of joy (*laetum...honorem*) expressed here and throughout this episode (34, 40, 58, 100, 107)[25] connote the effects of the communal ritual celebration, namely, solidarity and hope for success in the future, and sharply contrast with Aeneas' earlier (private) grief at the death of his father.

The transition from private funeral to public celebration reaches its climax with the description of the games. The close connection between games and funeral is indicated by the fact that they take place on the ninth day of the funeral rites, that is, on the day of their conclusion. In addition, Aeneas initiates the ceremony by using formulae that evoke the words of a priest before the onset of ritual to ensure purity: *ore fauete omnes et cingite tempora ramis* [be silent all and wreathe your brows with leaves] (71) (Williams 1960: 55).[26] Elements of hero-cult once again surface as Anchises' spirit, in the form of a snake tasting the offerings at the tomb, seems to be sharing in the feast. The appearance of the snake stuns Aeneas (90), who is unsure as to the significance of the portent (95–96). In narratives of hero-cult, physical encounters with the hero are

[24] Before he leaves Sicily, Aeneas founds the temple of Venus of Eryx but also assigns to the tomb of Anchises a priest and a sacred grove (759–61).

[25] The word is also often repeated during the games as well as during the narrative of the *lusus Troiae* (183, 210, 236, 283, 304, 515, 531, 577, 667).

[26] The offerings presented at the tomb of Anchises evoke the Roman sacrificial ceremony of *suouetaurilia*. See Bailey 1935: 294 and Williams 1960: 63. Hellenistic elements of *apotheosis* are also at work here (see Williams 1960: 48).

always rife with fear and danger. The appearance of a snake in particular, always a terrifying creature, is often taken to be a manifestation of the hero (Burkert 1985: 206). Moreover, the strengthening of the communal bond being forged through the ritual is also evident in the narrative's emphasis on the effacement of socioeconomic distinctions among the participants. We see stress placed on the act of participation and not on the type of offerings contributed by each (*quae cuique est copia* [as each can afford], 100).[27]

As a number of scholars have pointed out, at the games we observe an imitation of the contests enacted on the battlefield. Within the controlled space of ritual contest, the threat of violence among the members of the community is averted by the distribution of prizes to all contestants, even when it may seem inappropriate, as in the case of Nisus and Euryalus (335–61). Aeneas thus emerges eager to impose unity, even if at times this unity may appear artificial. His actions cultivate among the contestants a sense of belonging to the community that is required by those ready to die for it in battle. Yet the potentiality of violence among members of the group is strikingly present, though eventually averted by sacrificial substitution, as becomes apparent in the case of Entellus, who sacrifices a bull in the place of a human victim.[28] The themes of unity, solidarity, and continuity are also manifest in the concluding segment of the games, the *lusus Troiae*. We are told that the skill displayed by the boys as they execute their mock battle formations gives joy to the spectators:

> excipiunt plausu pauidos gaudentque tuentes
> Dardanidae, ueterumque agnoscunt ora parentum.                    (575–76)

> The Dardans welcome the anxious boys with applause and rejoice,
> as they gaze, to recognize in them the features of their old fathers.

Once again, the feelings of joy are grounded in the recognition of the continuity between fathers and sons. The importance of this continuity between the new generation and the world of the dead and the tradi-

---

[27] The fact that funerals can be a site of competition among members of the community is amply attested. See, in particular, Ovid's description of the *Parentalia* in *Fast.* 2.533–46, where he advocates the necessity of presenting humble offerings to the dead, the implication being that excessive offerings were common.

[28] On the complexities of the use of sacrifice and sacrificial substitution in *Aeneid* 5, see Hardie 1993: 32–33, 52 and Feldherr 2002.

tions it represents is also, as we have seen, a feature of Greek hero-cult. The prominence of the *lusus Troiae* in the rites surrounding Anchises' death and afterlife therefore emphasizes the positive role of the young in the new community that is being forged and celebrated. At the same time, Vergil's *lusus*, an aetiology for the contemporary practice of the *lusus Troiae*, serves multiple purposes: on the one hand, it creates a link between this new community that will eventually lead to the foundation of Rome and the new civic identity that Augustus seeks to promote. On the other, it reinforces the notion of continuity between past and present by affirming a common ancestry that is revived and celebrated afresh under the new Augustan regime.[29]

## 2. The Trojan Women

The exclusion of women from the affirming and unifying ceremonies described earlier results in their secession from the community. Ritual lamentation and mourning provide the context within which the women's rebellion becomes possible. *Aeneid* 5 displays women's inability and/ or refusal to espouse the values celebrated by the men during Anchises' funeral rites. Far from sharing the same feelings of joy as the men, women appear unable to overcome the grief and sorrow of the past and to look forward to their new home. This inability is, of course, closely linked to their exclusion from the rites performed by the men. Their ritual role as mourners privileges their relationship with the dead, which gives rise to the divisive feeling of rage at the losses they have incurred, a rage that turns against their own people.

Female mourning is an activity normally associated with the private realm of the household. Nevertheless, in their lament for Anchises' death, the women voice specific views and goals regarding the fate of their community. When we first encounter the Trojan women in the narrative, they are gathered by the ships, lamenting the death of Anchises:

> at procul in sola secretae Troades acta
> amissum Anchisen *flebant cunctaeque* profundum
> pontum aspectabant *flentes*: heu tot uada fessis

[29] The *lusus Troiae* was revived by Sulla and encouraged by Augustus. See Williams 1960: 145–47.

et tantum superesse maris, *uox omnibus una.*
*urbem orant*; taedet pelagi perferre laborem.                          (613–17)

But far apart on the lonely shore the Trojan women
*wept* for Anchises' loss, *and all, as they wept*, gazed on
the deep ocean: Alas, for worn out people what waves remain,
what wastes of sea, such is *the one cry of all.*
*It is a city they wish for*; they have had enough of the sea's hardships.

Though engaged in a primarily female task, mourning for the dead,
their actions mirror those of the men: they too view Anchises' loss as a
communal one and appear united (*cunctae*) in their sense of loss and grief.
At the same time, however, just as had happened with the men earlier,
the death of Anchises emerges as linked with their mission: the parallel
is carefully drawn in the repetition of *flebant* and *flentes*, the former referring to Anchises' death and the latter to the vast expanses of the sea that
lie ahead. The women therefore express an active interest in the common
goal and articulate as a group their view of its viability.

Yet the vision that the women express is markedly different from that
of the men, as it is grounded in grief, loss, and the past: the city they
envision (through the voice of Iris impersonating Beroe)[30] is a replica of
Troy and resembles Buthrotum:

quis prohibet muros iacere et dare ciuibus urbem?
o patria et rapti nequiquam ex hoste Penates,
nullane iam Troiae dicentur moenia? nusquam
Hectoreos amnis, Xanthum et Simoenta, uidebo?                          (631–34)

Who forbids us to cast up walls and give our citizens a city?
O fatherland, O household gods, in vain rescued from the foe,
shall no walls from now on be called Troy's? Shall I nowhere
see the rivers of Hector, Xanthus and Simois?

The women share in the communal vision that requires the foundation
of a city for all (*dare ciuibus urbem*). But their vision, fixed in the past and

[30] Nugent (1992: 281) rightly argues that Iris does not express the desire of all
women when she urges them to burn the ships. The women indeed waver about
the method that Iris advocates, and appear torn between the loss of the past
and the hope for the future (654–56).

the recreation of Troy, contrasts strongly with Aeneas' forward gaze to
the new city and its new institutions. It is thus obsession not with private loss but with communal loss and suffering that causes the women
to articulate their own plan over that of the men. The women are then
propelled to violent action that leads to perversion of the rites they had
so faithfully observed:

> '... quin agite et mecum infaustas exurite puppis.
> nam mihi Cassandrae per somnum uatis imago
> ardentis dare uisa faces: 'hic quaerite Troiam,
> hic domus est,' inquit 'uobis.' iam tempus agi res,
> nec tantis mora prodigiis. en quattuor arae
> Neptuno; deus ipse faces animumque ministrat.'                    (635–40)

> '... Come and burn with me these accursed ships.
> For in my sleep the ghost of the prophetess Cassandra
> seemed to give me blazing firebrands: 'Here seek Troy,'
> she said 'here's your home.' Now is the time to act;
> nor delay befits such portents. Here, four altars
> to Neptune; the god himself lends the firebrands and the courage.'

Interfering with the burning of the fire at the altars outside the framework of ritual ceremony (*infensum ui corripit ignem* [seized with force the
deadly flame], 641) is a defilement of normal ritual practice. It is precisely the sacrilegious nature of the act that stuns the women (*arrectae
mentes stupefactaque corda / Iliadum* [startled are the minds of the Trojan
women, their hearts bewildered], 643–44), causing Pyrgo to intervene
and inform them that the woman inciting them to violent action cannot
be Beroe.[31] Yet Iris' flight to heaven (657–58) ignites the hearts of the
women as well as the ships:

> tum uero attonitae monstris actaeque *furore*
> conclamant rapiuntque *focis penetralibus* ignem;
> pars *spoliant aras*, frondem ac uirgulta facesque
> coniciunt. *furit* immissis Volcanus habenis
> transtra per et remos et pictas abiete puppis.                    (659–63)

---

[31] In her speech she reminds the women, and the reader, that they are in the process of performing funeral rites (651–52).

> Then indeed stunned by the marvels and driven *by frenzy*,
> they cry aloud, and some snatch fire *from the hearths within*;
> others *strip the altars*, and throw on leaves and twigs
> and brands. With free rein Vulcan *rages*
> amid thwarts and oars and hulls of painted pine.

The women's fury is a result of their intense grief over the losses the community has incurred during the quest for Italy. The goddess fuels this grief so that it becomes rage, which leads to destruction as they set fire to the ships. The women's rage also results in sacrificial corruption, as they now follow Iris' sacrilegious example. The women's frenzy becomes one with the frenzy of the fire that consumes the ships, the uncontrollable fire being a concrete manifestation of the women's lack of self-control. The language describing the women's frenzied state bears great resemblance to that used to describe the more specifically bacchic rage of Amata and her followers in *Aeneid* 7 (*attonitae Baccho . . . matres* [the mothers . . . frenzied by Bacchus], 580).[32] More distinctly maenadic characteristics surface in the description of the women's flight after Ascanius chastises them:

> ast illae diuersa metu per litora passim
> diffugiunt, siluasque et sicubi concaua furtim
> saxa petunt; piget incepti lucisque, suosque
> mutatae agnoscunt excussaque pectore Iuno est.          (676–79)

> But the women scatter in fear over the shores this way and that,
> and stealthily seek the woods and the hollow rocks anywhere
> they can find them; they loathe what they began and the light of day;
> now changed, they know their kin, and Juno is shaken from their breasts.

The women's movement recalls that of bacchants who abandon the civilized world for the world of the wild. Their flight comes at the moment of sanity, however, which is incongruent with standard maenadic practice, where women flee to the wild in their madness only to return to their homes after the frenzy has subsided. Maenadic flight signals the

---

[32] The Trojan women's bacchic behavior as a result of Iris' interference is not surprising given the many similarities between her and Allecto, on which see Putnam 1965: 88–90.

abandonment of the female space and marks a transgression of the women's roles as wives and mothers. In this particular instance, however, it is the women's traditional role as ritual mourners that encroaches on public space. Through their lamentation they express their collective will to oppose the plans of the men. The use of bacchic imagery to express the women's return to sanity rather than their madness emphasizes their transgression, because it describes their rage as the product of distorted female rites. Their bacchic flight symbolizes the fact that they have lost their place in the community once they have turned against it. The women are thus permanently delegated to the wild; their ties to the community are severed, and their flight prefigures their subsequent exclusion from Aeneas' Rome. Their exclusion is thus a result of both their attachment to the past, exemplified by their ritual status as mourners, and their inability to understand and share in the positive effects of public death ritual.[33]

The women's encroachment on the public sphere is vividly captured by Ascanius:

> primus et Ascanius, cursus ut *laetus* equestris
> ducebat, sic acer equo *turbata* petiuit
> castra, nec exanimes possunt retinere magistri.
> 'quis *furor* iste nouus? quo nunc, quo tenditis,' inquit,
> 'heu miserae ciues? non hostem inimicaque castra
> Argiuum, *uestras* spes uritis. en, ego *uester*
> Ascanius!' galeam ante pedes proiecit inanem,
> qua ludo indutus belli simulacra ciebat.                    (667–74)

> And first Ascanius, as *joyfully* he led the equestrian
> course, eagerly sought with his horse the *bewildered*
> camp, nor can his breathless masters hold him back.
> 'What strange *madness* is this?' he says, 'Where now, where are you going,
> my wretched *citizens*? It is not the foe, not the hostile Argive
> camp you burn, but *your own* hopes. I am *your own*
> Ascanius! And before his feet he tossed the empty helmet
> which he was wearing as he roused in sport the imitation of battle.

---

[33] This inability is, of course, as we have noted, also a result of their exclusion from the life-affirming, positive rituals.

The public nature of the women's actions is evident in Ascanius' appeal to them as *ciues* and his effort to reestablish the connection between the women and the rest of the community by the repetition of *uestras* and *uester*.[34] Furthermore, Ascanius' description as *laetus* evokes the earlier episode of the games and the emotions of joy and solidarity that ritual generates among the members of the community. By contrast, the women's perversion of their role as ritual mourners negates the beneficial effects of properly executed ritual.

That the women's collective action is critical to the future of Aeneas' mission is evident in Aeneas' emotional reaction:

> at pater Aeneas casu *concussus* acerbo
> nunc huc ingentis, nunc illuc pectore curas
> mutabat uersans, Siculisne resideret aruis,
> *oblitus fatorum*, Italasne capesseret oras.                    (700–704)

> But father Aeneas *stunned* by the bitter blow
> now this way, now that, within his heart turned over
> his cares, whether, *forgetful of fate*, he should settle
> in Sicilian fields, or aim for Italian shores.

Aeneas here resembles much more the women stupefied by Iris' words and actions than the leader who earlier in the book had showed a deft ability to ease tensions among his people. Aeneas' reaction also eloquently and poignantly demonstrates how communal unity, reinforced through the elaborate description of the commemoration of Anchises' death, is always fragile. The earlier sentiments of joy now forgotten, Aeneas contemplates doing what the women want. It takes the intervention of Nautes and Anchises himself to convince him otherwise and thus to undo the damage the women have done. The outcome of these deliberations is the abandonment of the women in Sicily along with the elderly men.[35] Yet this city, like Buthrotum, is chained to the past: it is a new Troy (756).

[34] Nugent (1992: 280) notes that Ascanius' gesture demonstrates the divide between men and women: the male in his armor is unrecognizable in the domestic space. On Ascanius as Euripides' Pentheus within the maenadic context, see Oliensis 2001: 58–59.

[35] On the decision to leave the women in Sicily, see also Nugent 1992: 283. Interestingly, the women are granted civic status: *transcribunt urbi matres*, 750.

The women appear limited in their capacity to understand the collective mission and are therefore denied participation in it. What is more, their traditional role as ritual mourners is shown to endanger communal unity and the success of Aeneas' mission.

In Book 9 (473–502), the Trojan army displays a reaction similar to that of Aeneas as a result of the lament of Euryalus' bereaved mother.[36] In this instance too, female grief exhibits bacchic attributes: the woman is said to be mad (*amens*, 478), and her cries (*femineo ululatu*, 477) appropriate the maenadic cry so frequently used by maenads. She abandons the female space and its attendant activities (476) and moves to the ranks of battle (*agmina . . . / petit*, 478–79), while bemoaning the fact that the reality of war prevents her from performing burial rites for her son (485–89). The great impact of her lament on the Trojan army is recorded in detail: the soldiers' spirit is shaken (*concussi animi*, 498), and sorrowful moaning arises among all (*maestusque per omnis / it gemitus*, 498–99). Euryalus' mother, however, far from stirring the men's grief into action and revenge, undermines their ability to continue the fight. We are told that their strength for battle diminishes (*torpent infractae ad proelia uires*, 499), while the woman kindles lamentation like fire among them (*incendentem luctus*, 500) before she is removed. Once again we see that female lamentation can be pernicious, diminishing men's effectiveness to fulfill the common goal.

In conclusion, in Book 5 Vergil employs the use of hero-cult in Greek tragedy but inverts and transforms it in order to expose the cracks at the seams of communal unity and the new civic identity it seeks to affirm. In Greek tragedy, according to Richard Seaford, the violence that often ensues as the result of death ritual, in the form of reciprocal vengeance, is eventually replaced by hero-cult. As a form of funerary ritual that eliminates the divisiveness caused by death, the institution of hero-cult transfers the emotions of private funeral to a collective participation in

---

According to Servius *ad loc.*, *transcribere* is a technical term denoting citizenship. See Williams 1960: 184.

[36] On Euryalus' mother's appearance despite the statement that all of the women stayed in Sicily, see Nugent 1992: 272–74. On her lament, see also Nugent 1999: 254–56. Note that here too, as in the case of Dido, Fama helps spread female lamentation (see Hardie 1994: 159–60).

the lament over a hero and thus promotes civic unity. Vergil inverts this pattern from Greek tragedy: the greater portion of the book celebrates the positive, unifying effects of death ritual, cast as a tribute for the dead Anchises, whose spirit is able to benefit the community. As a common *pater* to all, he provides a renewed strengthening of communal bonds under the shared vision of a future in Italy. This unity, however, appears to be incomplete because it excludes other groups from the community, namely, the women. As a result, communal unity is shown to be threatened not by loyalties to autonomous households (as is the case in Greek tragedy) but by the women, whose opposition takes the guise of a transgression of their role as ritual mourners. Violence thus erupts at the conclusion of the funeral games, a violence that divides the community into male and female and destabilizes Aeneas' (and, by implication, the community's) resolve to fulfill their mission. The inversion of the Greek tragic pattern underscores the fragility of the new civic identity and its ability to stop reciprocal violence. Aeneas' final act, the killing of Turnus, cast as an act of memory and grief for the loss of Pallas (*saeui monimenta doloris* [reminders of savage grief], 12.945) may thus be seen as yet another confirmation of the problematization of public death ritual in the *Aeneid*.

PART II

# EMPIRE

# 6 Heroic Identity: Vergil's Ajax

IN THE PREVIOUS CHAPTERS, WE HAVE SEEN THAT THE NEXUS OF ritual and allusive intertexts is part of a larger tragic intertext operative in the *Aeneid*, bringing into sharp relief problems surrounding communal unity, national identity, social hierarchy, and gender protocols. In the following pages, I focus on the epic hero and propose that the delineation of his identity relies heavily on Greek tragedy's construction of heroic identity. I argue further that this "tragic" notion of heroism in the *Aeneid* is intimately connected with the problems facing ideas regarding Roman leadership in Vergil's time. The poet's skillful mobilization of the allusive intertext of Sophocles' *Ajax*, one of Greek tragedy's most notable explorations of the contours of heroic identity, reveals that the heroic self is constantly questioned and redefined in the *Aeneid*. As with the problem of ritual, so in the case of the hero the mobilization of the tragic intertext is bound up with the tragedy's political and ideological goals. Similarly, a detailed examination of the deployment of the tragic intertext from this perspective illuminates the role of the *Aeneid* as a national epic of Rome and its empire, as well as its much-contested relationship to Augustan ideology.

Though overemphasized as a feature of Greek tragedy,[1] the concept of the tragic hero may still serve as a good measure of the poem's tragic intertext, since it may readily be juxtaposed with that of the epic hero. In a highly influential essay, Jean-Pierre Vernant posits that tragedy is a particular stage in the development of the categories of action and agent (Vernant 1988b: 71). In contrast to epic and lyric, tragedy, as *mimesis*

---

[1] On the dangers arising from such an emphasis, see Jones 1962: 13.

*praxeos*, presents individuals engaged in action (ibid.: 44). The tragic decision is thus defined by the simultaneous presence of a "self" (*ethos*) and the
operation of something greater, that is, divine force (*daimon*), so that the
same character appears as both agent, the cause of his actions, and as acted
upon, "engulfed in a source that is beyond him and sweeps him away"
(77). For Vernant, tragedy dramatizes the tensions arising when human
and divine constitute categories distinct enough to be set in opposition
while still remaining conceptually inseparable. As a result, the subject is
an agent whose autonomy is inconsistent and limited because it is vaguely
defined (82). The collusion of human and divine responsibility and their
simultaneous opposition may also be argued for a number of Vergilian
heroes, especially Dido and Turnus, who grapple with similar issues and
choose to resolve them in what can be called a "tragic" manner.

Furthermore, issues of self-definition and identity, right action, and
moral judgment are all crucial in the cases of Dido and Turnus, who
both find themselves in conflict with and unable to adapt to the social
and political systems that Aeneas' new order will launch. Vergil explores
these issues of identity by mobilizing a tragic subtext that colludes with
and is reinforced by the Homeric allusive intertext. In particular, the
personae of Dido and Turnus are constructed through systematic allusion to the figure of Ajax, the preeminent Homeric hero and protagonist
in Sophocles' tragedy. This dual literary pedigree of the Greek hero provided Vergil with ample means to activate and sustain a tragic subtext
within the epic without compromising – at least explicitly – its generic
integrity. I will trace in detail Ajax's allusive presence in the *Aeneid* as
well as the Homeric and tragic intertexts at work in Vergil's epic. It is
necessary first, however, to define more precisely the host of meanings
that the figure of Ajax encompasses in Homer and in Sophocles, an analysis that will be central to my discussion of Dido and Turnus.


## I. HOMERIC AND SOPHOCLEAN AJAX

By comparison to the volume of scholarship devoted to other heroes of the
Homeric poems, Ajax has received little treatment. This is perhaps due
to the fact that Homer himself treats the second-best of the Achaeans[2]

---

[2] Cf. *Il.* 2.768. See also Nagy 1999: 27.

in a rather peculiar way; although the hero figures prominently in a few important instances of the narrative (especially the embassy to Achilles and the fight over the body of Patroclus), in contrast to other Homeric heroes he is given no *aristeia* (Whitman 1958: 169).

Ajax is the protagonist in two famous stories in the post-Iliadic tradition: he defended the corpse of Achilles, and he went mad after the loss of the contest for the arms of Achilles to Odysseus. The poet of the *Iliad* relates neither of these; yet scholars have suggested that they provide a framework within which the Homeric Ajax may be viewed: his role in the defense of Patroclus' body in Book 17 may have been adapted from his famous retreat while bearing the dead Achilles (Edwards 1991: 132), and in Book 23 the wrestling match with Odysseus prefigures the "judgment of the arms."[3]

In the *Iliad*, Ajax has been recognized by scholars as the figure most consistently associated with the idea of *aidos*, that is, responsibility to others and a sense of their importance to oneself. As an ideal prescribing the perfect alignment of personal and communal interests, the concept of *aidos* is crucial for a full appreciation of the problems surrounding the pursuit of personal interest and individual honor in the epic. Ajax's sense of individual honor finds expression in promoting the common enterprise at Troy. Achilles, by contrast, consumed by self-interest, negates the common goal and causes death and destruction for his community (Bradshaw 1991: 111–12).

Ajax's extraordinary physical strength and his unfailing commitment to the communal cause are symbolically expressed in the description of his enormous sevenfold shield, which receives extensive treatment in *Iliad* 7:

> Αἴας δ᾽ ἐγγύθεν ἦλθε φέρων σάκος ἠΰτε πύργον,
> χάλκεον ἑπταβόειον, ὅ οἱ Τυχίος κάμε τεύχων,
> σκυτοτόμων ὄχ᾽ ἄριστος, Ὕλῃ ἔνι οἰκία ναίων,
> ὅς οἱ ἐποίησεν σάκος αἰόλον ἑπταβόειον
> ταύρων ζατρεφέων, ἐπὶ δ᾽ ὄγδοον ἤλασε χαλκόν.          (219–23)[4]

---

[3] Whitman 1958: 169; Richardson (1993: 245–46) states that the match between the two is inconclusive due to Achilles' intervention. Odysseus refers to this episode in *Od.* 11.543–64. Richardson argues that if it is indeed true that the match is related to the contest of the arms, Achilles' decision maintains a balance between the two opponents broken by the later contest.

[4] *Il.* 7.219 is repeated at 11.485 and 17.128.

> Now Aias came nearby, carrying like a tower his shield
> of bronze and sevenfold ox-hide, which Tychios wrought for him with
>     much toil,
> Tychios, who had his home in Hyle, far the best of all leather-workers,
> who had made him the glistening shield of sevenfold ox-hide
> from strong bulls, and upon it hammered an eighth layer of bronze.

The attributes of the shield are readily transferred to Ajax himself in Odysseus' greeting to him in their encounter in the Underworld (*Od.* 11.556: τοῖος γάρ σφιν πύργος ἀπώλεο [such a great tower of strength you were lost to us]).[5] The name of Ajax's son, Eurysaces, offers further evidence for the shield's exceptional qualities and for its particular connection with the hero. In the aristocratic value system of the Homeric epics, where nobility and valor are transmissible by heredity, the naming of Eurysaces after his father's shield renders this piece of defensive weaponry a constitutive force in the construction of Ajax's identity as well as of the identity of his son.[6]

Scholars have located the central issues of the tragedy in the conflict between Ajax's fixed behavioral code and the ever-fluctuating reality of societal structures.[7] Ajax is a hero of raw physical strength faced with the fragility of his intellectual powers and, though fully cognizant of the demands of the new reality before him, ultimately incapable of embracing the moral relativism it requires. Sophocles manipulates the traditional story of the conflict in terms of the hero's blindness and self-deception, by adding and dramatically intensifying Ajax's return to sanity and full consciousness of his choice of suicide (Rose 1995: 64). Ajax's plight is cast as an insoluble problem that can be resolved only through his self-removal from a society in which he no longer has a place. His raw, heroic nature is balanced by an intellectual recognition of the forces dictating a readjustment of his behavioral code. He finds suicide the only means by which he can maintain dignity without yielding to these forces (Knox 1961: 19–20; Sicherl 1977: 88–91).

---

[5] In the *Iliad* Helen refers to him in similar terms at 3.229; cf. also *Il.* 6.5 and 7.211.

[6] The importance of hereditary valor is reflected in Sophocles' play both in the scene where Ajax hands over the shield to Eurysaces and in Ajax's words that his son, if he is indeed his, will not be scared by the appearance of blood. See also Goldhill 1986: 187.

[7] See, for instance, Knox 1961; Sicherl 1977; and Bradshaw 1991.

The tragic essence of Sophocles' Ajax cannot be fully appreciated without constant reference to Homer. The hero's tragedy lies in his violation of *aidos*, the very virtue he champions in the *Iliad*, that is, the strong sense of honor that a deep commitment to the community affords. His slaying of the cattle (which in his madness he mistakes for the Achaean leaders) and his subsequent suicide mark a disgraceful betrayal of the loyalties he so fervently safeguarded in the *Iliad*. Ajax's tragic isolation, therefore, is rendered more poignant in view of his Homeric portrayal as the hero most conscious of the communal goals and of the value of camaraderie. Sophocles expresses Ajax's qualities in Iliadic language, and thus constructs a hero larger than life.[8] The play's emphasis on his self-sufficiency stands in sharp contrast with the Homeric image of the man who was the bulwark of his people, who was defined by and in turn contributed to the protection and preservation of his social milieu. Concurrently, the death of the hero, though resulting from his isolation, nevertheless has a profound effect on his dependents. Since Tecmessa's and the Salaminians' survival wholly rests on his (896–902), Ajax's life ends with a further disregard for the immediate familial and civic ties that have hitherto defined his existence.

Ajax, however, cannot be merely reduced to an embodiment of the old heroic ideal that is to be admired but not emulated (Bradshaw 1991). The complexity of his ethical quandary affords no such easy solution. On the contrary, Ajax's moral superiority despite his extremism is powerfully revealed in the second half of the play, in which the gulf separating the hero from his enemies becomes all too apparent.[9] The play offers no comparable moral force to counterbalance Ajax's loss within the value

[8] See Knox 1961: 21, although I do not share Knox's view that the Homeric ideal, at least the one that Ajax represents, is that of the individual hero who is unable to conform to the rules of society (22). On the contrary, Achilles' anger is chastised throughout the poem – and indeed by Ajax himself in his speech in Book 9 – as a paradigm of the destructive consequences of such individualistic behavior, and, as we have seen, Ajax's conduct in battle and elsewhere serves as a positive contrast to that of Achilles. Bradshaw (1991: 118–19) is more to the point when he argues that in Sophocles' tragedy, Ajax assumes an Achillean temperament.

[9] For a good discussion of Ajax's enemies, see Goldhill 1986: 157–60, where he convincingly argues that even Odysseus, who appears as the model statesman in the play, is still far from heroic when compared to Ajax.

system of the new reality (which reflects the realities of fifth-century Athens), and the problem of moral and social evaluation that it poses therefore becomes unsettling because it is ultimately unresolved.[10]

The constant negotiation between Homeric tradition and contemporary reality thus constitutes the backdrop against which the ethical problems posed in the drama are played out. As Goldhill (1986: 161) puts it:

> The problem of the evaluation of humans and humans' conduct in a social setting is developed through the complex network of strands and strains of Homeric and contemporary values, associations, distortions. It is this interpenetration of ideas, this dialectic, whereby the values and characterization of the heroic past and contemporary world clash with, undermine, illuminate each other that makes the moral and social evaluations of Sophoclean drama so complex. The concern with right action and moral judgement in Sophocles' drama is developed through the interrelations of the tragic and Homeric texts. The 'unsettling, questioning process' of this 'intertextuality,' then, informs Sophoclean tragedy. Sophocles may be read for and/or against but never without Homer.

This intertextual relationship between the Homeric tradition and Sophocles' drama in turn constitutes the backdrop against which Vergil orchestrates the interpenetration of epic and tragic allusive intertexts in the construction of the figures of Dido and Turnus, to which I now turn.

## II. DIDO

Critics since the time of Servius have recognized that Dido's meeting with Aeneas in *Aeneid* 6 is patterned after Odysseus' brief meeting with Ajax

---

[10] Bradshaw (1991) argues a similar point, reading the figure of Ajax as an allegory for the city of Athens and as a paradigm for the values and problems that fifth-century Athens faced with regard to her allies. The question of resolution and restoration in the play is, of course, a wholly different matter. Leaving aside the problem of ritual corruption and resolution (on which see Sicherl 1977 and, more recently, Krummen 1998), which is beyond the scope of this Chapter, I simply refer here to the inadequacy of Odysseus as a heroic model to replace Ajax's loss in the play and by extension serve as a wholly satisfactory model for fifth-century Athenian society.

in *Odyssey* 11.543–67: both Dido and Ajax encounter in the Underworld the men responsible for their demise, and both treat them with the same dignified silence.[11] Critics have also long acknowledged that Dido's suicide shares many affinities with that of Sophocles' Ajax.[12] Yet the allusive presence of the Sophoclean Ajax at this important moment in the epic has been treated as an isolated, local[13] – and therefore limited – occurrence, while for many critics the allusion to the Homeric Ajax in Book 6 merely constitutes another instance of borrowing in the larger scheme of Homeric imitation in the *Aeneid*. In what follows, I will explore other intertextual debts to the Homeric and the Sophoclean Ajax in the Dido episode, aiming at challenging the view that the intertextual presence of the figure of Ajax is an isolated instance and locating it within the larger framework of intertextuality in the poem.[14] I argue that Vergil's allusive annotation of Ajax, both as a tragic persona and as a Homeric hero, has important repercussions, since it reveals that the tragic intertext in the *Aeneid* can operate in dialogue with the Homeric allusive intertext.

The unmistakable link between Dido and Ajax is their suicides (König 1970: 215–16; Lefèvre 1978: 9–24; Tatum 1984: 446). Both die by the sword, and both attribute their impasse to the person who supplied them with the weapon (4.646–47 and *Aj.* 665).[15] Dido makes sure that her sister will be the first to find her body (634–40), just as Ajax prays to Zeus that his brother Teucer will be the first to find his (826–28). While Ajax traces the beginning of his downfall to the time when enmity first turned to friendship, Dido considers her encounter

---

[11] Servius on *Aen.* 6.468: *tractum autem est hoc de Homero, qui inducit Aiacis umbram Vlixis conloquia fugientem, quod ei fuerat causa mortis* [this, however, is taken from Homer, who shows the shade of Ajax avoiding the words of Ulysses because he was the cause of his death]. Both episodes have the same length (twenty-seven lines), a fact attesting to Vergil's careful allusive annotation. See also Norden 1926: 253 and Knauer 1964: 108–12.

[12] Wigodsky (1972: 95–97) identifies a number of useful parallels; Lefèvre 1978 has the most thorough collection of the evidence.

[13] For the term, see Hinds 1998: 129–35.

[14] Some of this has been attempted by Lyne (1987) and Tatum (1984). Feldherr (1999) also explores generic tensions between epic and elegy in the episode of the Underworld.

[15] See Tatum 1984: 446. On Ajax's sword, see Kane 1996; on Dido's, Basto 1984.

with Aeneas, a friendship turned into enmity, to be the catalyst that brought about the violation of her behavioral code. Moreover, specific verbal contact allusively links Dido's and Ajax's dying moments:

> dixerat, atque illam media inter talia ferro
> *conlapsam* aspiciunt comites, *ensem*que *cruore*
> spumantem *sparsas*que manus. it clamor ad alta
> atria: concussam bacchatur *Fama* per urbem.                    (4.663–66)

> She had spoken, and amid these words, her attendants saw her
> *falling* upon the blade, the *sword* foaming with blood
> and her hands *spattered*. A scream rises to the roofs of
> the palace; then *Rumor* runs frenzied through the shaken city.

> πέμψον τιν' ἡμῖν ἄγγελον, κακὴν φάτιν
> Τεύκρῳ φέροντα, πρῶτος ὥς με βαστάσῃ
> πεπτῶτα τῷδε περὶ νεορράντῳ ξίφει,...                          (826–28)

> Send a messenger to bring my sad *news* to Teucer,
> so that he may be the first to lift me
> when I have *fallen* upon this *sword freshly spattered*,...

Vergil observes the dramatic convention prohibiting depiction of violence "onstage," as the narrative at the decisive moment shifts the focus from Dido herself to her attendants, who see her collapse under the mortal blow.[16] Yet the poet's artistry in the description of Dido's suicide powerfully evokes Ajax's death onstage, and several propositions have been offered for its significance. Lefèvre argues that the figure of Ajax links Dido with the Greek world and serves to contrast her with Aeneas as a Roman (Lefèvre 1978: 24). Tatum draws attention to Dido's adherence to the value of *fama*, which he finds to be corresponding to Ajax's strong sense of *time* (Tatum 1984: 446–51). It is important to recognize, however, that the link between Dido and Ajax is even more complex than these scholars allow: Ajax commits suicide after violating the value

---

[16] Servius on *Aen.* 4.664: *non induxit occidentem se, sed ostendit occisam. et hoc tragico fecit exemplo, apud quos non videtur quemadmodum fit caedes, sed facta narratur* [he does not show her killing herself, but presents her dead. And this he did after the tragic example, where it is not seen how the slaying occurs but is reported after it has happened].

he championed when alive, that of *aidos*; Dido takes her life after having violated a value very similar to Ajax's *aidos*, that is, *pudor*. Both fall
prey to madness, and both experience isolation from their communities.
The extremism accompanying the final stages of their lives and the kinship between their personal value systems are painstakingly portrayed in
the Vergilian narrative. Most important, both find themselves unable to
negotiate an alternative heroic identity when faced with the demands of
a new sociopolitical reality.

Dido's heroic stature is established as comparable to that of Aeneas
early in the poem; this status is closely related to her role as a public and
political figure. Critics have noted that the queen serves as Aeneas' double in many respects (see, for instance, Rudd 1990: 160). Venus' account
of Dido's story to her son in Book 1 presents the Carthaginian queen as a
woman of virtue, ability, foresight, and courage, and thus claims Aeneas'
and the reader's sympathy and admiration. Dido took brave and decisive
action when she removed herself and her people from the authority of her
ruthless brother and successfully established a new and prospering city.[17]
The queen's first appearance in the poem (1.503–508) exhibits her ener-
getic, caring, and just leadership, while the compassion with which she
receives the shipwrecked Aeneas attests to her sense of *humanitas* (Monti
1981: 20). With her image as a gifted leader thus established, the narrative of Book 4, in true tragic fashion, shifts the focus to the workings
of Dido's mind. The opening of the book shows the queen oscillating
between her attraction to the newcomer and the importance of *pudor* in
her personal system of values (4.24–29). Dido fervently asserts her loyalty
to her dead husband, Sychaeus, linking the concept of *pudor* with the
Roman ideal of *uniuira*, an ideal grounded within the larger value system
of the entire community.[18] Anna, however, by emphasizing the political

---

[17] On the political aspect of the enterprise, see Monti 1981: 22.

[18] Rudd (1990: 154–59) and Monti (1981: 53–59) propound the view that Dido's
failure to uphold the ideal of *uniuira* was not a crime by Roman standards.
Monti recognizes, however, that it came close to being a moral obligation. But
even if one concedes that Dido did not violate a moral standard that was upheld
in real life (like her literary models, Catullus' Ariadne, Euripides' Medea, and
Ajax), her perception of her action as wrong suffices to justify her feeling of
isolation, which will eventually push her to suicide. I am also in disagree-
ment with Pavlock (1990: 78), who comments that the poet implies that Dido's

gains that a union with Aeneas would secure, appeals to the queen's strong commitment to the welfare of her city, and therefore effectively alleviates her sister's concerns. Dido's sense of personal honor arises from a steadfast adherence to communal values.

Since Dido's identity is constructed around the ideal of *pudor*, the question of right action and moral judgment that she faces may not be considered apart from her role as a champion of her city's welfare and prosperity.[19] Scholars in search of Dido's "tragic" flaw or *hamartia* usually place emphasis on the violation of her oath to remain loyal to Sychaeus[20] or present the queen as a woman in conflict over her private love for Aeneas and her duty to Carthage (Wiltshire 1989: 90–93, 108–109). While to a certain degree Dido's passion necessitates a choice between clashing polarities (husband vs. lover, private vs. public), when she finally succumbs to that passion she does so in the belief that she is putting her personal desire at the service of her city and people. Her "marriage" to Aeneas is not simply a lovers' union; it also guarantees the permanency of Aeneas' political alliance.[21] Dido's actions are determined through constant reference to her community, and in this regard she is different from the female heroines to whom she is allusively connected: while for Euripides' Medea and Catullus' Ariadne the abdication of familial and communal ties does not significantly affect the survival of their communities, in the case of Dido it is precisely her inadvertent rupturing of the bonds with her people that results in the annihilation of her city. *Pudor* has always been the guiding principle in her actions, public and private: when she later confronts Aeneas about his imminent departure, she refers to *pudor* and *fama* as constitutive elements in Carthage's foreign relations (4.320–23, see Monti 1981: 40), and in her subsequent monologue (534–52) she displays yet again the high value she places on her reputation as an honorable and devoted leader, who, until

persistence in remaining faithful to Sychaeus is ultimately unnatural. Even if this is true, it does not preclude the possibility that Dido herself did not see it in the same way, and I believe it is disproved when the queen is shown with Sychaeus in Book 6.

[19] Monti (1981) has amply demonstrated this much-neglected aspect of Dido's identity.

[20] Williams 1962: 45; 1968: 384–85; Moles 1984, 1987; Harrison 1989: 11–13.

[21] Dido may indeed neglect the construction of the city (4.86–89), but Aeneas has taken over (4.259–61).

Aeneas' arrival, refused to jeopardize her city's independence with a political union that would ensure safety from foreign peril.

Dido's high valuation of *pudor* and extraordinary attachment to her community are qualities she shares with Ajax, the champion of *aidos*. Vergil thus invests Dido with the attributes of a male hero – the male hero par excellence – while he simultaneously casts her as unmistakably female by mobilizing the allusive framework of erotic poetry.[22] The poet's manipulation of these allusive intertexts brings these two facets of Dido's identity to the foreground in order to intensify the loss she incurs with Aeneas' departure. The queen's "female" side is evident in her first confrontation with Aeneas (4.305–30; 365–87): allusion casts the queen as Ariadne pleading with Theseus (Catullus 64.132–201) and as Medea upbraiding Jason in Euripides (*Med.* 465–519) and Apollonius (*Argon.* 4.355–90). At the same time, Dido's reasoning is steeped in the political vocabulary of reciprocity and exchange, when she in effect charges Aeneas with a breach of *fides* (Monti 1981: 39). Aeneas abandons Carthage after exacerbating the hostility between Dido and her political adversaries. Dido, like Ajax, perceives her loss as irreparable, as she finds herself in a world where loyalties unexpectedly shift when friends turn to enemies. As a female heroine, she cannot conceive of life without the object of her desire. As a "male" leader, she is surrounded by angry and predatory neighbors. Dido's "female" and "male" identities are further complicated through allusion to Sophocles' *Ajax*. Surprisingly, the verbal contact is not between Dido and Ajax but between Dido and Tecmessa:

> *si* bene quid de te merui, fuit aut tibi *quicquam*
> *dulce* meum, miserere domus labentis . . .                                 (4.317–18)

> if I deserved any favor from you at all, or *if anything* about me
> gave you *pleasure*, pity my sinking household . . .

> ἀλλ' ἴσχε κἀμοῦ μνῆστιν· ἀνδρὶ τοι χρεὼν
> μνήμην προσεῖναι, τερπνὸν εἴ τί που πάθοι.                                 (520–21)

> Think of me also; a man should remember,
> *if* he received *any pleasure*.

---

[22] On Dido and allusion to love poetry, see Tatum 1984: 440–44; Griffith 1995; and Feldherr 1999. On Dido's "male" and "female" attributes, see West 1980.

The similarity of the two women's situation provides a prima facie justification for the presence of the allusion. Tecmessa contemplates the
dangers awaiting her in the event of Ajax's death. She appeals to her
past devotion and loyalty to him as his wife and reminds him of his
responsibility toward his *philoi* in an effort to persuade him not to commit suicide.[23] Tecmessa's entreaties (485–524) insist on the marital bond
between Ajax and herself and display her entire dependence on him:
without Ajax's protection she faces slavery and possibly death. By stressing the reciprocity central to the relations between husband and wife,
Tecmessa constructs herself as a legitimate wife, although her actual
status as spear-bride is probably less clear than her rhetoric here implies
(Ormand 1999: 110–19). Dido too appeals to a commitment she views
as binding.[24] Allusion to this particular segment of the play therefore
serves to underscore the ambiguity of Dido's position as Aeneas' wife
and illuminates the queen's self-portrayal as a spear-bride facing cap-
tivity (325–26 and 330). At the same time, Dido, like Ajax, grapples
with a real ethical and political dilemma. She has to learn to live with
Aeneas as an enemy and to negotiate the political and personal significance of the injury to her *pudor*.[25] Aeneas' departure threatens Dido in
both her "male" and "female" capacities. Her eventual refusal to entertain any moral relativism in finding a solution to her predicament, however, decidedly aligns her with Ajax.

State of mind is a crucial issue in both Sophocles and Vergil. Dido's
and Ajax's infringement upon the moral principles they have always

---

[23] The scene in the Greek play is modeled after *Il.* 6.390–502. Kirkwood (1965:
56–59) has demonstrated the affinity of the two texts and has drawn attention
to their contrasts, which he deems more significant than their similarities for
the interpretation of the tragedy.

[24] On the "marriage" of Dido and Aeneas, see Williams 1968: 378–83 and Rudd
1990: 153–54.

[25] The allusion to this passage, however, also points to Ajax's peremptory dis-
missal of Tecmessa's pleas and invites comparison to Aeneas' behavior toward
Dido. To be sure, Aeneas does not display Ajax's self-absorption. But we are
dealing with the same conflict between love and duty, where duty must prevail.
It is also interesting how the critics writing on *Ajax* and on the *Aeneid* are at
pains to justify the cruelty displayed by the heroes toward the women. See Poe
1987: 43–45 and Austin 1955: 105–106.

striven to uphold is portrayed as madness caused by divine intervention. Madness alone can account for the disavowal of loyalties: Ajax, the bulwark of the Achaeans, turns against his superiors; Dido forfeits her promise to her dead husband and endangers her city. Divine cruelty is a theme paramount in both texts. Athena's callousness in the Greek play is matched by the business like cruelty of Venus and Juno in the *Aeneid*.[26] Madness is caused by forces external working side by side with forces residing within. Dido and Ajax, formerly wholly invested in the world outside, are now faced with an inner disturbance. As they turn into creatures of the night, their internal anguish stands in sharp contrast to the world around them: Ajax's *mania*, which causes him to slay the cattle, occurs at night time (Padel 1995: 66–70); similarly, Dido's *furor* intensifies during the night (80–83), especially in the poignant moment when the queen's turmoil is pitted against night's quiet rest (522–32). Dido's and Ajax's suicides are not attributable to a bout of madness, however; on the contrary, their mental agony leads them to a new consciousness and enables them to gain clearer vision. Dido and Ajax gauge their options and decide on a solution with remarkable intellectual clarity.

Madness may be temporary, but the isolation it generates is permanent. Dido immediately apprehends her political isolation (320–21, 325–26); loneliness torments her in nightmares (466–68); her nocturnal anxiety revolves around the fear of alienation:

> 'en, *quid ago*? rursusne procos *inrisa* priores
> experiar, Nomadumque petam conubia supplex,
> quos ego sim totiens iam dedignata maritos?
>
> . . .
>
> quis me autem, fac uelle, sinet ratibusue superbis
> *inuisam* accipiet? . . .
>
> . . .
>
> quid tum? sola fuga nautas comitabor ouantis?
> an Tyriis omnique manu stipata meorum

---

[26] *Aen.* 4.90–128. The scene is very different in tone from the humorous divine exchanges in Apollonius, *Argon.* 3.1–166, where divine frivolity contrasts with human suffering. On this scene, see also Chapter 3, pp. 93–95.

inferar et, quos Sidonia uix urbe reuelli,
rursus agam *pelago* et uentis dare uela iubebo? ...'                    (4.534–46)[27]

"*See, what shall I do?* Shall I try again my former suitors,
only to be *laughed at*? Beg the Numidians for marriage,
whom so often I have scorned as husbands?

...

Who, suppose that I wished it, will suffer me or take me,
*hated so*, aboard their proud ships? ...

...

What then? Shall I by myself accompany those exulting sailors in flight?
Or go against them along with the entire band of my Tyrians,
and drive again out *to sea* and bid set sail to the winds those
whom I barely tore away from the city of Sidon?

Ajax voices similar concerns as soon as he regains his senses:

κεῖνοι [sc. the Atreidae] δ' ἐπεγγελῶσιν ἐκπεφευγότες,

...

καὶ νῦν τί χρὴ δρᾶν; ὅστις ἐμφανῶς θεοῖς
ἐχθαίρομαι, μισεῖ δέ μ' Ἑλλήνων στρατός,
ἔχθει δὲ Τροία πᾶσα καὶ πεδία τάδε.
πότερα πρὸς οἴκους, ναυλόχους λιπὼν ἕδρας
μόνους τ' Ἀτρείδας, πέλαγος Αἰγαῖον περῶ;                          (454–61)

they [sc. the Atridae], having escaped, are *laughing at* me;

...

and now *what* must *I do?* I who obviously am *hated*
by the gods, *hated* by the army of the Greeks,
and hated by all of Troy and by these plains?

---

[27] The Vergilian passage also alludes to Medea's speech (Euripides, *Med.* 502–15).
The main difference between Dido and Medea, however, is that in Medea's case
her isolation is more the result of both her "difference" from the other Greek
women (she is a foreigner and a witch) and the crimes she has committed against
her family. Moreover, her wounded pride generates further aggression against
her enemies, whereas Ajax's and Dido's reasoning ends in self-destruction that is
perceived as adherence to a superior moral code. Of course, the allusive material
of this passage (*Aen.* 4.522–52) also points to *Argon.* 3.744–801 and Catullus
64.176–83, on which see Pavlock 1990: 81–82.

Shall I cross the Aegean Sea and go home, leaving behind
the station of the ships and the sons of Atreus to themselves?

In both passages the realization of the state of isolation is paired with
a newly found awareness.[28] Dido ponders a series of different courses of
action: to renew relations with her African suitors is unfeasible in view of
her former treatment of them and their present hostility; to sail with the
Trojans to Italy is dismissed on the basis of their ungratefulness for her
generosity and compassion toward them (537–39). Unable to uproot her
people a second time, she comes to the conclusion that she has severed
ties with both her people and her enemies. Ajax in his self-questioning
also weighs possible options, which he similarly dismisses: to return
home dishonored (460–65) or to attack the Trojans and die in battle
(466–70). In both cases the characters' attempts to formulate the alternatives to heroic suicide convince them of their impossibility:[29]

> ἀλλ' ἢ καλῶς ζῆν ἢ καλῶς τεθνηκέναι
> τὸν εὐγενῆ χρή.                                              (479–80)

the noble man must live honorably
or die honorably.

quin morere ut merita es, ferroque auerte dolorem.          (4.547)

no, die as you deserve, end your pain with the sword.

The problem of Dido's and Ajax's state of mind is closely connected
with the planning and execution of their suicides. Scholarship on *Ajax*
has focused on the hero's famous *Trugrede* (646–92) and in particular
on the question of whether or not Ajax changes his mind and decides
against killing himself.[30] Likewise, critics have debated whether or not

---

[28] Tatum (1984: 447) comments that both Dido and Ajax now express themselves
through monologue.

[29] Knox 1961: 17 on *Ajax*, but the same can be argued for Dido as well. See also
Heinze (1915: 136n.1 [= 1993: 115]), who points to Sophocles' *Aj.* 460. On the
alternative courses of action that Ajax rejects, see Winnington-Ingram 1980:
28 and Poe 1987: 42. On Dido's, see Pöschl 1962: 85–87; Monti 1981: 56–57;
and Pavlock 1990: 81–82.

[30] See Knox 1961; Sicherl 1977; Winnington-Ingram 1980: 46–56; and Poe 1987:
50–71.

Dido had resolved on death at the moment when she first voices the possibility (308, 323)[31] and, if indeed she has, why she delays in implement-
ing it. In both instances, Ajax's *Trugrede* and Dido's speeches (416–36,
478–98, 534–52) are filled with ambivalence and double entendres,[32] and
in both cases the characters reveal an obsession with death.

The Greek hero's words mark a recognition of the ever-fluctuating
nature of reality, and the moral relativism this entails, which, of course,
cannot be reconciled with his concept of personal honor (Knox 1961: 16;
Sicherl 1977: 81–91; Winnington-Ingram 1980: 52). He begins with a
general statement on the action of time (646–49), followed by the realization that he himself takes part in this temporal order (650–52). It
seems that it is a new Ajax speaking when he reveals that he is softened
by Tecmessa's words. But his choice of diction also indicates that there is
deep irony behind these statements (Knox 1961: 15). Ambiguity is also
present when he proceeds to describe how he will perform ritual cleansing, which could refer either to a willingness to return to normalcy or
to the ritual washing of his dead body (654–59).[33] The hero then goes
on to express in tangible terms what his hard-won knowledge of the
law of time and change entails, that is, a reconciliation with the Atridae
(666–67): "give in to the gods and show reverence to the sons of Atreus."
Again, irony lies behind his word choice: one should show reverence not
to humans but to gods.[34] By the time he addresses Tecmessa, therefore,
Ajax's decision has been made. His words to her constitute the final
arrangements before his death.

---

[31] Austin (1955: 99) argues that Dido decides on suicide only when she has lost all
hope, *contra* Pöschl 1962: 85. That Dido, in employing a *Trugrede*, clearly intends
to deceive Anna (478–98) further confirms the parallel between Dido and the
tragic Ajax.

[32] See Pöschl 1962: 83–85, where he directly links these features to Greek tragedy but does not identify the kinship with Sophocles' *Ajax*. On the ambiguity
in Ajax's *Trugrede*, see Knox 1961: 11–13; Sicherl 1977; and Padel 1995: 71.

[33] Knox 1961: 11 and Sicherl 1977: 78. Along the same lines one may read that his
plan to "hide" his sword can mean either that he will simply get rid of it or that he
will bury it in his body (Sicherl 1977: 79–80), though I find this reading strained.

[34] Noted by the ancient scholiast. See also Knox 1961: 34 n.85 and Winnington-
Ingram 1980: 49.

Dido declares that she is intent on death at the moment she first confronts Aeneas, but does not actually commit suicide until after Aeneas' departure from Carthage. In the meantime (and here she differs from Ajax) she oscillates between alternatives: love and hate, life and death,[35] social decorum and personal desire. Guilt over the violation of her oath to Sychaeus, disillusionment over a love lost, consciousness of her alienation from her people, the daunting prospect of humiliation and mockery by her enemies are all present in her thoughts. But she too, like Ajax, finally comes to an important recognition: the rift between her past and present states brings into question her ability and willingness to continue her existence. The presence of Aeneas has caused an irrevocable disruption of life as she knew it, and her inability to reclaim a meaningful existence in the new terms that his departure imposes pushes her to opt for death. The sinister omens she receives (453–65) and the magic ritual to which she resorts defy every hope that normal life will be resumed (474–521).[36]

The curses Dido and Ajax cast against their enemies only serve to confirm their failure to come to reconciliation with their social milieu. When Dido sees Aeneas sneaking off before dawn, her reaction is violent. Oscillating between madness and sanity, she contemplates once again different courses of action (590–629). She ends her monologue by calling upon the Sun, the Furies, and Hecate to avenge her death. Similarly, in Sophocles' play, Ajax ends his life with a terrible curse on the Atridae. Vergil allusively manipulates Dido's curse so that its first part alludes to the one uttered by the dying Ajax, while its conclusion is intertextually linked to a curse pronounced by Teucer later in the play. The allusive kinship between these three passages is remarkable.[37]

Dido's curse:

> *Sol*, qui *terrarum* flammis opera omnia *lustras*,
> tuque harum interpres curarum et conscia Iuno,
> nocturnisque Hecate triuiis *ululata per urbes*

---

[35] Pöschl 1962: 86–87. See also Pavlock 1990: 82 on the ambivalence that dominates Dido's speeches.

[36] Pavlock (1990: 83) suggests that Vergil, by connecting Dido with the forces of magic, exposes her ambivalent relation to civilized values.

[37] Heinze 1915: 136 n.2 (= 1993: 115–16) identifies the allusion to *Aj*. 835 and Catullus 64.193.

et *Dirae ultrices* et di morientis Elissae,
accipite haec, meritumque malis aduertite numen
et nostras audite preces...

...

...nec, cum se sub leges pacisque iniquae
tradiderit, regno aut optata luce fruatur,
sed *cadat* ante diem mediaque *inhumatus* harena
haec precor, hanc uocem extremam cum sanguine fundo.
tum uos, o Tyrii, *stirpem* et *genus* omne futurum
exercete odiis, cinerique haec mittite nostro
munera. nullus amor populis nec foedera sunto.                    (4.607–24)

O *Sun*, with your rays *survey* all the deeds of the *earth*,
and you, Juno, the mediator and witness of these cares,
and Hecate, whose name is *wailed* by night *at the city* crossroads,
and *avenging Furies*, and gods of *dying* Elissa,
hear me, turn your divine anger to the wicked deeds
that deserve it, and hear my prayers...

...

...and when he's entered the terms of an unjust peace,
let him not enjoy his kingdom or the life he longs for,
but let him *fall* before his time and lie *unburied* on the sand.
This is my prayer, this last cry I pour out with my blood.
Then, you, my Tyrians, turn your hatred upon *his children*
and all *their race* to come, make this offering
to my ashes. Let there be no love, no treaty between our peoples.

## Ajax's curse to the Atridae:

ἴτ', ὦ ταχεῖαι ποίνιμοί τ' Ἐρινύες,
γεύεσθε, μὴ φείδεσθε πανδήμου στρατοῦ.
σὺ δ', ὦ τὸν αἰπὺν οὐρανὸν διφρηλατῶν
Ἥλιε, πατρῴαν τὴν ἐμὴν ὅταν χθόνα
ἴδῃς, ἐπισχὼν χρυσόνωτον ἡνίαν
ἄγγειλον ἄτας τὰς ἐμὰς *μόρον* τ' ἐμὸν
γέροντι πατρὶ τῇ τε δυστήνῳ τροφῷ.
ἦ που τάλαινα, τήνδ' ὅταν κλύῃ φάτιν,
ἥσει μέγαν κωκυτὸν ἐν πάσῃ *πόλει*.                               (843–51)

> Come, swift *avenging Erinyes*,
> feed on the whole army, do not spare it.
> But you, oh *Sun*, who drives your chariot through high heaven,
> when you <u>see</u> my home *land*,
> check your golden rein
> and announce my ruin and my <u>death</u>
> to my old father and my unhappy mother.
> Indeed, poor woman, when she hears this news
> she will utter *wailing through* all *the city*.

After Ajax's death, his brother Teucer, embroiled in a quarrel with the Atridae, pronounces a curse against whoever would attempt to remove Ajax's son from his father's dead body:

> ...εἰ δέ τις στρατοῦ
> βίᾳ σ' ἀποσπάσειε τοῦδε τοῦ νεκροῦ,
> κακὸς κακῶς ἄθαπτος ἐκπέσοι χθονός,
> γένους ἅπαντος ῥίζαν ἐξημημένος,...                            (1175–78)

> ...and if any of the army
> tries to tear you by force away from this corpse,
> may that man be <u>cast</u> out of the earth *unburied*,
> wickedly as befits a wicked man, with the *root* of all his *race* cut off,...

Ajax's curse on the Atridae at once constitutes a rejection of the world of change and a reaffirmation of his own ethical code. Ajax refuses to renegotiate his heroic values in the face of the new reality before him, while his extreme individualism seems out of place in a community defined by reciprocity, compromise, and exchange. Ajax's loss, however, is keenly felt in the latter portion of the play in the petty bickering of the Atridae over the hero's dead body. Teucer's curse, a counterpart to the earlier one uttered by Ajax himself and which reaffirms the old enmities (839–40), underscores this loss.[38] Neither the new ethical code of relativism (which Odysseus recognizes and advocates) nor Teucer's fervent defense of his brother's cause is a match for the higher moral dignity of Ajax's heroic persona.

---

[38] Kamerbeek 1963: 226. Lloyd-Jones and Wilson 1990 obelize the lines, but, as is obvious from the present discussion, they are perfectly apropos in this segment of the narrative.

Dido, in her curse against Aeneas, turns to her people, confirming once again that the Trojan hero harmed not only her person but also her city. By addressing the Tyrians and proclaiming the future enmity between her people and his, the queen too, like Ajax, reaffirms the values that defined her previous existence by momentarily renewing the ties with her community. Dido identifies with her city in her call for the perpetuation of an enmity that is closely linked with her inability to renegotiate her ethical code in the face of the new reality that Aeneas' mission presents. At the same time, the intertextual connection with Teucer's curse over Ajax's dead body intensifies the certainty of the queen's death and of a future devoid of Dido's heroic values. Dido's intransigence contrasts sharply with Aeneas' ability to adapt to the demands of his new destiny.

The extremism with which Dido and Ajax view reality, their predicament, and their options forces them to turn the sword inward on themselves, thus completing their severing of the external ties of *pudor* and *aidos*. Dido's isolation as she takes her life is mitigated only by her allusive bond to Ajax, since the reader is informed of the presence of her *comites* after the fact. Similarly, Ajax's last farewell is not directed to his loved ones but to the permanent and immovable landscape of his homeland and of Troy. The play's dramaturgy accentuates the hero's isolation. In an extraordinary gesture that defies dramatic convention, the Chorus are removed from the stage and the mortal blow takes place in full view.

Ajax's solitude is lamented by the Chorus:

> ... οἷος ἄρ' αἱμάχθης,
> ἄφαρκτος φίλων·
> ἐγὼ δ' ὁ πάντα κωφός, ὁ πάντ' ἄϊδρις,
> κατημέλησα.                                            (909–12)

> ... all alone then you bled,
> unguarded from your friends;
> and I, completely deaf, completely ignorant,
> took no care.

Anna's dirge allusively assumes the role of the Chorus:

> his etiam struxi manibus patriosque uocaui
> uoce deos, sic te ut posita, crudelis, abessem?
> exstinxti te meque, soror, populumque patresque
> Sidonios urbemque tuam.                              (4.680–83)

Did I build this pyre with my own hands and with my voice call upon
our fatherland's gods, so that, as you lie thus on it, I, cruel one, may
    be away?
You have destroyed yourself and me together, sister, the people
and the nobles of Sidon and your city.

Anna's words confirm that Dido's death is a matter not solely of personal
but also of political importance; in the same fashion, the Chorus recognize the importance of the leader for the life of the army:

ὤμοι, κατέπεφνες, ἄναξ,
τόνδε συνναύταν, τάλας·...                                              (901–902)

alas my lord, you have killed me
your fellow sailor, poor man; . . .

When Aeneas meets Dido in the Underworld (6.450–76), the queen's
moral restoration (as she treats Aeneas with indifference and takes her
place next to her husband) celebrates the heroic ideals she represents and
confirms that her death marks an important loss for the epic's hero and
his mission. Scholars have long recognized that the encounter of the two
lovers, though inspired by Homer, underscores the "tragic" issues delin-
eated in Book 4. This "tragic" quality has been mainly located in the
passage's intertextual debt to Book 4 (Austin 1977: 163). Vergil, however, also manipulates the Homeric text, expanding the allusive space[39]
to include Sophocles' *Ajax*, and invites us to tease out the implications of
the allusive interplay of all three texts.[40]

More specifically, in Homer Odysseus seeks reconciliation with the
slain hero, yet he displays a certain self-absorption in that he neither
offers an apology (he instead attributes the unfortunate incident to Zeus'
hatred) nor takes the time to persuade Ajax to speak or listen.[41] Aeneas,
on the contrary, recognizes his share of responsibility for Dido's plight
(*funeris heu tibi causa fui?*, 458), is deeply shaken by her death, and follows

---

[39] For the term, see Pucci 1998: 43–44.

[40] Other allusive intertexts operative in this passage are discussed by Tatum
(1984) and Feldherr (1999).

[41] Jebb (1907: xlii) argues that the Homeric Odysseus is similar to that of
Sophocles. While it is true that in Homer Odysseus is moved by pity at the
sight of Ajax, here he seems more interested in the implications of his loss for
the Achaean army than in the hero's untimely death (*Od.* 11.556–60).

her in tears.[42] Aeneas' sympathy does not merely constitute a display of *pietas*; it also indicates a sincere hope that a final reconciliation with Dido will take place, a hope eventually frustrated by the queen's cold silence. In this light, Aeneas' attitude owes something to that of Odysseus in Sophocles' *Ajax*, who, out of sympathy for the fragility of the human condition (e.g., 121–26), ensures proper burial for the lost hero and champions his restoration. By casting Aeneas as a foil to the tragic (and not the Homeric) Odysseus, Vergil sharply contrasts Odysseus' success with Aeneas' failure in this respect.

The inclusion of the Odyssean model thus serves multiple purposes: Dido's heroic persona is completely restored when she assumes a place by her husband, a restoration that affirms the importance of the heroic ideals she embodies and emphasizes that they no longer have a place in Aeneas' new world. Furthermore, the intertextual fusion of the Homeric and the tragic Ajax in Dido's persona is paired with a conflation of the Homeric and the Sophoclean Odysseus in the persona of Aeneas. In Homer, Odysseus' unsuccessful attempt at a reconciliation with Ajax parallels Aeneas' failure to achieve reconciliation with Dido. At the same time, Aeneas' pity and *pietas* towards Dido in Book 6 evoke the tragic Odysseus, who displayed a similar attitude toward the plight of his foe, convinced the obstinate Atridae to allow his body to be buried, and almost single-handedly effected the restoration of Ajax's heroic status among the Greek army at the end of the play. The active role that the tragic Odysseus played in the hero's restoration is juxtaposed with Aeneas' absence in the process of Dido's restoration, poignantly underscored by his utter surprise at seeing her among the shades in the world below. Aeneas is completely severed from the dangers that the queen's attachment poses for his mission, but this also implies that the new state he is about to create will be deprived of the heroic ideals that she champions.

## III. TURNUS

Much like Dido, Turnus' figure also problematizes established notions of heroic identity and proper behavior in the face of ethical dilemmas

---

[42] This contrast is noted by Tatum (1984: 445).

circumscribed by ineluctable Fate and evolving social structures. In the case of Turnus, Vergil deploys allusive material from the Iliadic and the Sophoclean Ajax in order to achieve specific narrative strategies: a series of allusions to a pair of Homeric episodes establish the hero's prowess as a warrior as well as his extraordinary talent in military defense. Once annotation[43] to Ajax is launched through reference to the epic's code-model (Homer), the tragic *Ajax* enters the intertextual map, creating a new allusive space that necessitates a renegotiation of the hero's identity in view of the new (tragic) allusive material.[44] The reader is now forced to admit that another model, Sophocles' tragedy, is at work. These allusive subtexts operate in conjunction, but they also intensify and reinforce one another: the Homeric material invites the reader to revisit and reinterpret it in light of the tragic appropriations, while the tragic is mobilized by and relies on the Homeric in order to fulfill its interpretative potential. More important, the Homeric material is put to work in the service of a broader pattern of narrative allusion that is in effect tragic.[45]

Furthermore, Turnus' intertextual connection with the figure of Ajax permits a reading of his *furor* and *violentia* as facets of the poem's articulation of a new definition of heroic (and, by extension, Roman) identity and the tensions and conflicts that such a redefinition necessarily generates. The linking of Ajax and Turnus therefore establishes a Homeric archetype of military excellence for the Vergilian hero, while his association with the Greek hero most conscious of the communal goal calls into question his image as an egotist who causes death and destruction to his community in order to avenge his own wounded pride. As a result, Turnus' *furor* and *violentia* are fueled by a desire to fulfill his responsibility toward his people, a responsibility inextricably linked to his own sense of honor. The tragic Ajax displays a similarly misplaced determination that leads him to madness, disillusionment, and death. Turnus, however, like Sophocles' Ajax and, of course, Dido, engages in action

---

[43] On annotation as "footnote," see Hinds 1998: 1–5.

[44] See Conte 1986: 31 and Hinds 1998: 41–43 for a discussion of "code" model and "exemplary" model.

[45] A similar case is argued by Hinds (1998: 140) for Horatian and Ovidian allusion in Statius' *Achilleid*.

that pits him against the interests of his community and that results
in his complete isolation from it. Unable to adjust to the kind of moral
relativism that would enable a peaceful coexistence with the Trojans, he
also embodies a heroic ideal that, though laudable, can have no rightful
place in the Roman future. The tension between the celebration of this
ideal and the realization that social change has rendered it obsolete is
precisely the point of Sophocles' drama. Just as Ajax's tragedy relies on
the audience's knowledge of his Homeric past, so the Homeric qualities
of Turnus, painstakingly established earlier in the narrative, underscore
Vergil's engagement with similarly tragic issues.

The most impressive set of intertextual associations firmly linking
Turnus and Ajax is found in the first display of Turnus' warrior talent
as Book 9 draws to a close. In the absence of Aeneas, the Rutulian hero
is given a proper *aristeia* when he combats the host of the Trojans alone.
This segment of the narrative annotates its allusive debt to two Homeric
passages, each attesting to Ajax's talent in the face of overwhelming
odds. The first passage is from *Iliad* 11:

Ζεὺς δὲ πατὴρ Αἴανθ' ὑψίζυγος ἐν φόβον ὦρσε·
στῆ δὲ ταφών, ὄπιθεν δὲ σάκος βάλεν ἑπταβόειον,
τρέσσε δὲ παπτήνας ἐφ' ὁμίλου, θηρὶ ἐοικώς,
ἐντροπαλιζόμενος, ὀλίγον γόνυ γουνὸς ἀμείβων.
ὡς δ' αἴθωνα λέοντα βοῶν ἀπὸ μεσσαύλοιο
ἐσσεύαντο κύνες τε καὶ ἀνέρες ἀγροιῶται,
οἵ τέ μιν οὐκ εἰῶσι βοῶν ἐκ πῖαρ ἑλέσθαι
πάννυχοι ἐγρήσσοντες· ὁ δὲ κρειῶν ἐρατίζων
ἰθύει, ἀλλ' οὔ τι πρήσσει· θαμέες γὰρ ἄκοντες
ἀντίον ἀΐσσουσι θρασειάων ἀπὸ χειρῶν,
καιόμεναί τε δεταί, τάς τε τρεῖ ἐσσύμενός περ·
ἠῶθεν δ' ἀπονόσφιν ἔβη τετιηότι θυμῷ·
ὡς Αἴας τότ' ἀπὸ Τρώων τετιημένος ἦτορ
ἤϊε πόλλ' ἀέκων· περὶ γὰρ δίε νηυσὶν Ἀχαιῶν.                        (11.544–57)

But father Zeus sitting on high rose *fear* upon Aias.
He stood *stunned*, and cast the sevenfold ox-hide shield behind him,
and *drew back*, glancing at the crowd of men, like a wild beast,
turning about, retreating step by step only a little;
as when country men and their dogs drove

a tawny lion away from the fold of their cattle,
and will not let him take as prey the fattest of the oxen,
watching all night; yet he, hungry for meat,
charges on, but to no avail; for javelins thick and fast
dart against him from the bold hands of the men,
and the flaming torches, and at these *he recoils* though he is eager;
and at dawn he goes away *with sullen heart*;
so Aias, *sullen* at heart, drew back from the Trojans
much against his will; for he feared greatly for the ships of the Achaians.

The alluding text reads as follows:

...Turnus paulatim excedere pugna
et fluuium petere ac partem quae cingitur unda.
acrius hoc Teucri clamore incumbere magno
et glomerare manum, ceu saeuum *turba leonem*
cum *telis* premit *infensis*; at *territus* ille,
*asper, acerba tuens, retro redit* et neque terga
*ira* dare aut uirtus patitur, nec *tendere* contra
ille quidem hoc cupiens *potis est per tela uirosque*.
haud aliter retro *dubius* uestigia Turnus
*improperata* refert et *mens exaestuat ira*.                    (9.789–98)

...Little by little Turnus drew back from the fight
and made for the river and that place encircled by the water.
The Trojans pressed in on him with loud cries all the more fiercely
and massed their ranks; as when a *crowd of men* presses on
a savage *lion* with *menacing* spears; and he, *frightened*,
but still *fierce, glaring angrily, draws back*, yet his *rage*
and his courage do not let him turn his back; nor *is he able to make his way*
*through the men and their weapons*, eager though he is.
Just so Turnus *in doubt* traces back his steps
*unhurried* and *his heart is seething with rage*.

Turnus, like Ajax, is compared to a lion cornered and seemingly help-
less. The emphasis in both passages is on the hero's extraordinary ability in
defensive battle. Turnus' representation as a force of *violentia* in the poem
is sustained and reinforced by the emphasis on the beast's violence and
anger, while the Iliadic passage only stresses the feeling of terror inspired

by a divine power.[46] Vergil, however, by including a reference to the lion's *uirtus* (Schenk 1984: 208), further diverges from the Greek text, which only makes mention of the beast's physicality, hunger, and frustration. This addition imparts information on both the high quality of the hero's performance in battle and his moral compass. Moreover, the pairing of *ira* and *uirtus* as subjects of the same verb (*patitur*) suggests a deeper and more important connection between the two words. The lion's anger surfaces as a consequence of *uirtus*, a desire to continue fighting prescribed by the conventions of heroic behavior in a social setting. Vergil thus causes the boundaries between simile and narrative proper to collapse temporarily as he turns the narrative focus away from the lion and back on Turnus. The Rutulian's anger in this instance, aroused by his inability to live up to the heroic code by which he abides, emerges as natural and justified.

The conclusion of Turnus' retreat is drawn from another Homeric passage where Ajax is again the protagonist:[47]

> Αἴας δ' οὐκ ἔτ' ἔμιμνε· βιάζετο γὰρ βελέεσσι·
> δάμνα μιν Ζηνός τε νόος καὶ Τρῶες ἀγαυοὶ
> βάλλοντες· δεινὴν δὲ περὶ κροτάφοισι φαεινὴ
> πήληξ βαλλομένη καναχὴν ἔχε, βάλλετο δ' αἰεὶ
> κὰπ φάλαρ' εὐποίηθ'· ὁ δ' ἀριστερὸν ὦμον ἔκαμνεν
> ἔμπεδον αἰὲν ἔχων σάκος αἰόλον· οὐδ' ἐδύναντο
> ἀμφ' αὐτῷ πελεμίξαι ἐρείδοντες βελέεσσιν.
> αἰεὶ δ' ἀργαλέῳ ἔχετ' ἄσθματι, κὰδ δέ οἱ ἱδρὼς
> πάντοθεν ἐκ μελέων πολὺς ἔρρεεν, οὐδέ πη εἶχεν
> ἀμπνεῦσαι· πάντῃ δὲ κακὸν κακῷ ἐστήρικτο.                    (*Il.* 16.102–11)

Aias no longer held his ground; for he was pressed by the arrows.
The will of Zeus overcame him and the proud Trojans
with their weapons; and around his temples the shining helmet
was ringing terribly as it was struck; it was struck constantly
on the well-wrought cheekpieces; and he grew tired on his left shoulder,
always holding up firmly his gleaming shield; yet they could not
drive him away, though they pressed their weapons around him.
And his breath always came out painful, and much sweat

---

[46] The words in italics in each passage reflect these respective emphases.
[47] Hardie (1994: 245–46) also notes Ennius' adaptation of the Homeric passage.

was pouring down from every limb, nor could he catch
his breath at all, but from everywhere evil was piled on evil.

ergo nec clipeo iuuenis subsistere tantum
nec dextra ualet, iniectis sic undique telis
obruitur. strepit adsiduo caua tempora circum
tinnitu galea et saxis solida aera fatiscunt
discussaeque iubae capiti[48] nec sufficit umbo
ictibus; ingeminant hastis et Troes et ipse
fulmineus Mnestheus. tum toto corpore sudor
liquitur et piceum (nec respirare potestas)
flumen agit, fessos quatit aeger anhelitus artus.                    (9.806–14)

And the young man neither with his shield nor his right hand
can hold his ground; he is overwhelmed by the missiles thrown
     against him
from all sides. The helmet around his hollow temples echoes with
constant ringing and its strong bronze is cracked open by stones,
and the plumes are shaken out from its crest, nor does his shield's boss
withstand the blows: both the Trojans and Mnestheus with the force of
     lightning
step up with their spears. Then sweat runs over his whole body
and flows in a pitchy stream (he had no power to breathe)
and painful panting shakes his weary limbs.

Vergil's intertextual debt in this instance is to a crucial moment in the *Iliad*, the burning of the ships, a moment when the Greek fleet faces total destruction. The main point of comparison in both passages is Turnus' and Ajax's physical fatigue, the gradual loss of vigor that results in ultimate retreat. Turnus is welcomed by the friendly waters of the Tiber;[49] Ajax's withdrawal is followed by Hector's success in setting the Achaean ships on fire, an event that leads to the subsequent *aristeia* and

---

[48] The OCT text punctuates after *capiti*, thus taking *umbo* to mean the top of the helmet. I follow *Skutsch* (560) and Hardie (1994: 247), who take *capiti* with *iubae* and translate *umbo* as the boss of the shield.

[49] To be sure, Turnus' escape evokes the famous leap of the Roman hero Horatius Cocles: the Rutulian takes on the role of one of the most famous saviors of Rome. See Hardie 1994: 248–50.

death of Patroclus. Ajax here stands for the Greek army as a whole, his suffering exemplifying the communal suffering caused by Achilles' individualistic behavior (Janko 1992: 330). The two Homeric passages with Ajax as the main figure merge into one in the Latin, a powerful annotation of the allusive connection between Turnus and the Greek hero. As a result, the mobilization of the Homeric intertext, far from casting Turnus as a man pursuing personal gain, renders him a champion of the safety of the Latin community.[50]

This link between the Homeric Ajax and Turnus is anticipated by an allusive gesture framing both the beginning and the ending of the "Turnus narrative" of Book 9 with the figure of the Greek hero. When the reader first encounters Turnus in this book, Vergil footnotes Homer as his source for what follows by appropriating the epic motif of the invocation to the Muses.[51] Turnus, acting here as another Hector, prepares to set fire to the Trojan ships, which are saved from incineration by the aid of Cybele. At this critical moment for the Trojan fleet, Vergil interrupts the flow of the narrative to summon the Muses:

> Quis deus, o Musae, tam saeua incendia Teucris
> auertit? tantos ratibus quis depulit ignis?
> dicite: prisca fides facto, sed fama perennis.                    (9.77–79)

[50] The Homeric passage describing Ajax's retreat is also particularly relevant to the action of the Vergilian narrative, both structurally and contextually. In the *Iliad*, Hector's triumph over the worn-out Ajax at 16.113–22, which follows the passage quoted earlier, is undercut by the reader's knowledge that Patroclus is about to counterattack (Janko 1992: 292). Similarly, in the *Aeneid*, Turnus' retreat foreshadows his ultimate defeat at the poem's close (see Hardie 1994: 242–44). Moreover, this particular Iliadic incident is part of a series of duels between Hector and Ajax begun in Book 12, in which Ajax is represented as the bastion of the entire Achaean defense (Schadewaldt 1966: 69). In addition, the present confrontation between the two Iliadic heroes by Protesilaus' ship is connected with the fight in Book 11: the affinity between the two Homeric episodes rests not only on the predominance of the figure of Ajax in both instances but also on the utilization of the same narrative technique: the poet of the *Iliad* builds the expectation of a final combat that he consistently suspends for a later moment in the story (Schadewaldt 1966: 70), a technique also used by Vergil later in Book 12.

[51] Hinds (1998: 34–47) offers a very useful discussion on the uses of *topoi* as invoking the literary tradition in its entirety.

What god, O Muses, turned such a fierce blaze
from the Trojans? Who drove away such great a fire from their ships?
Tell me: belief in the event is old, but its fame is enduring.

Vergil's manipulation of a familiar Homeric motif serves as yet another reminder of the epic literary tradition to which his poetry ascribes. Of the six similar invocations found in the *Iliad*, however, Vergil mobilizes the one most appropriate to the larger allusive scheme of his narrative, the reworking of the Homeric burning of the ships:

Ἔσπετε νῦν μοι, Μοῦσαι Ὀλύμπια δώματ' ἔχουσαι,
ὅππως δὴ πρῶτον πῦρ ἔμπεσε νηυσὶν Ἀχαιῶν.          (*Il.* 16.112–13)

Tell me now, you Muses who have your homes on Olympos,
how fire first fell upon the ships of the Achaians.

This allusion not only places emphasis on Turnus' failure to burn the Trojan ships by juxtaposing it to Hector's success in the *Iliad*,[52] it also pauses the narrative to call attention to the fact that the Homeric passage at work in this instance belongs to the same narrative segment on which the final scene of Turnus' jump into the Tiber is modeled. Thus Turnus' first and last actions in the book are allusively linked, and, more importantly, by the time the narrative of Book 9 has come to a close, Turnus has been transformed from Hector to Ajax, from aggressor to defender.[53]

---

[52] For the inversion of the Homeric model, see Hardie 1994: 89. Vergil also inverts the order of the formula of invocation by posing first the question and then the request: the placement of the imperative *dicite* in the first metrical *sedes* followed by a pause places special emphasis on the request.

[53] This self-conscious pause is important for the authentication of the poem's place within the epic tradition as well as for securing the status of Homeric warrior for Turnus. Vergil here builds on the self-conscious manipulation of the "Muses" motif in Homer. As De Jong (2004: 45–53) has convincingly argued for the *Iliad*, calling upon the divine authority of the Muses does not demote the narrator's poetic activity; on the contrary, it calls attention to the poet's authority precisely because of his alignment with the divine. In the case of Vergil, the use of the "Muses" motif further serves to underscore the particular literary tradition within which the poet's activity takes place. The poet complements his imperative to the Muses with a phrase that confirms the literary aims of his annotation: the reason given for the invocation is continuity between past, present, and future (*prisca fides facto, sed fama perennis*, 79), achieved only

Aside from the Homeric Hector, Achilles, and Ajax, after whom Turnus' persona has hitherto been crafted, the figure of Sophocles' Ajax is added to the allusive map. In Book 10 Turnus shares the foreground of the action with Aeneas, as this portion of the epic contains the slaying of young Pallas, which provides the impetus for the poem's ending. Concurrently, the reader gains a deeper insight into Turnus' mind, since during the *aristeia* the narrative focus stays on him. This concentration on the inner workings of the hero's mind triggers in turn a shift in the models utilized in order to achieve this goal. The reader is thus invited to renegotiate the Homeric qualities of Turnus in light of the allusive tragic material. Moreover, this mobilization of the tragic intertext, far from constituting an isolated occurrence, persists until the end of the poem.

Before I discuss the systematic nature of Vergil's manipulation of the Sophoclean tragedy, it is instructive to trace how the shift in the allusive model occurs. Midway through Book 10, Turnus, tricked into following a phantom of Aeneas, is removed from the battlefield. As soon as he realizes what has happened to him, he utters a despondent soliloquy:

> 'omnipotens genitor, tanton me crimine dignum
> duxisti et talis uoluisti expendere poenas?
> quo feror? unde abii? quae me fuga quemue reducit?
> Laurentisne iterum muros aut castra uidebo?
> quid manus illa uirum, qui me meaque arma secuti?
> quosque (nefas) omnis infanda in morte reliqui
> et nunc palantis uideo, gemitumque cadentum
> accipio? quid ago? aut quae iam satis ima dehiscat
> terra mihi? uos o potius miserescite, uenti;
> in rupes, in saxa (uolens uos Turnus adoro)
> ferte ratem saeuisque uadis immittite syrtis,
> quo nec me Rutuli nec conscia fama sequatur.'          (10.668–79)

through the power of poetry, which the narrator owes to his association with the Muses. The emphasis on the epic task therefore reinforces simultaneously Vergil's epic heritage and Turnus' Homeric pedigree. The importance of the allusive play at work here is further emphasized by Vergil's use of the same device in the opening of the book's section dealing with Turnus' *aristeia* proper (see 9.525–28 and *Il.* 11.218–20). On the double reworking of the Homeric model and on the firing of the tower, see Hardie 1994: 171.

'Almighty father, did you think me deserving of so great
a disgrace and wish me to incur such a punishment?
Where am I taken? From where have I left? What flight pulls me back
    and how?
Will I see the walls or the camp of Laurentum again?
What of the group of men who followed me and my standards?
Did I leave all of them (unspeakable) to a heinous death
and now do I see them scattered and hear their groans
as they fall? What am I to do? What earth would now gape
deep enough for me? Rather, you winds, take pity on me;
dash this ship on the reefs, on the rocks (from my heart I beg you)
and cast it on some savage sandbanks, where neither the Rutulians
nor rumor privy to my shame may follow me.

Critics have acknowledged the kinship between Turnus' predicament and that of Sophocles' Ajax, as well as the similar manners in which they choose to face it.[54] But how is the situation that Turnus faces more tragic than Homeric? And how does one determine that the model at work is no longer Homer's Ajax but that of Sophocles? Tragic discourse engages the simultaneous presence of the categories of human agency and divine will and grapples with the tension between active and passive, intention and constraint;[55] Turnus' predicament and behavior in this instance neatly fit this definition of the tragic hero. Manipulated by Juno and Jupiter and deceived into chasing Aeneas' phantom, Turnus soon becomes painfully aware that he is caught between his own personal code of ethics and the divine at work.

There are indeed many points of contact between Turnus and Sophocles' Ajax in this instance. Ajax was also deceived by a deity as to the identity of his enemies. In the passage quoted earlier, Turnus' address to Jupiter first contains a realization of his *crimen*, that is, his absence from the line of duty; when the hero speaks of punishment, he refers to the dishonor that accompanies such action. Initially fearing that he

---

[54] See Pöschl 1962: 107–108 and Schenk 1984: 114. The latter, however, condemns the hero for exceeding the Homeric norm of "*Selbstwertgefühl.*" See also Harrison (1991: 231), who compares Turnus' monologue to those uttered by "disturbed and abandoned heroines such as Medea and Ariadne."

[55] Vernant 1988b: 79 on the tragic hero.

will be unable to return, his thoughts next turn to his comrades. The
hero appears genuinely concerned for their safety, which he perceives as
his responsibility (*quid manus illa uirum qui me meaque arma secuti?*, 672):
this is a fine display of the Homeric quality of *aidos*, which we have seen
that Ajax embodies in Homer, and which Vergil so carefully established
for Turnus in Book 9.[56] We witness firsthand his profound desperation
and sorrow as he addresses the winds in his desolation and asks them to
aid him in his death. Turnus' dejected monologue ends with a reference
to his moral obligation to his people and to *fama*, the values that define
his place within his community and that he believes he has forfeited.
The same betrayal of the ideals that defined his existence presented
Sophocles' Ajax with no alternative other than suicide. Turnus readily
attempts the same:

> haec memorans animo nunc huc, nunc fluctuat illuc,
> an sese mucrone ob tantum dedecus amens
> induat et crudum per costas exigat ensem,
> fluctibus an iaciat mediis et litora nando
> curua petat Teucrumque iterum se reddat in arma.
> ter conatus utramque uiam, ter maxima Iuno
> continuit iuuenemque animi miserata repressit.          (10.680–86)

> So Turnus spoke, and his mind wavers now this way, now that,
> whether in madness he should throw himself on his sword
> at such disgrace and drive the cruel blade through his ribs,
> or plunge into the sea, make his way to the winding shore
> by swimming and once again return to the armed Trojans.
> Three times he tried each way; three times great Juno
> prevented him, and, pitying the young man in her heart, held him back.

Thus Turnus, like Dido, struggles between his "internal spontaneity . . . and
the destiny that is fixed for him in advance by the gods" (Vernant 1988b:
79). The hero's proposed recourse to action takes two forms, both of which
are tantamount to suicide: significantly, the first possibility he entertains
is suicide in the manner of the Sophoclean Ajax. Death is finally averted

---

[56] Pöschl (1962: 108) comments that Turnus here first acknowledges his "guilt,"
meaning his resistance to Aeneas. But I believe that it is clear that Turnus
blames himself for leaving his comrades to their fate, not for causing war
against Aeneas.

through divine interference, but nevertheless, both Turnus' perception of his relationship with his comrades and his resolve to overcome his impasse honorably serve to underscore his full adherence to the heroic code, which in turn counterbalances his cruelty in the slaying of young Pallas. The reader also gains a glimpse into the workings of the hero's mind and the fragility of his intellectual powers when pitted against divine will.

Vergil's reworking of the tragic Ajax in the figure of Turnus continues in full force in Book 12. Turnus now displays a fierce determination to adhere to a system of values no longer effective against Aeneas and the new order he represents. This determination, arising from the hero's deep commitment to the common interest, turns into a violent rage that is usually explained in terms of *furor*, the irrational, dehumanizing, and barbaric force of the epic that Aeneas (and Rome) must strive to vanquish. Book 12 opens with a powerful illustration of Turnus' *violentia*: the army's defeat (*infractos ... Latinos*, 1) is transferred to Turnus himself through a simile in which he is likened to a lion wounded (*saucius ille graui uenantum uulnere pectus*, 5) yet angered and dangerous (*fremit ore cruento*, 8).[57] The wound represents both the defeat in battle and the blow to Turnus' honor that the delay of the final confrontation with Aeneas causes. Yet the hero's violent rage is also linked to his allegiance to the value of *aidos*: he declares his readiness to shoulder the responsibility for his community and fight Aeneas in a duel that will determine the outcome of the conflict (*solus ferro crimen commune refellam*, 16).

Latinus and Amata make an attempt to avert Turnus from fighting what they know is a doomed war. According to the heroic code by which Turnus abides, commitment to the common enterprise goes side by side with commitment to one's family. Latinus, at the close of his appeal, reminds the hero of his responsibility his aged father:

> respice res bello uarias, miserere *parentis*
> *longaeui*, quem nunc *maestum* patria Ardea longe
> diuidit. (12.43–45)

---

[57] The best discussions of the simile are still, I think, those of Putnam (1965: 153–58) and Pöschl (1962: 109–11), who include in detail the links with Dido's wound in Book 4. On *eros* and war, Dido and Turnus, see in addition Putnam 1999. On the scene and its Homeric models, see Schenk 1984: 146–50. Also note how the world of the narrative and the world of the simile merge in the identification of Turnus with the lion, just as happened earlier in Book 9.

Consider war's changing fortunes. Take pity on your *old father*,
whom now his homeland Ardea keeps far away
*in sorrow.*

Commentators point to *Iliad* 22.38–76 as the model for this scene, where
Priam urges Hector, a hero famous for his familial loyalty (Bradshaw
1991: 118), not to fight Achilles, and compare Turnus' refusal to comply with the old man's request to that of Hector (Schenk 1984: 152–56).
Turnus' alignment with Hector's decision undeniably foreshadows his
ultimate death, while at the same time underscoring his valor. Despite
these obvious connections, however, the Homeric scene lacks the overwhelming presence of the divine *fata*, the predetermined outcome of the
duel, as in the Vergilian narrative. Within this context of divine constraint, Latinus urges Turnus to acknowledge the fluctuating nature of
fortune in war (*respice res bello uarias*, 43) and the necessity to yield.

The conflict between intention and constraint, the individual's personal sense of honor and the shifting demands of the communal goals,
mobilizes the emergence of the tragic intertext in Vergil's epic. Indeed,
verbal contact can be located between Latinus' words and Tecmessa's
address to Ajax in the Sophoclean play:

ἀλλ' αἴδεσαι μὲν πατέρα τὸν σὸν ἐν λυγρῷ
γήρᾳ προλείπων, . . .                                               (506–507)

but, show regard for your *father*, whom you're deserting
in *sorrowful old age*, . . .

As we have seen, Ajax's inability to adapt to the ever-fluctuating realities
of wartime politics is the Sophoclean play's chief crisis. In this particular
scene, Ajax, his hands still stained with the blood of the slaughtered
sheep, has just become aware of his actions. Tecmessa and the Chorus,
however, speak of him as suffering from *nosos* (mental derangement)
and therefore still presenting a danger to himself and others. Tecmessa
attempts to dissuade him from compromising himself and his family
any further. Her speech opens with a statement on the mutability of
fortune imposed on all humans by the divine, and she offers herself as an
example: once a princess, she is now a spear-bride wholly dependent on
her captor, with whom her loyalties now lie. She then goes on to appeal

to Ajax to honor his familial ties to herself, their son, and his father.
Tecmessa's words prefigure Ajax's own realization of the mutability of
fortune later in the play.

Turnus and Ajax both display a rage that feeds on their weakened
state, an internal madness that intensifies their separation from the external world. Ajax is "sick," while Turnus is a wounded lion. Like Ajax, who
refuses to give an answer to Tecmessa's pleas and thus further compromise the heroic code of honor, so Turnus in his reply to Latinus reaffirms
his decision to fight to the death in order to preserve his honor:

> quam pro me curam geris, hanc precor, optime, pro me
> deponas letumque sinas pro laude pacisci.
> et nos tela, pater, ferrumque haud debile dextra
> spargimus, et nostro sequitur de uulnere sanguis.          (12.48–51)

> the anxiety you feel for my sake, most noble one, I beg you
> for my sake to put aside and let me bargain death for honor.
> I too, father, can hurl weapons and no puny sword with my
> right hand, and from the wounds I give blood flows as well.

Both in Sophocles' play and in Vergil's epic the hero's "sick" rage,
which breeds a misguided confidence, is followed by the realization of
his ultimate failure and exclusion from his social milieu. As the narrative proceeds, Turnus' confidence is gradually depleted, but his loyalties
remain unfailing. At the moment he hears the wailing from the besieged
city, he comes to the realization that this war has taken a turn that will
eventually destroy his community. His words to his sister reflect the sorrow and grief of a leader unable to help his people, recalling thereby the
earlier moment of his removal from the battlefield in Book 10 as well as
the grim disillusionment of Sophocles' Ajax:

> exscindine domos (id rebus defuit unum)
> perpetiar, dextra nec Drancis dicta refellam?
> terga dabo et Turnum fugientem haec terra uidebit?
> usque adeone mori miserum est? uos o mihi, Manes,
> este boni, quoniam superis auersa uoluntas.
> sancta ad uos anima atque istius inscia culpae
> descendam magnorum haud umquam indignus auorum.      (12.643–49)

am I to suffer our homes be destroyed (this one thing is left)
and not refute Drances' charges with my right hand?
Shall I turn my back and will this country see Turnus on the run?
Is is so terrible to die? You, Shades, be kind to me,
since the goodwill of the gods above is turned away from me.
I shall come down to you, a soul unstained and innocent of this crime,
never unworthy of my great ancestors.

ἐγὼ δ' ὁ κείνου παῖς, τὸν αὐτὸν ἐς τόπον
Τροίας ἐπελθὼν οὐκ ἐλάσσονι σθένει,
οὐδ' ἔργα μείω χειρὸς ἀρκέσας ἐμῆς, . . .                              (437–39)

καὶ νῦν τί χρὴ δρᾶν; ὅστις ἐμφανῶς θεοῖς
ἐχθαίρομαι, μισεῖ δέ μ' Ἑλλήνων στρατός,
ἔχθει δὲ Τροία πᾶσα καὶ πεδία τάδε.                                   (457–59)

but I, his son, having come to the same land
of Troy with no less might
and having accomplished no lesser deeds with my hand . . .

and now what must I do? I who obviously am hated
by the gods, hated by the army of the Greeks,
and hated by all of Troy and by these plains . . .

Turnus, like Ajax, places himself within the family tradition and, like the
Greek hero, asserts that he has done his share dutifully; both conclude
that divine will is against them and that they have brought harm to their
people. This constitutes the acknowledgment of an inner defeat, more profound and disturbing than the defeat in battle; Turnus, like Ajax and like
Dido, experiences the loss of all that has hitherto defined his existence.

Tangible confirmation of this recognition comes immediately after-
ward, when Turnus is informed of Queen Amata's death and sees the
tower that he himself had built collapse in smoke and flames:

Ecce autem flammis inter tabulata uolutus
ad caelum undabat uertex turrimque tenebat,
turrim compactis trabibus quam eduxerat ipse
subdideratque rotas pontisque instrauerat altos.
'iam iam fata, soror, superant, absiste morari;
quo deus et quo dura uocat Fortuna sequamur.
stat conferre manum Aeneae, stat, quidquid acerbi est,

morte pati, neque me indecorem, germana, uidebis
amplius. hunc, oro, sine me furere ante furorem.'            (12.672–80)

But look, a whirling spire of flames was rolling
from floor to floor toward the sky and got hold of a tower,
a tower that he himself had built with beams fastened together
and he had put wheels underneath, and placed long gangways.
"Now sister, now fate has won, stop your delays;
let us go where god and cruel Fortune call.
I am resolved to fight Aeneas, resolved to bear any bitterness
in death, and you will not, my sister, see me disgraced
any longer. Let me first, I beg you, seethe in this rage."

Turnus' words again display his disillusionment but also his strong sense
of honor and pride, a pride similar to Dido's, which dictates that the
only possible way out of an impossible situation is an honorable and self-
inflicted death. Yet there is a further connection that involves the tower
itself. Turnus' first exploit in Book 9 (530–37) was to burn the tower of
the Trojans. Aeneas' action here corresponds to that of Turnus in Book 9
and "is part of a larger movement of inversion whereby the beleaguered
Trojans end up in the role of Homer's city-sacking Achaeans."[58] Moreover,
the tower's collapse serves as a metaphor for Turnus' own death (Pöschl
1962: 128), while at the same time it implies an identification of the hero
with the defensive structure. Vergil thus effectively links Turnus with
Ajax at this crucial moment of Turnus' disillusionment, by concretizing
and then inverting the Homeric metaphor of Ajax as a tower: as already
mentioned, Odysseus' address to Ajax in the Underworld appropriates
the image of the tower for the hero himself (see note 5 to this chapter).

Despite his recognition of the fate that awaits him, Turnus appears
determined not to yield but to abide by his code of honor until the
end. He appears unable to entertain any notion of moral relativism that
would permit him to adjust to the demands of the new order that the
gods have in store for the Latins and the Trojans. He shares the tragic
Ajax's (and Dido's) intransigence and extremism, which run contrary to
the demands of the individual's submission to the greater enterprise of

[58] Hardie 1994: 175. He also points out the allusions to the incident in Book 12.
See Hardie 1994: 173, 175.

Rome.[59] The tragedy of Ajax rests on his betrayal of the very values that he has championed in the *Iliad*, especially his loyalty to the common cause. Turnus too, because of his inability to conform to the new role his community is called on to play in Aeneas' Latium, finds himself in complete isolation, grasping at his outdated sense of honor and rushing to certain death as a result. Turnus thus embodies the clash between the necessity to adapt to a new social order and the inability to do so while still abiding by the (Homeric) heroic code. Since the foundation of the new Latium with Trojans and Italians in equal partnership marks both Rome's beginning and the rebirth of the Roman state under the Augustan regime, the Rutulian hero poignantly exemplifies the powerful tensions and conflicts inherent in the social and political changes these processes entail. Concurrently, Turnus' imminent death represents the loss of a vital moral force that necessitates the articulation of a comparable, if not superior, ethical code for Aeneas' Latium. Just as Odysseus in the Sophoclean play emerges as the alternative model to Ajax in the post-Achillean times and in the new sociopolitical reality of fifth-century Athens, so Aeneas constitutes the alternative to Turnus' outdated heroism in the new Latium and in the new reality of Augustan Rome.

Yet another allusion to the tragic Ajax distorts and confuses Aeneas' emergence as a superior moral force in the poem. Before the final confrontation between Aeneas and Turnus, intertextual evidence forces us to pause and ponder a rather unexpected connection between Ajax and the poem's hero. While Aeneas, his wound healed, prepares to reenter the fray, he imparts the following advice to his son:

> disce, *puer*, uirtutem ex me uerumque laborem
> *fortunam* ex aliis.                                    (12.435–36)

> *son*, learn valor from me and true toil;
> *fortune* from others.

Scholars have located the model in Sophocles' *Ajax*:[60]

> ὦ παῖ, γένοιο πατρὸς εὐτυχέστερος,
> τὰ δ' ἄλλ' ὁμοῖος· καὶ γένοι' ἂν οὐ κακός.           (550–51)

---

[59] For the imperial politics of Rome, see, for instance, Lyne 1983; Hardie 1986; Quint 1993: 21–96; and Gurval 1995.

[60] Macrobius (*Sat.* 6.1.58) states that Vergil's source was Accius' *Armorum iudicium* (*TRF* 156): *uirtuti sis par, dispar fortunis patris*. Jocelyn (1965: 128) interprets

*son*, may you be more *fortunate* than your father,
but in everything else like him; then you would be no coward.

The Vergilian reader may initially be puzzled by this allusion, since, apparently, the connection between a hero bent on suicide and the soon-to-be-victorious Aeneas is far from obvious.[61] Both Vergil and Sophocles in this instance appropriate the Iliadic Hector's farewell to his son. In this segment of the play, the Sophoclean Ajax evinces a stern arrogance, which sharply contrasts with Hector's modesty and fatherly ambition that his son may surpass him in valor (Kirkwood 1965: 58). The intersection of the Homeric and tragic in *Ajax* is also superbly manipulated by Vergil, as Aeneas too shares in this contrast with the Iliadic Hector. Furthermore, Sophocles' Ajax, in his preceding monologue, came to the agonizing realization that he had failed to succeed his father, Telamon, in honorable repute through lack of fortune; he now looks upon his son to win heroic accolades in the line of male succession (Winnington-Ingram 1980: 30–31). In this light, Aeneas' advice to Ascanius looks forward to a similar contingency. At the final moment of Turnus' supplication, the Trojan hero will in effect betray his own father's legacy (Putnam

this as spoken "not by an Ajax bent on suicide, but by an Ajax conscious of his *uirtus*, despite the decision given against him in the matter of Achilles' armour, and wishing to recover his reputation among men by a glorious deed in battle. Vergil's copy of Accius' sentence is more comprehensible on such an interpretation." *Contra* Wigodsky (1972: 95–97), who argues that the lines can be said to have been taken from the Greek text. See also Lefèvre 1978: 25. Whatever the context in Accius may be, the Vergilian text contains allusions to Sophocles' *Ajax*, which need to be interpreted in their own right. Lyne (1987: 4–12) also argues that the model for Aeneas here is the tragic Ajax. I believe that the evidence presented here adds force to this argument. For Aeneas as *ductor Rhoeteius* and implications of apotheosis, as well as a justification for the killing of Turnus, see Rowland 1992.

[61] Fowler 1919: 86 well illustrates the reader's puzzlement: "All the commentators, down to Mr. Page, tell us that Virgil is 'copying' the famous lines in Sophocles' *Ajax* ... Virgil may have been thinking of them, but he must have seen that the circumstances of Ajax and Aeneas were very different. Ajax had been mad: he is the protagonist of a tragedy; Aeneas had no special cause to lament his misfortunes, nor was it his habit to do so. We need not go to the Greeks for what is a truly Roman sentiment. In the family, the Roman boy learnt to live a manly life, and to face life's painful struggles with a good heart: what *fortuna* might mean for him he might learn from any other teacher, from his experience of the world."

1965: 192–94). As a result, he falls prey to anger and *furor*, the uncivilized forces he has tried to combat and conquer throughout the epic. The Aeneas of the final scene of the poem, who in his avenging wrath kills Turnus the suppliant, is as much a deluded hero as the blinded Ajax who brought death to the sheepfolds of the Achaeans. The tragic Ajax as intertextual subtext aligning Aeneas with Dido and Turnus further complicates and problematizes his heroic identity. Aeneas, the model hero of a new social order, may be said in this instance to share Ajax's misplaced adherence to a moral code no longer viable, as well as the fragility of his state of mind.

In the scene of the final duel between the two heroes, the figure of Ajax returns as a foil to Turnus. Aeneas strikes Turnus' breastplate and shield with his spear:

> uolat atri turbinis instar
> exitium dirum hasta ferens orasque recludit
> loricae et clipei extremos *septemplicis* orbis;          (12.923–25)

> the spear flies like a black whirlwind
> bringing grim death and and pierces the rim
> of the corselet and the outermost circles of the *sevenfold* shield;

The word *septemplicis* is a *hapax* in the Vergilian corpus. Similarly, Ajax's shield is the only shield in the *Iliad* that has seven ox-hide layers (see note 4 to this chapter), and it is the same one that Ajax entrusts to his son in Sophocles' tragedy when he asks to be buried along with his other weapons:

> ἀλλ' αὐτό μοι σύ, παῖ, λαβὼν τοὐπώνυμον,
> Εὐρύσακες, ἴσχε διὰ πολυρράφου στρέφων
> πόρπακος ἑπτάβοιον ἄρρηκτον σάκος, . . .          (574–76)

> but, son, take this from which you have your name,
> Eurysaces, hold it, wielding it by the well-sewn
> handle, my unbreakable *sevenfold* shield, . . .

In the Greek play, the shield serves as a reminder of Ajax's heroic past: his enormous physical power, his talent in military defense, and his role in the Trojan war as a bastion of the entire Achaean army. It is a visible symbol of both his bodily strength and his *aidos*, and hence a constitutive element of his identity as a hero. The allusive appropriation of Ajax's shield in the scene of Turnus' final defeat achieves a similar goal: it is a reminder of the Rutulian's past services and loyalty to his people and of his inadvertent betrayal of his community's enterprise. In this light, Turnus' actions, like Dido's, are not motivated by self-interest, as scholars usually argue. To be sure, he has a personal stake in the matter; but, like Dido, he believes that his personal interest coincides with the common goal. As in the case of Sophocles' Ajax, his tragedy lies in his realization that the two have ceased to be identical and his inability to reconcile his own sense of honor with the demands of this new reality.

All the preceding allusions, Homeric and tragic, intersect in this final scene as Turnus once again takes on Ajax's attributes.[62] The rich allusive texture of the Sophoclean play puts the Homeric material to work as a backdrop against which the tragedy of Ajax is to be measured. Similarly, the Vergilian epic appropriates Homeric material in order to establish Turnus as a valiant warrior, but utilizes the tragic Ajax in order to reveal his moral agony and the fragility of his state of mind in the face of divine manipulation (Juno) and opposition (Jupiter). The appropriation of the Homeric epics sufficiently enables Vergil to celebrate the ideals of the Homeric (and Roman) behavioral code as well as to endow his poem with the luster and authority that its literary pedigree implies. But in the case of Turnus, as in the case of Dido, the Homeric material serves to deploy a systematic tragic intertext, without which it would be impossible to appreciate the profound problems, tensions, and conflicts inherent in the sociopolitical changes that Aeneas' new order and, by extension, Augustus' Rome bring to bear.

---

[62] As Aeneas hesitates over the suppliant Turnus, he catches sight of the baldric that the Rutulian had taken from the young Pallas (12.940–44). The use of the word *infelix* attributed to the baldric constitutes another tragic gesture: see Conington 1884, 3: 484 (quoting Heyne on 12.940): "this passage is quite in accordance with the feeling expressed in Greek tragedies, that what was given by, or taken from, an enemy, brought ill fortune with it. In *Iliad* 22.322 a chance is given to Achilles' weapon, because Patroclus' armor does not fit Hector. Hector, according to Sophocles, was dragged around the walls of Troy by the belt which Ajax had given him, while Ajax killed himself with the sword of Hector."

# 7   Contesting Ideologies: Ritual and Empire

THE RITUAL AND TRAGIC INTERTEXTS OF THE *AENEID* NEED TO
be considered side by side with the Homeric intertext and its role not
only in the literary valuation or understanding of the epic but also as a
vehicle for the expression and promotion of Augustan ideology. My analysis has privileged the tragic/ritual intertext and its contingent implications, which emphasize ideological anxieties vis-à-vis the ability of the
new Augustan order to achieve lasting peace. It is important to stress,
however, that my readings must also be appraised within the poem's
overall ideological framework, as this emerges from the poem's other
intertexts as well as from the poem's reception.

The simultaneous existence of different and opposing ideologies within
a text that has become synonymous with Augustan ideology is not surprising considering the most recent advances in the field of political theory, which have brought to bear the complex nature of ideology and the
intense processes of negotiation, suppression, and manipulation that take
place therein.[1] Gramsci was the first to view ideology not as monolithic
and static but as a dialogic and dynamic phenomenon, in which opposing
voices define its content even if they are ultimately suppressed (Bell 1992:
190). For Gramsci, ideology is not directed to the subordinated classes
but aims at the self-understanding of the dominant class. Bourdieu, by
contrast, focuses on the subordinated groups, which he views as complicit.
For Bourdieu, these groups neither submit passively nor adopt freely the

---

[1] An introduction to theories of ideology can be found in Eagleton 1991. Bell
(1992: 187–96) gives a good and concise summary of the main schools of
thought on ideology.

tenets of the dominant class. Their consent is an act of misrecognition by which the dominated accept the values of the dominant class and apply its criteria to their own practices, even when these values and criteria go against their own interests (Bourdieu 1977: 114–15; Bell 1992: 190). Other theorists, such as Merquior, further qualify Bourdieu's notion of complicity by pointing out that consent is not an uncritical internalization of the values of the dominant class or belief in their legitimacy (Merquior 1979: 35). The same self-awareness may be claimed for the people of the dominant class: one may very well hold ideological views and be perfectly aware that they are ideological (Eagleton 1991: 60). Acquiescence is thus not passive but rather a product of negotiation.

This theoretical approach posits that ideology is the result of a tension between opposing and conflicting ideological stances and emphasizes that ideologies exist in specific historical moments and in relation to other ideologies (Bell 1992: 191). Viewed in this light, the unequal distribution of power that ideology necessarily promotes also implies a greater distribution of power than would exist in relationships defined by brute force. Ideology seeks legitimization and complicity, and in doing so it is a much more flexible and fluid mechanism than previously thought (Bell 1992: 193). Within this framework, the subject is seen as an actor, an agent who both generates and consumes the ideological message. As Catherine Bell puts it, "the actor emerges as divided, decentered, overdetermined, but quite active" (1992: 192).

Ritual practice constitutes a locus where such ideological negotiations are enacted and where ideologies are shaped. Ritual acts embody specific power relations, producing and objectifying hierarchies, structures, and beliefs (Bell 1992: 196). As is the case in ideological discourses, in rituals too objectification results in a misrecognition of their source and the arbitrariness of their claims. In other words, rituals are believed to originate and derive from powers and realities beyond the community, such as god or tradition, connected with the organization of nature and the cosmos. The participants therefore misrecognize the set of relationships and hierarchies they experience embodied in ritual acts and practices as originating from a body outside that of the community, thereby embracing them and accepting them as binding, unchanging, and eternal.

The Romans were no strangers to such objectification, boasting their origins from the gods: both Rome's founding fathers, Aeneas and

Romulus, had divine parentage, and both were deified after their death. Livy's preface lends voice to the interconnection between objectification, misrecognition, and ideology:

This allowance is made to the ancients to render more venerable the origins of cities by mixing human things with divine; and if any people are to be permitted to sanctify their origins and refer to the gods as their founders, such is the military glory of the Roman people that, when they say that their father and the father of their founder is no other than Mars, the nations of the earth submit to it just as they submit to their imperial power.[2]

The passage simultaneously endorses Rome's divine parentage and exposes it as an act of misrecognition of the source of its imperial power.[3] In this statement, we can see both the ideological import of Rome's divine origins and an awareness of its function as such. The intersection of imperial success and misrecognition is evident in Livy's passage, where Romans' claims to divine authority acquire validity because of their military might. The Romans themselves participated in this act of objectification, since they believed that their military and imperial success was a direct result of their religiosity.[4]

Livy's passage also brings to the foreground, the notion of consent, a key element in the dissemination of ideology. Participants in rituals accept the power structures enacted and promoted therein (Bell 1992: 207). At the same time, each participant brings to ritual activities "a self-constituting history that is a patchwork of compliance, resistance, misunderstanding, and redemptive personal appropriation of the hegemonic order" (Bell 1992: 208). A Roman, for instance, participating in a ritualized activity, such as the dedication of a temple or a public rite,

---

[2] Livy, *praef.* 7: *Datur haec uenia antiquitati ut miscendo humana diuinis primordia urbium augustiora faciat; et si cui populo licere oportet consecrare origines suas et ad deos referre auctores, ea belli gloria est populo Romano ut cum suum conditorisque sui parentem Martem potissimum ferat, tam et hoc gentes humanae patiantur aequo animo quam imperium patiuntur.*

[3] Compare Ovid, *Ars* 1.637: *expedit esse deos, et, ut expedit, esse putemus* [it is expedient that gods exist, and, since it is expedient, let us believe that gods exist]. Although Ovid makes this statement as advice for successfully gaining the affections of a lady, he goes even further than Livy in exposing religion's utilitarianism.

[4] Cicero, *De natura deorum* 2.3.8; *De haruspicum responsis* 19; see also Orlin 2007: 76.

may assert that he or she accepts the official authority sponsoring these activities, yet he or she may still be hostile to that authority.

Augustus was keenly aware of the importance of cult and ritual as a means of consolidating his power by generating popular consent. During his reign, both in Rome and in the provinces, opportunities to participate in public life through the practice of religion and cult became available for the first time to people belonging to lower social strata. One such opportunity was presented through the reorganization of the administrative division of Rome into 14 *regiones* and 265 *vici* (wards); each *vicus* and its leaders (*vicomagistri*) were in charge of the cult of Lares at the crossroads, which included festivals and games and afforded participation to women and slaves. Previously, the cult's management had belonged to the *collegia*, associations consisting of members of the lower social classes, and was often the source of threats against the established order.[5] As a result, Augustus was able to transform a locus of turmoil into an instrument offering visible contribution to the new order[6] and thus generating consent to his regime.

Yet one's active participation in the ideological program of a certain order may not necessarily imply a wholesale acceptance of that order. That was certainly true in Augustan Rome, as the civil unrest of 6 CE makes plain (Dio Cassius 55.27.1; Galinsky 1996: 308). One of the ways in which Augustus used religion and ritual as a means to facilitate the process of reconciliation was the revitalization of the Arval Brotherhood. The group's cultic responsibilities were both public and private: its main task appears to have been the performance of public sacrifices to ensure agricultural fertility. By becoming a member of this group, Augustus joined the ranks of Rome's most illustrious families, many of whom had fought against him during the civil wars, and thus reached out to his former opponents. Membership in the group also afforded the possibility

---

[5] The *collegia* had been outlawed and reinstated several times during the Republic, until Augustus permanently banned them in 22 BCE. For further details on the vicissitudes of the fate of the *collegia* and their connection to riots, see Galinsky 1996: 300. See also Zanker 1988: 118–35.

[6] Galinsky 1996: 300–312. Augustus was able to do the same thing beyond the city of Rome by establishing the *collegia* of the *augustales* in Italy and the western part of the empire, associations devoted to the cult of the *princeps* (see Galinsky 1996: 310–12).

of "negotiated consent" (Bell 1992: 210–11), as can readily be seen in the case of Messalla Corvinus. A former supporter of Antony who had fought with Augustus in Actium, he resigned in protest from his office as prefect of Rome in 26 BCE but remained Augustus' Arval Brother (Galinsky 1996: 292). His dissent was thus qualified by his allegiance to Augustus through their shared religious affiliation.

Augustus' religious reform and moral legislation cast him as the revitalizer and champion of tradition precisely because ritual acts derive their power and effectiveness from their relevance to the beliefs, needs, and experiences of the civic body. The massive building program he launched is a case in point. It chiefly involved the restoration of temples, most of which had lapsed into a state of decay and disrepair during the time of civil wars. Although restoration plans were already at work in late Republican times, Augustus was justified in claiming that he truly transformed the religious landscape of Rome (Suetonius, *Aug.* 28.3). A professed adherence to tradition became the perfect vehicle for his new ideological message. For instance, new anniversary dates were given to many of the restored temples, rescheduled in such a way as to coincide with the *princeps'* birthday or other events significant for him or his policies (Galinsky 1996: 301). Accordingly, the gamut of ritual acts performed within the vicinity of these temples – festivals, ceremonies, and games – were rendered powerful because they purported both to restore a tradition considered lost and to emphasize the privileged position the Augustan regime claimed within that tradition.

This dual role of ritual as both constituting of and constituted by ideology complicates the idea of consent as synonymous with acquiescence. In this light, consent is negotiated (Bell 1992: 210–18) and reflective of the fragility of the objectification, authority, and traditionalism associated with ritual power. In other words, ritual requires only that its participants consent to forms, while it simultaneously allows the possibility of resistance to the authority it seeks to solidify. As Bell puts it, "negotiated compliance offers manifold opportunities for strategic appropriation, depending on one's mastery of social schemes, even to the point of subversion" (1992: 215). Such resistance in turn permits varying nuances in the ideological message that the dominant ritual activities project onto the social body.

As we have seen, Augustus himself was deeply aware of the power of ritual to promote his policies and cement his status as *princeps*, and ritualized celebration early on formed a big component of his policy. A similar connection can also be seen at work in the *Aeneid*, composed in the early years of Augustus' rise (29–19 BCE): in Chapter 5, for instance, we saw that Ascanius and the Trojan youths perform a *lusus Troiae*, a public spectacle revived in the time of Augustus, linking Aeneas' present with the future of Rome. Other such examples abound in the epic: the description of Latinus' palace in Book 7, described as *augustum* (7.170), points to a group of buildings that Augustus will build (see Zetzel 1997: 195–96); in Book 8, Augustus' triple triumph after Actium in 29 BCE commemorates one of the most spectacular events in Rome that marked the end of civil wars.[7] At the same time, Augustus himself appropriated symbols from the *Aeneid* to proliferate his ideological program. In the Ara Pacis, a monument dedicated in 9 BCE, the identification of Augustus with Aeneas is made explicit by their similar representation: both figures have veiled heads; Augustus participates in a procession on the south side, while Aeneas can be viewed around the corner in a similar pose and performing a sacrifice (Hardie 1993: 21; Zanker: 1988: 201–10).

Within this framework, the mobilization of the ritual intertext in the *Aeneid* may therefore be explained as another means for the reproduction of the nascent social and political order of Augustus. Greek tragedy employs ritual to a similar effect: it dramatizes ideological battles (Seaford 1994: 363–67) while ultimately affirming and justifying Athenian hegemony over its allies (Tzanetou forthcoming). The *Aeneid*'s use of the ritual/tragic intertext can thus be seen as one of a host of narrative strategies deployed to assert a specific type of power relations, the promotion of the principate and the justification of the power of Augustus as *princeps*. Similarly, as we have seen, the notion of repetition, so closely associated with both narrative and ritual, also permits the attainment of mastery and empowerment and thus promotes the ideological message of Augustus (Quint 1993: 50–53). Another such strategy, is, of course, the mobilization of the Homeric intertext.

The present study of the ritual and tragic intertexts, however, does not allow for such a unilateral interpretation of Vergil's poem, but paints a rather more complicated picture. My analysis demonstrates that the

---

[7] On Vergil's manipulation of historical events in this instance, see Miller 2000: 410–14.

ritual intertext of the *Aeneid* focuses on the fragility of ritual and the breakdown of ritual practices, exposing the artificiality of the power relations contained therein. As a result, the tragic/ritual intertext illustrates that the creation of ideology is a process whereby consent is negotiated and qualified. The reconciliation scene between Jupiter and Juno may serve as a case in point. By emphasizing the vulnerability of ritual and the precariousness of the idea of *concordia*, the episode showcases Juno's "negotiated consent" to Jupiter's plan. Juno's terms as well as her eventual agreement reveal how it is possible to agree with an ideological program and simultaneously challenge its terms and legitimacy.[8] Similarly, the ritual intertext's depiction of Turnus as a *devotus* complicates his representation as the enemy "other" who is justly conquered. In casting Turnus as a version of one of the great heroes of the Republic, P. Decius Mus, the ritual intertext contests his "Homeric" identities as a second Hector or a second Achilles and reveals them as constructs of an ideological process that aims to justify Augustan supremacy.[9] As a result, the ideological nature of the poem stands exposed, and the ritual/tragic intertext becomes a way of registering opposition, anxiety, and repression.

The simultaneous existence in the *Aeneid* of the ideological positions of acquiescence and opposition to the Augustan regime is not simply another way of expressing the all-too-familiar axiom of the "two voices" of the epic, or to assert the privileging of the voice of resistance and pessimism over that of endorsement and optimism. Using a similar view of ideology, Duncan Kennedy, in an insightful essay, suggests that the terms "pro-" and "anti-Augustan" commonly used to describe political and ideological attitudes during this historical period possess neither a stable nor a clearly defined meaning. Focusing on language and discourse, he argues that at historical moments when power is on the move or being challenged, any ideologically charged word may be aligned to a variety of meanings and reflect different types of power relations. Accordingly, each "meaning" competes with others for supremacy (Kennedy 1992: 35). For Kennedy, Vergil writes in a period during which the fragmented discourse of the Republic is reorganized and the *princeps* gradually takes the

---

[8] Other scholars have shared this view. For a complete bibliography, see my discussion in Chapter 3 of this volume.

[9] On Turnus as a *devotus*, see Chapter 2, pp. 56–71.

form of an institution that will provide society with stable meaning. We should therefore look upon Augustus not as a person, Kennedy argues, but as an idea (Kennedy 1992: 35). The same ideological work is achieved through ritualization, which depersonalizes authority by assigning power to an office or formal status, not to a person (Bell 1992: 211).

I argue that the *Aeneid*, a text about the birth of a new nation and a new order, enacts a similar reorganization of reality. The ritual/tragic intertext's emphasis on the fragility of the epic's purported ideological proposition, however, suggests the indeterminacy of the notion of "Augustanism." In other words, it draws attention to the fact that the very idea of what it means to be "pro-Augustan" is still in the process of being defined. Each intertext operative in the epic, then, may be seen as vying with the other for supremacy and meaning. I propose that the ritual/tragic intertext and the Homeric intertext participate with equal force in this "reorganization" of civic discourse and the struggle for social stability. In the end, Augustus wins not only the civil war but also the battle over discourse and ideology. But my reading indicates that such a victory is not to be found in the text of the *Aeneid*. The poem's reception as pro-Augustan is undeniable. At the same time, given the ideological contests enacted within the text, this reception is better explained as a *result* of the triumph of the ideological program of Augustus, not as one of its causes.

The previous proposition need not imply that one should ignore or devalue those moments in the *Aeneid* that openly endorse Augustus' ideas or programs; but one need be aware that many of these "pro-Augustan" moments may have become important to Augustus only as a consequence of the poem's canonical, pro-Augustan status. A useful example can be seen, again, in the reconciliation scene between Jupiter and Juno in *Aeneid* 12. As Orlin (2007) convincingly argues, Jupiter's proposition to Juno ascribes the provenance of Roman religion to a single divine source, Jupiter, presented in the guise of divine revelation, despite the fact that Romans consistently resisted depicting their religious system as delivered by the gods (74). Orlin goes on to argue that the view of Roman religion projected here is similar to that behind Augustus' program of temple restoration. Roman temples served not only as venues for ritual activity but also "as monuments in which Roman memories and Roman history resided" (83) and thus helped create a unified sense

of identity encompassing both Romans and Italians. Vergil's revolution-
ary rewriting of Roman religious history found expression in Augustus'
religious program (92). This "collusion" between the text of the *Aeneid*
and Augustan ideology is arguably not the origin but the result of a long
process of redefinition of civic discourse and national identity.

The dialogue of the epic's literary intertexts is thus better understood
as enacting a dialogue between competing ideological positions. The
Homeric intertext enables the processes of misrecognition that Bourdieu
considers so important for the creation of ideology, by reinforcing the
positive, heroic values the epic promotes, such as the notion of "empire
without end." At the same time, the poem's tragic intertext, with its
emphasis on ritual corruption and loss, eloquently demonstrates that
"empire without end," desirable though it may be, comes at a price that
individuals and even communities may not or should not wish to pay.[10]
In this way, consent to Augustus' ideological program is qualified, appropriated, negotiated, while the individual emerges as actively engaged in
the creation of ideological meaning. The *Aeneid* thus appears as a divided
text in search for stability, for institutions that are both humane and
able to control the forces of irrationality and destruction that have shat-
tered the Roman social and political fabric. Attention to the ideological
negotiations operative in the poem elucidates our understanding of its
most puzzling quandaries as well as of the complexities surrounding the
formation and proliferation of Augustan ideology.

[10] Anchises' famous bequest to Aeneas (6.851–53) read against Aeneas' killing of
Turnus may be adduced as evidence for such an argument, and critics have often
done so. See, for instance, Putnam's eloquent argumentation (1965: 192–201).

# Bibliography

Alcock, S. E. 1997. "The Heroic Past in a Hellenistic Present." In *Hellenistic Constructs: Essays in Culture, History, and Historiography*. P. Cartledge, P. Garnsey, and E. Gruen, eds. Berkeley: 20–34.

Alexiou, M. 2002. *The Ritual Lament in Greek Tradition*. Revised by D. Yatromanolakis and P. Roilos. 2nd edition. Lanham.

Allan, W. 2000. *The* Andromache *and Euripidean Tragedy*. Oxford.

Anderson, W. S. 1969. *The Art of the* Aeneid. Englewood Cliffs, NJ.

Austin, R. G. 1955. *P. Vergili Maronis Aeneidos Liber Quartus. Edited with a Commentary*. Oxford.

———— 1964. *P. Vergili Maronis Aeneidos Liber Secundus. Edited with a Commentary*. Oxford.

———— 1977. *P. Vergili Maronis Aeneidos Liber Sextus. Edited with a Commentary*. Oxford.

Bailey, C. 1935. *Religion in Virgil*. Oxford.

———— 1947. *Titi Lucreti Cari De Rerum Natura. Libri Sex. Edited with Prolegomena, Critical Apparatus, Translation and Commentary*. 3 vols. Oxford.

Bandera, C. 1981. "Sacrificial Levels in Virgil's *Aeneid*." *Arethusa* 14: 217–39.

———— 1990. "From Virgil to Cervantes: Literature Desacralized." *Helios* 17: 109–20.

Barchiesi, A. 1978. "Il lamento di Giuturna." *MD* 1: 99–121.

———— 1994. "Rappresentazioni del dolore e interpretazione nell' *Eneide*." *A&A* 40: 109–24.

Barton, C. A. 1993. *The Sorrows of the Ancient Romans: The Gladiator and the Monster*. Princeton.

Beard, M. 1980. "The Sexual Status of Vestal Virgins." *JRS* 70: 12–27.

———— 1994. "The Roman and the Foreign: The Cult of the 'Great Mother' in Imperial Rome." In *Shamanism, History, and the State*. N. Thomas and C. Humphrey, eds. Ann Arbor: 164–90.

———— 1995. "Re-reading (Vestal) Virginity." In *Women in Antiquity: New Assessments*. R. Hawley and B. Levick, eds. London: 166–77.

Beard, M., et al. 1998. *Religions of Rome*. 2 vols. Cambridge.

Bell, C. 1992. *Ritual Theory, Ritual Practice*. New York.

Bierl, A. 1994. "Apollo in Greek Tragedy: Orestes and the God of Initiation." In *Apollo: Origins and Influences*. J. Solomon, ed. Tuscon: 81–96.

Bourdieu, P. 1977. "Symbolic Power." In *Identity and Structure: Issues in the Sociology of Education*. D. Gleeson, ed. Driffield: 112–19.

Bowie, A. M. 1993. "Religion and Politics in Aeschylus' *Oresteia*." *CQ* 43: 10–31.

Boyle, A. J. 2006. *An Introduction to Roman Tragedy*. London.

Bradshaw, D. J. 1991. "The Ajax Myth and the Polis: Old Values and New." In *Myth and the Polis*. D. C. Pozzi and J. M. Wickersham, eds. Ithaca: 99–125.

Brooks, P. 1984. *Reading for the Plot: Design and Intention in Narrative*. New York.

Brown, A. L. 1984. "Eumenides in Greek Tragedy." *CQ* 34: 260–81.

Bruhl, A. 1953. *Liber Pater. Origine et expansion du culte dionysiaque à Rome et dans le monde romain*. Paris.

Burke, P. F., Jr. 1974a. "The Role of Mezentius in the *Aeneid*." *CJ* 69: 202–209.

———— 1974b. "Mezentius and the First-Fruits." *Vergilius* 20: 28–29.

Burkert, W. 1966. "Greek Tragedy and Sacrificial Ritual." *GRBS* 7: 87–121.

———— 1979. *Structure and History in Greek Mythology and Ritual*. Berkeley.

———— 1983. *Homo Necans: The Anthropology of Ancient Greek Sacrificial Ritual and Myth*. Translated by P. Bing. Berkeley. First published as *Homo Necans. Interpretationen altgriechischer Opferriten und Mythen*. Berlin, 1972.

———— 1985. *Greek Religion*. Translated by J. Raffan. Cambridge, MA. First published as *Griechische Religion der archaischen und klassischen Epoche*. Stuttgart, 1977.

Clausen, W. 1987. *Virgil's* Aeneid *and the Tradition of Hellenistic Poetry*. Sather Classical Lectures, vol. 51. Berkeley.

Cole, S. G. 2004. *Landscapes, Gender, and Ritual Space: The Ancient Greek Experience*. Berkeley.

Conacher, D. J. 1987. *Aeschylus'* Oresteia: *A Literary Commentary*. Toronto.

Conington, J. 1884. *P. Vergili Maronis Opera. The Works of Virgil, with a Commentary by John Conington*. Fourth edition, revised, with corrected orthography and additional notes by H. Nettleship. 3 vols. London.

Conte, G. B. 1986. *The Rhetoric of Imitation: Genre and Poetic Memory in Virgil and Other Latin Poets*. Translated by C. Segal. Cornell Studies in Classical

Philology 44. Ithaca. First published as *Memoria dei poeti e sistema letterario: Catullo, Virgilio, Ovidio, Lucano.* Turin, 1974 and as *Il genere e i suoi confini: cinque studi sulla poesia di Virgilio.* Turin, 1980.

Day Lewis, C. 1952. *The* Aeneid *of Virgil.* Oxford.

De Jong, I. J. F. 2004. *Narrators and Focalizers: The Presentation of the Story in the* Iliad. 2nd edition. Bristol.

Des Bouvrie, S. 1997. "Euripides' *Bakkhai* and Maenadism." *Classica et Mediaevalia* 48: 75–114.

Dodds, E. R. 1960. *Euripides* Bacchae. *Edited with Introduction and Commentary.* Oxford.

Douglas, M. 1966. *Purity and Danger: An Analysis of the Concepts of Pollution and Taboo.* London.

Duckworth, G. E. 1940. "Turnus as a Tragic Character." *Vergilius* 4: 5–17.

———— 1957. "The *Aeneid* as a Trilogy." *TAPA* 88: 1–10.

Dumézil, G. 1970. *Archaic Roman Religion.* Translated by P. Krapp. 2 vols. Chicago. First published as *La Religion romaine archaïque suivi d' un appendice sur la religion des Etrusques.* Paris, 1966.

Dyson, J. T. 2001. *King of the Wood: The Sacrificial Victor in Virgil's* Aeneid. Norman.

Eagleton, T. 1991. *Ideology: An Introduction.* London.

Edgeworth, R. J. 1986. "The Dirae of *Aeneid* XII." *Eranos* 84: 133–43.

Edmunds, L. 2001. *Intertextuality and the Reading of Roman Poetry.* Baltimore.

Edwards, M. W. 1991. *The* Iliad: *A Commentary. Volume V: Books 17–20.* Cambridge.

Eitrem, S. 1933. "Das Ende Didos in Vergils *Aeneis.*" In *Festskrift til Halvdan Koht.* Oslo: 29–41.

Erasmo, M. 2004. *Roman Tragedy: Theatre to Theatricality.* Austin.

Farrell, J. 1991. *Vergil's* Georgics *and the Traditions of Ancient Epic: The Art of Allusion in Literary History.* New York.

Fedeli, P. 1983. *Catullus'* Carmen 61. Amsterdam.

Feeney, D. C. 1984. "The Reconciliations of Juno." *CQ* 34: 179–94. Reprinted with corrections in Harrison 1990: 339–62.

———— 1991. *The Gods in Epic: Poets and Critics of the Classical Tradition.* Oxford.

———— 1998. *Literature and Religion at Rome: Cultures, Contexts, and Beliefs.* Cambridge.

Feldherr, A. 1997. "Livy's Revolution: Civic Identity and the Creation of the *Res Publica.*" In Habinek and Schiesaro 1997: 136–57.

———— 1998. *Spectacle and Society in Livy's History.* Berkeley.

———— 1999. "Putting Dido on the Map: Genre and Geography in Vergil's Underworld." *Arethusa* 32: 85–122.

———— 2002. "Stepping Out of the Ring: Repetition and Sacrifice in the Boxing Match in *Aeneid* 5." In *Clio and the Poets: Augustan Poetry and the Traditions of Ancient Historiography.* D. S. Levene and D. P. Nelis, eds. Leiden: 61–79.

Fenik, B. C. 1960. *The Influence of Euripides on Vergil's Aeneid.* Ph.D. dissertation, Princeton University.

Fernandelli, M. 1996a. "Invenzione mitologica e tecnica del racconto nell'episodio virgiliano di Polidoro (*Aen.* 3.1–68)." *Prometheus* 22: 247–73.

———— 1996b. "Presenze tragiche nell'Ilioupersis virgiliana: su *Aen.* 2, 768–794 e Eur. *Andr.* 1231–1283." *MD* 36: 187–96.

———— 2002. "Come sulle scene: *Eneide* IV e la tragedia." *Quaderni del Dipartimento di filologia, linguistica e tradizione classica A. Rostagni.* 19: 141–211.

Finley, M. I. 1978. *The World of Odysseus.* New York.

Foley, H. P., ed. 1981. *Reflections of Women in Antiquity.* New York.

———— 1985. *Ritual Irony: Poetry and Sacrifice in Euripides.* Ithaca.

———— 2001. *Female Acts in Greek Tragedy.* Princeton.

Fordyce, C. J. 1977. *P. Vergili Maronis Aeneidos Libri VII–VIII. With a Commentary.* Oxford.

Fowler, D. 1987. "Vergil on Killing Virgins." In Whitby et al. 1987: 185–98.

———— 1989. "First Thoughts on Closure: Problems and Prospects." *MD* 22: 75–122.

———— 1997. "Second Thoughts on Closure." In Roberts et al. 1997: 3–22.

Fowler, W. W. 1919. *The Death of Turnus: Observations on the Twelfth Book of the Aeneid.* Oxford.

Fraenkel, E. 1950. *Aeschylus* Agamemnon. *Edited with a Commentary.* 3 vols. Oxford.

Fries, J. 1985. *Der Zweikampf. Historische und literarische Aspekte seiner Darstellung bei T. Livius.* Beiträge zur klassischen Philologie 169. Königstein / Ts.

Galinsky, K. 1996. *Augustan Culture: An Interpretive Introduction.* Princeton.

Gillis, D. 1983. *Eros and Death in the Aeneid.* Centro Ricerche e Documentazione sull' Antichita' Classica Monografie 9. Rome.

Girard, R. 1977. *Violence and the Sacred.* Translated by P. Gregory. Baltimore. First published as *La violence et le sacré.* Paris, 1972.

Goff, B. 1990. *The Noose of Words: Readings of Desire, Violence and Language in Euripides' Hippolytos.* Cambridge.

———— 2004. *Citizen Bacchae: Women's Ritual Practice in Ancient Greece.* Berkeley.

Goldhill, S. 1984. *Language, Sexuality, Narrative: The* Oresteia. Cambridge.

———— 1986. *Reading Greek Tragedy.* Cambridge.

Gotoff, H. C. 1984. "The Transformation of Mezentius." *TAPA* 114: 191–218.

Gould, J. 1973. *"Hiketeia." JHS* 93: 74–103.

Graf, F. 1997. *Magic in the Ancient World.* Translated by F. Philip. Cambridge, MA. First published as *Idéologie et pratique de la magie dans l' antiquité Gréco-Romaine.* Paris, 1994.

Gransden, K. W. 1976. *Virgil.* Aeneid. *Book VIII.* Cambridge.

Griffith, R. D. 1995. "Catullus' *Coma Berenices* and Aeneas' Farewell to Dido." *TAPA* 125: 47–59.

Griffiths, F. T. 1979. "Girard on the Greeks / The Greeks on Girard." *Berkshire Review* 14: 20–36.

Grimm, R. E. 1967. "Aeneas and Andromache in *Aeneid* III." *AJP* 88: 151–62.

Gruen, E. S. 1990. *Studies in Greek Culture and Roman Policy.* Berkeley.

Gurval, R. A. 1995. *Actium and Augustus: The Politics and Emotions of Civil War.* Ann Arbor.

Habinek, T., and Schiesaro, A. 1997. *The Roman Cultural Revolution.* Cambridge.

Hardie, P. R. 1984. "The Sacrifice of Iphigeneia: An Example of 'Distribution' of a Lucretian Theme in Virgil." *CQ* 34: 406–12.

———— 1986. *Virgil's* Aeneid: *Cosmos and Imperium.* Oxford.

———— 1991. "The *Aeneid* and the *Oresteia*." *PVS* 20: 29–45.

———— 1993. *The Epic Successors of Virgil: A Study in the Dynamics of a Tradition.* Cambridge.

———— 1994. *Virgil.* Aeneid. *Book IX.* Cambridge.

———— 1997a. "Closure in Latin Epic." In Roberts et al. 1997: 139–62.

———— 1997b. "Virgil and Tragedy." In *The Cambridge Companion to Virgil.* C. Martindale, ed. Cambridge: 312–26.

Harrison, E. L. 1972–73. "Why Did Venus Wear Boots?" *PVS* 12: 10–25.

———— 1989. "The Tragedy of Dido." *EMC* 33: 1–21.

Harrison, S. J. 1990. *Oxford Readings in Vergil's* Aeneid. Oxford and New York.

———— 1991. *Vergil.* Aeneid 10. *With Introduction, Translation, and Commentary.* Oxford.

Heinze, R. 1915. *Vergils epische Technik.* Leipzig. Translated into English as *Virgil's Epic Technique* by H. Harvey, D. Harvey, and F. Robertson. Berkeley, 1993.

Henrichs, A. 1979. "Greek and Roman Glimpses of Dionysus." In *Dionysus and His Circle: Ancient through Modern*. C. Houser, ed. Cambridge, MA: 1–11.

Henry, E. 1989. *The Vigour of Prophecy: A Study of Virgil's* Aeneid. Carbondale.

Highet, G. 1972. *The Speeches in Vergil's* Aeneid. Princeton.

Hinds, S. 1998. *Allusion and Intertext: Dynamics of Appropriation in Roman Poetry*. Cambridge.

Horsfall, N. 2000. *Virgil,* Aeneid 7. *A Commentary*. Leiden.

Hübner, W. 1970. *Dirae im römischen Epos. Über das Verhältnis von Vogeldämonen und Prodigien*. Hildesheim.

Jacobson, H. 1987. "Vergil's Dido and Euripides' Helen." *AJP* 108: 167–68.

Jal, P. 1961. "*Pax Civilis-Concordia*." *REL* 39: 210–31.

Janko, R. 1992. *The* Iliad*: A Commentary. Volume IV: Books 13–16*. Cambridge.

Jebb, R. C. 1907. *Sophocles. The Plays and Fragments. With Critical Notes, Commentary and Translation in English Prose. Part VII. The* Ajax. Cambridge.

Jocelyn, H. D. 1965. "Ancient Scholarship and Virgil's Use of Republican Latin Poetry II." *CQ* 15: 126–44.

Johnson, W. R. 1976. *Darkness Visible: A Study of Vergil's* Aeneid. Berkeley.

Jones, J. 1962. *On Aristotle and Greek Tragedy*. London.

Kamerbeek, J. C. 1963. *The Plays of Sophocles. Commentaries. Part I. The* Ajax. Leiden.

Kane, R. L. 1996. "Ajax and the Sword of Hector. Sophocles, 'Ajax' 815–822." *Hermes* 124: 17–28.

Keith, A. 2000. *Engendering Rome: Women in Latin Epic*. Cambridge.

Kennedy, D. 1992. " 'Augustan' and 'Anti-Augustan': Reflections on Terms of Reference." In *Roman Poetry and Propaganda in the Age of Augustus*. A. Powell, ed. Bristol: 26–58.

Kirkwood, G. 1965. "Homer and Sophocles' *Ajax*." In *Classical Drama and Its Influence: Essays Presented to H. D. F. Kitto*. M. J. Anderson, ed. London: 53–70.

Knauer, G. N. 1964. *Die* Aeneis *und Homer. Studien zur poetischen Technik Vergils mit Listen der Homerzitate in der* Aeneis. *Hypomnemata* 7. Göttingen.

Knox, B. M. W. 1961. "The *Ajax* of Sophocles." *HSPh* 65: 1–37.

Knox, P. E. 1997. "Savagery in the *Aeneid* and Virgil's Ancient Commentators." *CJ* 92: 225–33.

König, A. 1970. *Die* Aeneis *und die Griechische Tragödie. Studien zur imitatio-Technik Vergils*. Ph.D. dissertation, Freien Universität Berlin.

Krummen, E. 1998. "Ritual und Katastrophe: Rituelle Handlung und Bildersprache bei Sophokles und Euripides." In *Ansichten griechischer Rituale. Geburtstags-Symposium für Walter Burkert. Castelen bei Basel 15. bis 18. März 1996.* F. Graf, ed. Stuttgart: 296–325.

Kyriakou, P. 1997. "All in the Family: Present and Past in Euripides' *Andromache.*" *Mnemosyne* 50: 7–26.

LaPenna, A. 1967. "Amata e Didone." *Maia* 19: 309–18.

Leach, E. W. 1971. "The Blindness of Mezentius (*Aeneid* 10.762–768)." *Arethusa* 4: 83–89.

Lebeck, A. 1971. *The* Oresteia: *A Study in Language and Structure.* Washington, DC.

Lee, M. O. 1979. *Fathers and Sons in Virgil's* Aeneid: *Tum Genitor Natum.* Albany.

Lefèvre, E. 1978. *Dido und Aias. Ein Beitrag zur römischen Tragödie.* Akademie der Wissenschaften und der Literatur. Mainz.

Leigh, M. 1993. "Hopelessly Devoted to You: Traces of the Decii in Virgil's *Aeneid.*" *PVS* 21: 89–110.

Levene, D. S. 1993. *Religion in Livy.* Leiden.

Lloyd, R. B. 1954. "On *Aeneid* III, 270–80." *AJP* 75: 288–99.

Lloyd-Jones, H., and N. G. Wilson, eds. 1990. *Sophoclis Fabulae.* Oxford.

Loraux, N. 1987. *Tragic Ways of Killing a Woman.* Translated by A. Foster. Cambridge, MA. First published as *Façons tragiques de tuer une femme.* Paris, 1985.

———— 1998. *Mothers in Mourning. With the Essay Of Amnesty and Its Opposite.* Translated by C. Pache. Ithaca. First published as *Les mères en deuil.* Paris, 1990.

Lyne, R. O. A. M. 1983. "Vergil and the Politics of War." *CQ* 33: 188–203.

———— 1987. *Further Voices in Vergil's* Aeneid. Oxford.

———— 1989. *Words and the Poet: Characteristic Techniques of Style in Vergil's* Aeneid. Oxford.

Mackie, C. J. 1992. "Vergil's Dirae, South Italy, and Etruria." *Phoenix* 46: 352–61.

Manuwald, B. 1985. "Improvisi aderunt. Zur Sinon-Szene in Vergils *Aeneis.*" *Hermes* 113: 183–208.

Merquior, J. G. 1979. *The Veil and the Mask: Essays on Culture and Ideology.* London.

Miles, G. B. 1995. *Livy: Reconstructing Early Rome.* Ithaca.

Miller, J. F. 2000. "*Triumphus in Palatio.*" *AJP* 121: 409–22.

Mitchell, R. N. 1991. "The Violence of Virginity in the *Aeneid.*" *Arethusa* 24: 219–37.

Mitchell-Boyask, R. N. 1993. "Sacrifice and Revenge in Euripides' *Hecuba*." *Ramus* 22: 116–34.

———— 1996. "*Sine Fine*: Vergil's Masterplot." *AJP* 117: 289–307.

Moles, J. 1984. "Aristotle and Dido's *Hamartia*." *G&R* 31: 48–54.

———— 1987. "The Tragedy and Guilt of Dido." In Whitby et al. 1987: 153–61.

Monti, R. C. 1981. *The Dido Episode and the* Aeneid: *Roman Social and Political Values in the Epic.* Mnemosyne Supplement 66. Leiden.

Muecke, F. 1983. "Foreshadowing and Dramatic Irony in the Story of Dido." *AJP* 104: 134–55.

Nagy, G. 1999. *The Best of the Achaeans: Concepts of the Hero in Archaic Greek Poetry.* Revised edition. Baltimore.

Nelis, D. 2001. *Vergil's* Aeneid *and the* Argonautica *of Apollonius Rhodius.* ARCA 39. Leeds.

Norden, E. 1926. *P. Vergilius Maro Aeneis Buch VI.* Leipzig.

Nugent, S. G. 1992. "Vergil's 'Voice of the Women' in *Aeneid* V." *Arethusa* 25: 255–92.

———— 1999. "The Women of the *Aeneid*: Vanishing Bodies, Lingering Voices." In Perkell 1999: 251–70.

Oakley, S. P. 1985. "Single Combat in the Roman Republic." *CQ* 35: 392–410.

————. 1998. *A Commentary on Livy. Books VI–X.* Oxford.

O'Hara, J. J. 1993. "Dido as 'Interpreting Character' at *Aeneid* 4.56–66." *Arethusa* 26: 99–114.

Oliensis, E. 2001. "Freud's *Aeneid*." *Vergilius* 47: 39–63.

Orlin, E. 2007. "Augustan Religion and the Reshaping of Roman Memory." *Arethusa* 40: 73–92.

Ormand, K. 1999. *Exchange and the Maiden: Marriage in Sophoclean Tragedy.* Austin.

Padel, R. 1995. *Whom Gods Destroy: Elements of Greek and Tragic Madness.* Princeton.

Palmer, R. E. A. 1974. *Roman Religion and Roman Empire: Five Essays.* Philadelphia.

Panoussi, V. 1998. *Epic Transfigured: Tragic Allusiveness in Vergil's* Aeneid. Ph.D. dissertation, Brown University.

Parker, R. 1983. *Miasma: Pollution and Purification in Early Greek Religion.* Oxford.

Pascal, C. B. 1990. "The Dubious Devotion of Turnus." *TAPA* 120: 251–68.

Paschalis, M. 1997. *Virgil's* Aeneid: *Semantic Relations and Proper Names.* Oxford.

Pavlock, B. 1990. *Eros, Imitation, and the Epic Tradition.* Ithaca.

Pease, A. S. 1935. *Publi Vergili Maronis Aeneidos Liber Quartus.* Cambridge, MA.

Perkell, C. 1981. "On Creusa, Dido, and the Quality of Victory in Virgil's *Aeneid.*" In Foley 1981: 355–77.

———— 1997. "The Lament of Juturna: Pathos and Interpretation in the *Aeneid.*" *TAPA* 127: 257–86.

———— 1999. *Reading Vergil's* Aeneid: *An Interpretive Guide.* Norman.

———— 2001. "Purity and Closure in *Aeneid* 12." Paper presented at the annual meeting of the American Philosophical Association.

Pichon, R. 1913. "L' épisode d' Amata dans l' *Enéide.*" *REA* 15: 161–66.

Poe, J. P. 1987. *Genre and Meaning in Sophocles'* Ajax. Beiträge zur klassischen Philologie 172. Frankfurt.

Pöschl, V. 1962. *The Art of Vergil: Image and Symbol in the* Aeneid. Translated by G. Seligson. Ann Arbor. First published as *Die Dichtkunst Vergils: Bild und Symbol in der* Aeneis. Innsbruck / Wien, 1950.

Pucci, J. M. 1998. *The Full-Knowing Reader: Allusion and the Power of the Reader in the Western Literary Tradition.* New Haven.

Putnam, M. C. J. 1965. *The Poetry of the* Aeneid: *Four Studies in Imaginative Unity and Design.* Cambridge, MA.

———— 1994. "Virgil's Danaid Ekphrasis." *ICS* 19: 171–89.

———— 1995. *Virgil's* Aeneid: *Interpretation and Influence.* Chapel Hill.

———— 1998. *Virgil's Epic Designs: Ekphrasis in the* Aeneid. New Haven.

———— 1999. "*Aeneid* 12: Unity in Closure." In Perkell 1999: 210–30.

Quinn, K. 1968. *Virgil's* Aeneid: *A Critical Description.* London.

Quint, D. 1993. *Epic and Empire: Politics and Generic Form from Virgil to Milton.* Princeton.

Raval, S. 1998. Pudibunda Ora: *Gender, Sexuality, and Voice in Ovid's* Metamorphoses. Ph.D. dissertation, Brown University.

Reckford, K. J. 1961. "Latent Tragedy in *Aeneid* VII, 1–285." *AJP* 82: 252–69.

———— 1981. "Helen in *Aeneid* 2 and 6." *Arethusa* 14: 85–99.

Redfield, J. 1975. *Nature and Culture in the* Iliad: *The Tragedy of Hector.* Chicago. Expanded edition. Durham, 1994.

Renger, C. 1985. *Aeneas und Turnus. Analyse einer Feindschaft.* Studien zur klassischen Philologie 11. Frankfurt.

Richardson, N. 1993. *The* Iliad: *A Commentary. Volume VI: Books 21–24.* Cambridge.

Richlin, A. 1992. "Reading Ovid's Rapes." In *Pornography and Representation in Greece and Rome*. A. Richlin, ed. Oxford: 158–79.

Roberts, D., et al. 1997. *Classical Closure: Reading the End in Greek and Latin Literature*. Princeton.

Rose, P. W. 1995. "Historicizing Sophocles' *Ajax*." In *History, Tragedy, Theory: Dialogues on Athenian Drama*. B. Goff, ed. Austin: 59–90.

Rowland, R. J., Jr. 1992. "*Ductor Rhoeteius*: Vergil, *Aeneid* 12.456." In Wilhelm and Jones 1992: 237–43.

Rudd, N. 1990. "Dido's *Culpa*." In Harrison 1990: 145–66.

Saylor, C. F. 1970. "Toy Troy: The New Perspective of the Backward Glance." *Vergilius* 16: 26–28.

Schadewaldt, W. 1966. *Iliasstudien*. Darmstadt.

Scheid, J. 1992. "The Religious Roles of Roman Women." In *A History of Women: From Ancient Goddesses to Christian Saints*. P. S. Pantel, ed. Cambridge, MA: 377–408.

Schein, S. L. 1984. *The Mortal Hero: An Introduction to Homer's* Iliad. Berkeley.

Schenk, P. 1984. *Die Gestalt des Turnus in Vergils* Aeneis. Beiträge zur klassischen Philologie 164. Königstein / Ts.

Schlesier, R. 1993. "Mixtures of Masks: Maenads as Tragic Models." In *Masks of Dionysus*. T. H. Carpenter and C. A. Faraone, eds. Ithaca: 89–114.

Schultz, C. E. 2006. *Women's Religious Activity in the Roman Republic*. Chapel Hill.

Schwenn, F. 1915. *Die Menschenopfer bei der Griechen und Römern*. Religionsgeschichtliche Versuche und Vorarbeiten 15, 3. Giessen. Reprinted Berlin, 1966.

Scodel, R. 1998. "The Captive's Dilemma: Sexual Acquiescence in Euripides *Hecuba* and *Troades*." *HSPh* 98: 137–54.

Seaford, R. 1989. "Homeric and Tragic Sacrifice." *TAPA* 119: 87–95.

——— 1994. *Reciprocity and Ritual: Homer and Tragedy in the Developing City State*. Oxford.

Segal, C. P. 1966. "*Aeternum per saecula nomen*, The Golden Bough and the Tragedy of History: Part II." *Arion* 5: 34–72.

——— 1971. *The Theme of the Mutilation of the Corpse in the* Iliad. Mnemosyne Supplement 17. Leiden.

——— 1978–79. "Pentheus and Hippolytus on the Couch and on the Grid: Psychoanalytic and Structuralist Readings of Greek Tragedy." *CW* 72: 129–48.

———— 1990. "Violence and the Other: Greek, Female, and Barbarian in Euripides' *Hecuba*." *TAPA* 120: 109–31.

———— 1997. *Dionysiac Poetics and Euripides'* Bacchae. Expanded edition with a new afterword by the author. Princeton.

Sharrock, A. 2000. "Intratextuality: Texts, Parts, and (W)holes in Theory." In *Intratextuality: Greek and Roman Textual Relations.* A. Sharrock and H. Morales, eds. Oxford: 1–39.

Sicherl, M. 1977. "The Tragic Issue in Sophocles' *Ajax*." In *Greek Tragedy.* T. F. Gould and C. J. Herrington, eds. *Yale Classical Studies* 25. Cambridge: 67–98.

Sommerstein, A. H. 1989. *Aeschylus* Eumenides. Cambridge.

Sorum, C. E. 1995. "Euripides' Judgment: Literary Creation in *Andromache*." *AJP* 116: 371–88.

Spaeth, B. S. 1996. *The Roman Goddess Ceres.* Austin.

Spence, S. 1991. "Cinching the Text: The Danaids and the End of the *Aeneid*." *Vergilius* 37: 11–19.

———— 1999. "The Polyvalence of Pallas in the *Aeneid*." *Arethusa* 32.2: 149–63.

Stevens, P. T. 1971. *Euripides* Andromache. *Edited with Introduction and Commentary.* Oxford.

Storey, I. C. 1989. "Domestic Disharmony in Euripides' *Andromache*." *G&R* 36: 16–27.

Stübler, G. 1941. *Die Religiosität des Livius.* Amsterdam.

Suzuki, M. 1989. *Metamorphoses of Helen: Authority, Difference, and the Epic.* Ithaca.

Swanepoel, J. 1995. "*Infelix Dido*: Vergil and the Notion of the Tragic." *Akroterion* 40: 30–46.

Tatum, J. 1984. "Allusion and Interpretation in *Aeneid* 6.440–76." *AJP* 105: 434–52.

Thomas, R. F. 1986. "Virgil's *Georgics* and the Art of Reference." *HSPh* 90: 171–98.

———— 1988. "Tree Violation and Ambivalence in Vergil." *TAPA* 118: 261–73.

———— 1998. "The Isolation of Turnus." In *Vergil's* Aeneid: *Augustan Epic and Political Context.* H.-P. Stahl, ed. London: 271–302.

Thompson, J. B. 1984. *Studies in the Theory of Ideology.* Berkeley.

Thornton, A. 1984. *Homer's* Iliad: *Its Composition and the Theme of Supplication.* Göttingen.

Toynbee, J. M. C. 1971. *Death and Burial in the Roman World.* Ithaca.

Treggiari, S. 1991. *Roman Marriage:* Iusti Coniuges *from the Time of Cicero to the Time of Ulpian.* Oxford.

Tupet, A.-M. 1970. "Didon Magicienne." *REL* **48**: 229–58.

Tzanetou, A. forthcoming. *City of Suppliants: Tragedy and the Athenian Empire.* Austin.

Van Gennep, A. 1960. *The Rites of Passage.* Translated by M. B. Vizedom and G. L. Caffee. Chicago. First published as *Les rites de passage.* Paris, 1909.

Van Wees, H. 1992. *Status Warriors: War, Violence and Society in Homer and History.* Dutch Monographs on Ancient History and Archaeology, vol. 9. Amsterdam.

Vance, E. 1981. "Sylvia's Pet Stag: Wildness and Domesticity in Virgil's *Aeneid.*" *Arethusa* **14**: 127–37.

Vernant, J.-P. 1988a. "Tensions and Ambiguities in Greek Tragedy." In Vernant and Vidal-Naquet 1988: 29–48.

———— 1988b. "Imitations of the Will in Greek Tragedy." In Vernant and Vidal-Naquet 1988: 49–84.

———— 1988c. "The Masked Dionysus of Euripides' *Bacchae.*" In Vernant and Vidal-Naquet 1988: 381–412.

———— 1989. "Food in the Countries of the Sun." In *The Cuisine of Sacrifice among the Greeks.* M. Detienne and J.-P. Vernant, eds. Translated by P. Wissing. Chicago: 164–69. First published as *La cuisine du sacrifice en pays grec.* Paris, 1979.

Vernant, J.-P., and Vidal-Naquet, P. 1988. *Myth and Tragedy in Ancient Greece.* Translated by J. Lloyd. New York. First published as *Mythe et tragédie en Grèce ancienne.* Paris, 1972 and as *Mythe et tragédie en Grèce ancienne. Deux.* Paris, 1986.

Versnel, H. S. 1976. "Two Types of Roman *Devotio.*" *Mnemosyne* **29**: 365–410.

————1981. "Self-Sacrifice, Compensation, and the Anonymous Gods." In *Le sacrifice dans l'antiquité.* Entretiens Fondation Hardt **27**: 135–85.

Von Albrecht, M. 1970. "Zur Tragik von Vergils Turnusgestalt: Aristotelisches in der Schlußszene der *Aeneis.*" In *Silvae. Festschrift für Ernst Zinn zum 60. Geburtstag. Dargebracht von Kollegen, Schülern und Mitarbeitern.* M. von Albrecht und E. Heck, eds. Tübingen: 1–5.

Wagenvoort H. 1947. *Roman Dynamism: Studies in Ancient Roman Thought, Language and Custom.* Oxford.

Watson, L. 1991. Arae, *the Curse Poetry of Antiquity.* Leeds.

Weber, C. 2002. "The Dionysus in Aeneas." *CP* **97**: 322–43.

West, D. 1969. "Multiple Correspondence Similes in the *Aeneid.*" *JRS* 59: 40–49.

West, G. S. 1980. "Caeneus and Dido." *TAPA* 110: 315–24.

——— 1983. "Andromache and Dido." *AJP* 104: 257–67.

West, M. L. 1990. *Aeschyli Tragoediae cum incerti poetae Prometheo.* Stuttgart.

Whitby, M. et al. 1987. Homo Viator: *Classical Essays for John Bramble.* Bristol.

Whitman C. H. 1958. *Homer and the Heroic Tradition.* Cambridge, MA.

Wigodsky, M. 1972. *Vergil and Early Latin Poetry.* Hermes Einzelschriften 24. Wiesbaden.

Wilhelm, M. P. 1992. "Minerva in the *Aeneid.*" In Wilhelm and Jones 1992: 74–81.

Wilhelm, R. M., and Jones, H. 1992. *The Two Worlds of the Poet: New Perspectives on Vergil.* Detroit.

Williams, G. 1962. "Poetry in the Moral Climate of Augustan Rome." *JRS* 52: 28–46.

——— 1968. *Tradition and Originality in Roman Poetry.* Oxford.

Williams, R. D. 1960. *P. Vergili Maronis Aeneidos Liber Quintus.* Edited with a commentary. Oxford.

——— 1962. *P. Vergili Maronis Aeneidos Liber Tertius.* Edited with a commentary. Oxford.

Willink, C. W. 1986. *Euripides* Orestes. With introduction and commentary. Oxford.

Wiltshire, S. F. 1989. *Public and Private in Vergil's* Aeneid. Amherst.

Winkler, J. J., and Zeitlin, F. I. 1990. *Nothing to Do with Dionysos? Athenian Drama in Its Social Context.* Princeton.

Winnington-Ingram, R. P. 1980. *Sophocles: An Interpretation.* Cambridge.

Wissowa, G. 1912. *Religion und Kultus der Römer.* Handbuch der klassischen Altertums-wissenschaft. München.

Wlosok, A. 1976. "Vergils Didotragödie. Ein Beitrag zum Problem des Tragischen in der *Aeneis.*" In *Studien zum antiken Epos.* H. Görgemanns and E. Schmidt, eds. Beiträge zur klassischen Philologie 72. Meisenheim am Glan: 228–50.

Zanker, P. 1988. *The Power of Images in the Age of Augustus.* Translated by A. Shapiro. Ann Arbor. First published as *Augustus und die Macht der Bilder.* Munich, 1987.

Zarker, J. W. 1969. "Amata: Vergil's Other Tragic Queen." *Vergilius* 15: 2–24.

Zeitlin, F. I. 1965. "The Motif of the Corrupted Sacrifice in Aeschylus' *Oresteia.*" *TAPA* 96: 463–508.

———— 1984. "The Dynamics of Misogyny: Myth and Mythmaking in the *Oresteia*." In *Women in the Ancient World: The Arethusa Papers*. J. Peradotto and J. P. Sullivan, eds. Albany: 159–94.

———— 1996. *Playing the Other: Gender and Society in Classical Greek Literature*. Chicago.

Zetzel, J. E. G. 1997. "Rome and Its Traditions." In *The Cambridge Companion to Virgil*. C. Martindale, ed. Cambridge: 188–203.

# General Index

# Index of Texts Cited